T. W. Schulz
March 1972

INSTITUTIONS IN AGRICULTURAL DEVELOPMENT

INSTITUTIONS IN AGRICULTURAL DEVELOPMENT

 EDITED BY **MELVIN G. BLASE**

The Iowa State University Press / Ames, Iowa

Composed and printed by
The Iowa State University Press

First edition, 1971

International Standard Book Number: 0-8138-0855-3
Library of Congress Catalog Card Number: 72-137088

TO JOSEPH ACKERMAN

CONTENTS

PREFACE

THE International Rural Institutions Subcommittee of the North Central Land Economics Research Committee (NCR-6) initiated in 1967 the project leading to this book of readings. As part of the project most of the manuscripts were discussed in seminars and many were revised. The final product reflects the persistent efforts of the authors to set a high standard of quality.

This publication is one of several sponsored by the subcommittee and its predecessor, the World Tenure Subcommittee, in the post-World War II period. Others have included:

Ackerman, Joseph, and Marshall Harris, eds. *Family farm policy.* Chicago: University of Chicago Press, 1946.

Parson, Kenneth, Ray Penn, and Philip Raup, eds. *Land tenure.* Madison: University of Wisconsin Press, 1956.

Agrarian reform and economic growth in developing countries. Papers from a seminar on Research Prospectives and Problems, ED, ERS, USDA, March, 1962.

Clawson, Marion. *The land system of the United States,* Lincoln: University of Nebraska Press, 1968.

Clearly, the subcommittee's concern for obtaining insights into the development of viable rural institutions in developing countries has been of long standing.

The subcommittee wishes to express its appreciation to the authors and discussants who contributed to this volume. In addition, appreciation is expressed to June Johnson and John Becker who typed and proofread the manuscript, respectively.

EDITORIAL COMMITTEE

J. H. ATKINSON, *Purdue University*
FOLKE DOVRING, *University of Illinois*
TED L. JONES, *Ohio State University*
DON KANEL, *University of Wisconsin*
ARNOLD PAULSEN, *Iowa State University*
PHILIP M. RAUP, *University of Minnesota*
G. EDWARD SCHUH, *Purdue University*
ROBERT D. STEVENS, *Michigan State University*
WILLIAM A. WAYT, *Ohio State University*
GENE WUNDERLICH, *U.S. Department of Agriculture*

MELVIN, G. BLASE, *University of Missouri,*
Chairman and Editor

A U T H O R S

ATKINSON, J. H., Professor of Agricultural Economics
Purdue University

BLASE, MELVIN G., Associate Professor of Agricultural Economics
University of Missouri

BRANDAO, ERLY D., Agricultural Economist
Inter-American Development Bank

BREIMYER, HAROLD F., Professor of Agricultural Economics
University of Missouri

CHURCH, W. LAWRENCE, Assistant Professor of Law
University of Wisconsin

COUTU, A. J., Professor of Agricultural Economics
North Carolina State University

DORNER, PETER, Professor of Agricultural Economics and Director
of the Land Tenure Center
University of Wisconsin

FLETCHER, LEHMAN B., Professor of Economics
Iowa State University

GITTINGER, J. PRICE, Lecturer, Economic Development Institute
International Bank for Reconstruction and Development

HANNAH, H. W., Professor of Agricultural and Veterinary Medical
Law
University of Illinois

HARRIS, MARSHALL, Research Professor, Agricultural Law Center
University of Iowa

JONES, TED L., Professor of Agricultural Economics and Assistant
Director of the Fiscal Affairs of the Ohio Agricultural Re-
search and Development Center
Ohio State University

LONG, ERVEN J., Director of Research and Institutional Grants
*Agency for International Development, U.S. Department of
State*

LUYKX, NICOLAAS, Director of the Food Institute
East-West Center, Honolulu

MARTIN, C. J., Adviser on Planning Organization, Development
Services Department
International Bank for Reconstruction and Development

McDermott, J. K., Assistant Director of Research and Institutional Grants
Agency for International Development, U.S. Department of State

Merrill, William C., Associate Professor of Economics
Iowa State University

Moseman, A. H., Associate
Agricultural Development Council

Nicholls, William H., Professor of Economics and Director of the Graduate Center for Latin American Studies
Vanderbilt University

Ottoson, Howard W., Professor of Agricultural Economics and Director of the Agricultural Experiment Station
University of Nebraska

Paulsen, Arnold, Professor of Economics
Iowa State University

Pine, Wilfred H., Professor of Agricultural Economics
Kansas State University

Raup, Philip M., Professor of Agricultural Economics
University of Minnesota

Ruttan, Vernon W., Professor of Agricultural Economics and Director of the Economic Development Center
University of Minnesota

Schuh, G. Edward, Professor of Agricultural Economics
Purdue University

Shah, S. M., Director, Integrated Area Development
Ministry of Food, Agriculture, Community Development, and Cooperation, Government of India

Siffin, W. J., Professor of Political Science
University of Indiana

Stevens, Robert D., Professor of Agricultural Economics
Michigan State University

Thomas, D. W., Professor of Agricultural Economics and Director of International Programs in Agriculture
Purdue University

Wayt, William A., Professor of Agricultural Economics
Ohio State University

Witt, Lawrence, Professor of Agricultural Economics
Michigan State University

Wunderlich, Gene, Chief, Resource Institutions Branch
Natural Resource Economics Division, U.S. Department of Agriculture

INSTITUTIONS IN AGRICULTURAL DEVELOPMENT

1

ROLE OF INSTITUTIONS IN
AGRICULTURAL DEVELOPMENT

MELVIN G. BLASE

STUDENTS of economic development are increasingly appreciative of the complexity of the process. The literature abounds with theoretical abstractions and generalizations which, collectively, emphasize both macroeconomics and "strategies" for economic development. Convergence on a set of widely accepted principles has been so lacking that one may compare the current state of economic development theory to the pre-Keynesian period in the formulation of theory in national income determination. In such a state, piecemeal and ineffective policy panaceas can flourish. Empirical information more recently gathered and analyzed has begun to provide new insights into the effectiveness of development efforts, and the role of institutions is becoming clearer.

ROLE OF AGRICULTURE

Drawing on data for the 1950–1965 period, Adler et al., at the International Bank for Reconstruction and Development have called attention to two findings:

First, in the fifteen years from 1950 to 1965 the world economy grew at an unprecedented rate. World production just about doubled, and per capita income increased by more than 50 per cent. Second, all parts of the world took part in this growth. By far the more significant finding is the second, because, as far as we know from the record of the nineteenth and the first half of the twentieth centuries, it is the first time that

3

economic growth was not confined to some countries, or to one area, but was truly worldwide. . . . This finding should go a long way to put to rest the contention that economic development efforts of the poor countries, and with it development aid, have failed.[1]

In spite of the heterogeneous nature of the seventy-five countries included in the analysis, Adler has drawn several conclusions. These are: (1) the rate of capital formation was an important determinant of the rate of growth, (2) increasing exports were related to high rates of growth, (3) industrial development has been relatively easy and agricultural development more difficult, and (4) economic growth tended to be sporadic rather than steady. "Finally, and more generally, the experience of the post war period shows the complexity and many sidedness of the process of economic development, on the one hand, and how little we know and how much we still have to learn about it, on the other."[2]

Using step-wise regression and discriminant analysis techniques, Adelman and Morris have constructed a model to obtain a statistical explanation of economic and noneconomic forces which directly and indirectly determine a country's capacity for economic growth.[3] The model uses observations on thirty-nine indicators of economic, social, and political aspects of national development. Data for seventy-four developing, noncommunist nations, during the period 1957–1962 were analyzed. The discriminant function obtained to distinguish among three performance groups of countries based on their average annual rates of growth of real per capita Gross National Product included: (1) the degree of modernization of outlook, (2) the extent of leadership commitment to economic development, and (3) the degree of improvement in agricultural productivity. In addition, the authors traced out a network of influences among economic, social, and political variables which revealed the complexities of the growth process.

Flores has described the crucial role of agriculture more forcefully:[4]

> Finally, we know that in practice the all-around rate of growth that an under-developed economy can achieve depends first of all on what happens to its agriculture and then, in more advanced stages, on what happens to its construction industry: steel, cement, glass, etc. In very backward countries where agriculture accounts for about 50 per cent of the Gross National Product, while services account for 35 per cent and

---

[1] John H. Adler, "Poverty Amidst Wealth: Trends in The World's Economy," *"Finance and Development,* no. 45, International Monetary Fund and the World Bank Group, Washington, D.C., 1968, p. 30.
[2] Ibid., p. 32.
[3] Irma Adelman and Cynthia Morris, "An Econometric Model of Socio-economic and Political Change in Underdeveloped Countries," *Am. Econ. Rev.,* 58, no. 5 (December, 1968), 1184–1218.
[4] Edmundo Flores, "The Big Threat Is Not Hunger," *CERES FAO Rev.,* 2, no. 3 (May–June, 1969), 19–21.

industry for 15 per cent, as occurs in some Asian and African countries, this is particularly so.

TRENDS IN AGRICULTURAL OUTPUT

The similarity of emphasis on agriculture in these analyses is not surprising in light of past trends in agricultural output. The United States Department of Agriculture has estimated that agricultural output of the world at the end of the 1960s was 33 percent greater than the 1957–1959 base period. Table 1.1 indicates, however, on a per capita basis the increase was only 7 percent. Moreover, per capita agricultural production in developing countries has not displayed a strongly positive trend in spite of significant aggregate increases, as Figure 1.1 shows.

How do these conditions manifest themselves in the lives of people? In developing countries and in pockets of those that are developed, many of the poor are trapped in Malthusian enclaves. In the less-developed world people consume approximately 2,000 calories per day, for example, whereas in the United States approximately 3,000 calories per day are consumed on the average. In general, in the latter, the diet is of higher quality in terms of protein, as indicated in Table 1.2. This is illustrated by the developing countries' consumption of 400 pounds of grain per person yearly. Approximately 1,600 pounds of grain are used in the United States (see Figure 1.2). North Americans enjoy the luxury of a high animal-protein diet which requires large quantities of grain to be processed through livestock.

POPULATION TRENDS

Even if agricultural output were increasing rapidly at a steady rate around the world, there would still be concern because of world

TABLE 1.1 ● World Per Capita Agricultural Production, 1965–1970 (1957–1959 = 100)

Calendar Year	Developed	Less-Developed	World*
1965	107	102	104
1966	114	100	106
1967	115	103	107
1968	118	103	109
1969	116	104	107
1970	116	104	107

Source: Charles A. Gibbons, "1969 World Agricultural Production Indices," *Foreign Agriculture,* Foreign Agricultural Service, USDA, Washington, D.C., February 9, 1970, p. 7, and personal communication.
* Excludes Communist Asia.

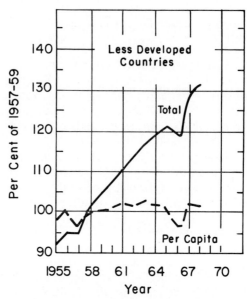

FIG. 1.1—Total and per capita agricultural production in developing nations.

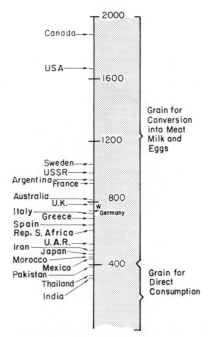

FIG. 1.2—Pounds of grain used per person per year, including grain used for food, feed, seed, and industrial purposes.

TABLE 1.2 ● Daily Per Capita Supply, 1961–1963

Region	Calories	Protein (gm)	
		Total	*Animal*
All undeveloped countries	2184	55	11
Latin America	2545	65	23
Africa	2209	58	10
Near East	2194	67	15
Asia and Far East	2079	50	8
North America	3090	91	64
European Econ. Comm.	2910	87	46

Source: David R. Wightman, "The Food Problem of Underdeveloped Countries," *Food aid and economic development,* Carnegie Endowment for International Peace in International Conciliation, New York, March, 1968, p. 7.

population trends. In a recent address, Robert S. McNamara, President of the World Bank Group, stated:

> I do not need, before this audience, to deal with the terrifying statistics of population growth as a whole which show that, although world population totaled one-quarter billion in the first century A.D. and required 1650 years to add another quarter billion, it added one billion in the next 200 years; a second billion in the following century, and a third billion in the next 30 years. It is now expected to add three more billion by the end of the century. By then, at present rates, it will be increasing one billion each eight years[5]

Perhaps more disturbing are the statistics concerning developing countries. Approximately 1½ billion people live in those countries now. By the year 2000, 3 billion are expected to live there. These statistics exclude mainland China for which population data are not available.[6] Thus, population is gaining so rapidly that many areas of the world can expect to continue living on the "razor's edge of subsistence," unless very dramatic changes are made with respect to economic development, especially in agriculture.

The pressure of population focuses attention on family planning, which offers a partial long-run solution but is plagued with many problems. *First,* the females who will contribute to the accelerated increase already exist and will come into childbearing age during the next twenty years. Consequently, the opportunity for stalling population growth by reducing the number of potentially reproductive members does not exist. But, there is a *second* complication to family planning. In many parts of the world, family size is not going to be controlled by the available techniques, whatever they may be.[7]

---

[5] Robert S. McNamara, Address to the Board of Governors, World Bank Group, Washington, D.C., September 30, 1968.

[6] Adler, "Poverty Amidst Wealth," p. 31.

[7] President's Science Advisory Committee, *The World Food Problem,* GPO, Washington, D.C. May, 1967, p. 14.

Minimum family size will be determined by the desire to have one surviving male heir to provide the equivalent of social security for the parents. To insure one male heir, on the average, at least four children must be born. This is because the probabilities are approximately 50 percent that a child will be a male and two males are required to insure that one survives. A *third* quite disturbing dimension involves urgent short-range problems. Most pressing is the occurrence of brain damage in infants. Preliminary medical research indicates an association between certain animal-protein deficiencies in infant diets and brain damage. Pediatricians Eichewald and Fry have reported:

> In this regard, observations on human infants have shown that inadequate feeding of pyridoxal phosphate, which serves as a coenzyme for most enzymatic reactions of amino acids, results in a series of changes in the physiological function of the brain and in the appearance of clinical symptoms. In the newborn baby, the ingestion of a diet deficient in this substance but otherwise adequate results within six weeks in hyper-irritability, convulsive seizures, abnormalities in development, and behavioral disorders. If this deficit continues for a sufficiently long period, irreversible alterations of cerebral function will occur, resulting in severe mental retardation.[8]

Consequently, in addition to but not as a substitute for family planning programs, there must be an adequate nutritional level provided to: increase the probability of survival of a male child so parents will be interested in limiting family size and to prevent possible brain damage in small children. Accomplishment of these objectives requires more than just increasing aggregate agricultural output. In fact, if attention is focused only on production a disservice will have been done.

ELEMENTS OF THE PROBLEM

Eicher has succinctly described some elements of the problem as follows:

> The supply approach to agricultural planning in many less-developed countries calls for a reappraisal. Advocates of this approach contend that the major bottleneck to agricultural development is on the supply side and that agricultural food production should be greatly expanded in most of these countries. But expanding agricultural production much above population growth rates has not and will not contribute to the overall growth of the economy because the effective demand is inadequate to purchase the increased production, and, as a result, the expanded output will lead to depressed farm prices and incomes. Therefore, effective demand constraints can play a critical role

---

[8] Heinz F. Eichewald and Peggy C. Fry, "Nutrition and Learning," *Science,* 163, no. 3868 (February 14, 1969): 645.

in determining priorities for agricultural development and more attention should be given to effective demand in the preparation of agricultural sector plans.[9]

The problem is more complex than merely producing more food. There are implications for changes in tenure institutions that affect income distribution, in factory and product markets, price policy-making, and a host of other institutions. Many of these changes have been gathered under the umbrella term of Second Generation Problems of the Green Revolution. Regardless of the terminology used, institutions in many developing countries must shed their rigidity and take on the mantle of responsiveness and flexibility.

SLUGGISH ECONOMIC GROWTH IN AGRICULTURE

Perhaps more than any other sector, agriculture in the developing countries is characterized by a circle of poverty. Low labor productivity results in low wages. Because wages are low, incomes are low; because incomes are low, savings are low; because savings are low, investments are low; because investments are low, labor productivity is low—and a full circle has been completed.

How can the circle be broken? In the book, *Asian Drama,* Myrdal argues that changes in institutions are essential. Discussing the book, Krishnaswamy says:

> Myrdal holds that development is not a mechanical process of adding to capital stock, human skills, technological knowledge and artifices but a matter of institutional change, of attitudes and behavior patterns, of all those intangible elements that distinguish a human society from a field of particles or a colony of ants. Changes in these intangibles can be brought about by an understanding of the springs of human action in the less-developed countries. And equally with the observable, measurable economic facts, the values governing the behavior and attitudes of individuals as well as groups become the subject for analysis and policy. To leave these out for reasons of exigency and analytical neatness is, according to Myrdal, tantamount to evading the issue.[10]

INSTITUTIONAL POINTS OF ENTRY

The word institution is plagued by being too all inclusive. In the first Fellow's Lecture presented to the American Agricultural Economic Association, T. W. Schultz defines an institution as a be-

[9] Carl K. Eicher, "Production Is Not Sacred," *CERES FAO Rev.,* 2, no. 3 (May–June, 1969): 36.
[10] K. S. Krishnaswamy, "Some Thoughts on a Drama," *Finance and Development,* no. 1, International Monetary Fund and the World Bank Group, Washington, D.C., 1969, p. 44.

havioral rule and continues: "It is my aim to consider particular political, including legal, institutions that in one way or another influence, or are in turn influenced by, the dynamics of economic growth."[11]

Schultz outlined three approaches which can be taken to the dynamics of economic growth with respect to institutions, as (1) one that omits or impounds institutions by abstracting from them, (2) one that treats institutions as subject to change exogenously, and (3) one that treats institutions as variables within the economic domain, variables that respond to the dynamics of economic growth. He opted for the latter and subsequently summarized his approach:

> Our theory is designed to explain those changes in institutions that occur in response to the dynamics of economic growth. The institution is treated as a supplier of a service which has an economic value. It is assumed that the process of growth alters the demand for the service and that this alteration in the demand brings about a dis-equilibrium between the demand and the supply measured in terms of long-run costs and returns. Although it is possible for the supply of the service of an institution to be altered independently of economic growth considerations, our theory cannot explain such a change in an institution; it can be used, however, to determine the resulting effects of such a change. . . . When agriculture acquires a growth momentum, as it recently has in many parts of Asia . . . the dynamics of that growth will induce farmers . . . to demand institutional adjustment. They will demand a larger supply of credit, with stress on its timeliness and terms, and they will organize cooperatives should these be necessary for this purpose. They will demand more flexibility in tenancy contracts. They will join with neighbors to acquire tube wells and to undertake minor investments to improve the supply of water. Both tenants and landowners will also use whatever political influence they have to induce the government to provide more and better large-scale irrigation and drainage facilities. These are all testable propositions. There is, so it seems to me, a growing body of evidence in support of each of these propositions.

This suggests that the evolution of institutions is a never ending process. But this does not justify overlooking them. On the contrary, it argues for a broad prospective with respect to those institutions that are strategic. The institutions discussed in this book all qualify as being potentially strategic at a given point in a nation's development and they all fall under the definition used here; they represent some form of social control over individual action.[12]

Deliberate exogenous efforts have been made to improve some of these institutions in developing countries. Part of the economic assistance provided by developed countries has been in the form of

---

[11] T. W. Schultz, "Institutions and the Rising Economic Value of Man," *Am. J. Agr. Econ.*, 50, no. 5 (December, 1968): pp. 1113–22.
[12] Others, not considered here but which might be added by some, are cooperative, transportation, medical, and religious institutions.

technical assistance. A substantial amount of this has been devoted to institution building projects. However, relative to the total assistance provided the portion allocated to the improvement of institutions has been small indeed. For example, between 1951 and 1968, the United States spent less than $150 million on university contracts for technical assistance in agriculture. Not all of these were of an institution building nature. However, even if they were, this is a small portion of the $42.5 billion of United States economic assistance to foreign nations during the period 1948–1966.[13]

Some efforts, originating from both exogenous and endogenous sources, to develop institutions that serve agriculture more effectively in developing countries have been quite productive. Several research institutions have been given high visibility recently due to their impacts via new crop varieties.[14] In a number of countries agricultural universities have been constructed or improved to the point where both the quantity and quality of their graduates have changed markedly.[15] In other instances credit systems have been improved, in still others, extension programs have been developed. It suffices to say that notable improvements have been made in some agricultural institutions.

CONCEPT OF LAYERED INSTITUTIONAL CONSTRAINTS

In a given country, institution building efforts tend to be centered on one or, at best, a few agricultural institutions. Unfortunately this focus frequently is placed on individual institutions without considering all those which have an influence on agricultural development. Consequently, there is frequently a lack of perspective concerning all institutions constraining the sector's development. Technical assistance and indigenous personnel alike are often frustrated when the development of one institution—designed to remedy a constraint within an economy—does little more than provide an opportunity for another poorly developed institution to substitute as the effective constraint. Consequently, the layering of institutional constraints often misleads individuals who feel the elimination of one institutional barrier represents a panacea for transforming traditional agriculture.

Hill perceived the multi-institutional nature of the problem when he wrote:

> If developing countries are substantially to increase agricultural production on a sustained basis, they too must provide the institutions . . . that make it possible for farmers to adopt improved practices,

---

[13] Ira Baldwin et al., *Building Institutions to Serve Agriculture*, Committee on Institution Cooperation, Purdue University, Lafayette, Ind., 1968, p. 222.
[14] Lester R. Brown, "The Agricultural Revolution in Asia," *Foreign Affairs*, 56, no. 4 (July, 1968): 688–712.
[15] Baldwin, *Building Institutions*, pp. 49–64.

and incentives that will induce them to do so. . . . My list includes: (1) development of educational and training institutions, (2) development of adequate agricultural research institutions and experiment stations, (3) development of effectively functioning supply lines, including a supply of credit, and of storage, transportation, and marketing facilities, (4) development of incentives to encourage increased production, (5) development of an effective extension service. A book could be written on each of these topics.[16]

Finally, Wells underscores the consequences of piecemeal approaches, "Unfortunately, however, the adoption of one or only a few technical improvements in a few selected locations does not materially increase aggregate productivity or overall production as a whole."[17]

INSTITUTIONS CONSIDERED

Clearly many institutions affect the agricultural sector of a developing nation: some are closely identified with agriculture while others are more pervasive. The former include tenure institutions, extension programs, and agricultural research institutions; the latter include such things as legal systems and national planning institutions. A more important distinction, however, is in the nature of institutions themselves. As social controls over individual action, some take the form of paralegal entities built on customs and mores. Still others take form in physical facilities and staffs to man them. These too have legal and cultural roots. However, because one type of institution is more visible than another is not to say it is more important. In fact the reverse may be more nearly the case. Regardless, both types are discussed in subsequent chapters. All share the common characteristic of having the potential for producing a product needed in order for a traditional agriculture to be transformed into a highly productive, modern one.[18] Conceptually, therefore, the services of

---

[16] F. E. Hill, "Developing Agricultural Institutions in Underdeveloped Countries," *Agricultural Sciences for the Developing Nations*, Albert H. Moseman, ed., Publication 76, American Association for the Advancement of Science, Washington, D.C., 1964, p. 142.

[17] O. V. Wells, "Some Problems of Agricultural Development," *Am. J. Agr. Econ.*, 51, no. 5 (December, 1969): 1041.

[18] T. W. Schultz, "Economic Growth from Traditional Agriculture," *Agricultural Sciences . . .*, Albert H. Moseman, ed., Publ. 76, American Association for Adv. of Science, Washington, D.C. 1964. Schultz has commented on the importance of agricultural inputs of institutions serving farmers, "The high-payoff sources are predominantly improvements in the quality of agricultural inputs; these inputs can be acquired by farmers only from nonfarm firms and from agencies engaged in agricultural research, extension work and schooling. It is therefore necessary to develop ways and means of improving the quality not only of the material reproducible inputs, but also of human agents en-

these institutions have differing marginal value productivities when viewed as production inputs for agricultural firms. It follows, then, that priorities can be placed on changes needed first in the level and mix of these outputs and second in the institutions which produce them.[19] These priorities should be assigned in accord with the extent to which each of the latter acts as a constraint to increasing agricultural output. This, however, is highly dependent upon the relative stages of development of the relevant institutions in a given country. Consequently, the calculus of priority determination with respect to needed changes in institutions must be accomplished separately for each unique national situation.[20] But this does not reduce the need for a comprehensive view with respect to the most important institutions to which consideration must be given. To provide such a view is the objective of this book.

---

gaged in farming. Thus far, in our attempts to assist poor countries in modernizing their agriculture, we have been vague and uncertain with regard to these sources of economic growth, and where we have happened to concentrate on the correct objective, we have with few exceptions failed to do things in the right order and in ways that would institutionalize the process."

[19] Melvin G. Blase, "Discussion, Why Technical Assistance Is Ineffective," *Am. J. of Agr. Econ.*, 50, no. 5 (December, 1968): 1341–1344.

[20] This is not to say that there are no orderings of institutions which are not intuitively obvious. Costly experience has demonstrated, for example, that the development of research institutions should precede that of extension programs; however, the question of priorities for institution building is much too complex to be left to intuition if the needed consideration is given to the full range of alternative institutions.

2

LAND TENURE INSTITUTIONS

PETER DORNER

IF THE QUESTION were simply whether land tenure institutions are important in the development process, an affirmative answer would appear obvious. They are part of a larger institutional system. Without such a system there is chaos; associated living in civilized society disappears and man reverts to that Hobbesian condition of war by all against all, where "the life of man is solitary, poor, nasty, brutish, and short." Institutions give some stability to human relations by providing security of expectation with respect to accepted procedures of human interaction and response.

No reasonable argument can be made in terms of some "inexorable forces of history" requiring particular forms of land tenure institutions. Development has occurred under a wide variety of land tenure systems. However, transformation of an agrarian system into an industrial economy requires a vast change in many institutions, including those of land tenure.

Moore's analysis deals with these issues at a very broad and general level (29). He identifies three main historical routes from the preindustrial to the modern world: (1) the bourgeois revolutions (which led to the combination of capitalism and Western democracy), (2) the capitalist and reactionary form or the revolution from above (culminating in twentieth century fascism of which Germany and Japan are cases), and (3) the communist revolutions of Russia and China. A crucial step toward the modern world, according to Moore, is "separating a large section of the ruling class from direct ties with the land, a separation that has taken place sooner or later in every industrialized country." The preindustrial agrarian structures are inconsistent with the requirements of making this great change from

an agrarian system to an industrial society. Additionally, according
to Moore, the way in which the agrarian structure is changed has
an important bearing on the resulting political system.

Except for the new countries—[1]which never labored under a
traditional agrarianism—this transformation process has frequently
been violent and disorderly. But historical analysis provides few clues
as to whether a particular nation is today approaching such an up-
heaval or whether its rate of progress in transforming its institutions
is sufficient to avoid a revolution. In fact, the revolutions associated
with this transformation have sometimes occurred very early in the
process of industrialization, while at other times they were long de-
layed. Why this should be so poses an interesting question for historical research.

Land tenure institutions constitute the legal and contractual or
customary arrangements whereby people in farming gain access to
productive opportunities on the land. These tenure arrangements
determine the ability of individuals to gain access to these opportunities, and define in part the nature, dimensions, and future security
of such opportunities. In short, land tenure institutions determine
the pattern of income distribution in the farm sector (6, 11, 37).

But land tenure institutions do not exist in isolation. The
dimensions and future security of opportunities are critically affected
by labor, capital, and product markets (27, 35). Thus, the land
tenure system interrelates with a wide range of other institutions.
This has led to two conceptualizations of the reform issue: (1) land
reform, a narrower concept referring primarily to tenure institutions
and the land market, and (2) agrarian reform, a concept that includes
appropriate modification and support for a much wider range of
activities. These interconnections make it difficult to confine the
analysis to land tenure institutions and their influence on development.

And what do we mean by development? The economic literature
identifies growth and development with the rate of increase in output
per capita. This formulation tends to deemphasize the income distribution consequences of the development process. The focus is on
output and supply. Since land tenure arrangements are most immediately and directly associated with the creation and accessibility
of income-earning opportunities and their distribution, they are
given only passing mention in much of the economic literature on
development.[2] This emphasis on production and growth in per

---

[1] Even the United States, however, had its Civil War which has been interpreted as reflecting this transformation (9, 29).
[2] The production consequences of changed tenure structures are less direct
and must be measured in a long-run context.

capita output is incomplete and needs to be supplemented by other measurements. The allocation of investment funds is affected in a very direct way by the pattern of income distribution.

A different perspective of development is gained by viewing it as a process of creating economic opportunities and upgrading human skills and capacities required for their exploitation (10, 15, 19). But Viner's statement still seems to hold: "Were I to insist, however, that the reduction of mass poverty be made a crucial test of the realization of economic development, I would be separating myself from the whole body of literature in this field." (48)

The manner in which increased production is achieved, and the number of people who participate and reap some benefits from the experience, may be as important as the production increase itself. Where jobs in industry are scarce, work on the land offers the only prospect for productive opportunities for most people. Agricultural production may not increase as rapidly or dramatically if it is achieved by the slow and painful process of getting millions of rural people firmly attached to viable and secure opportunities on the land. But it is likely to provide a more stable base for the country's economic and political development in the future (15, 39, 47). The connection between land tenure institutions and economic development is clear when the latter is seen as a process of creating opportunities and the human capacities needed to exploit them.

A wide diversity of land tenure forms is likely to exist in any given country. Although the tenure system in any country can usually be characterized by certain dominant forms, it is not homogeneous. Likewise, great diversity exists within the landlord and peasant classes. In the discussion that follows, some key influences that land tenure institutions may have on development will be illustrated. As will also be evident, the issues discussed are not all of key significance to all the developing countries.

INCOME DISTRIBUTION AND DEMAND CONSEQUENCES

The direct relationship between the land tenure system and income distribution in the farm sector has been discussed. If development is rapid and many new jobs are created in the industrial sector, then this relationship is less clear. When the industrial labor market provides effective alternatives, the bargaining power of those who occupy a weak position in agriculture is enhanced while that of the resource owner is weakened (22).

A common feature of many developing countries, however, is a very skewed distribution of land ownership and a relatively slow rate of growth in nonfarm employment. Consequently, those who own no land or own only a small parcel, or those who farm as tenants and sharecroppers have claim to only a meager income. Abundant labor supplies and lack of employment opportunities maintain this condition.

In a society having from 50 to 70 percent of its population in agriculture (a common feature of developing countries), per capita income of this majority is a key factor in determining the demand for goods and services. When most of them are poor, desperately poor, very little demand is generated.

Poor people are poor customers. They would eat more and eat better if they had more income. Poor people are even poorer customers for industrially produced goods. Food comes first. The extent of the market is too limited to support a variety of manufacturing industries and to reap the benefits of scale economies inherent in many industrial processes. This is especially significant in small countries and provides some of the advantages in economic integration (7).

There may be a degree of conflict between wider and more equal distribution of income and demand expansion on the one hand, and increased rates of saving and investment on the other. But this conflict is frequently more apparent than real. Kaldor's evaluation of the Chilean situation bears on this point. He concludes that "if luxury consumption could be reduced to a more modest proportion of the income of property owners, the proportion of savings in the national income could be considerably raised without lowering the standard of living of the mass of the population." (21, 2)

The skewed income distribution (which in the farm sector is directly related to the land tenure system) provides little demand expansion for industrial growth, and because of conspicuous consumption (especially of imported goods) on the part of high income recipients, high rates of saving and investment are not achieved. Even those investments that are made by high income recipients may be in areas that are not most critical for development.

Poor people are also poor customers for products in international trade. A recent USDA study analyzed growth in the world grain trade to 1970 and 1980 based on economic demands rather than on some projected nutritionally desirable diets (1). The demand for grain is a function of the rate of increase in production in the farm sector as well as in the rest of the economy. In other words, a change in the rate of agricultural output has a significant impact on total income (in nations where agriculture is the dominant form of economic activity) and therefore on consumption of agricultural commodities.

Clearly, peasants cannot get rich quickly by redistribution or any other means. Developing countries are too poor for that. But if they can get a little more income and expect that their efforts can yield them more in the future, a significant impact on demand will be left. Land tenure institutions are important means for providing security of expectations and are key determinants of income distribution in the farm sector.

ECONOMIC AND POLITICAL POWER DISTRIBUTION

Economic and political power are related positively to income levels. The rich have more power than the poor. Where the agrarian sector is large (in an economic sense) relative to the total economy, those who control the land resources are able to influence the political processes in a measure disproportionate to their numbers Thus, in addition to income distribution with its demand consequences, land tenure systems influence the political power structure and the goals and policies that are formulated through the political process (2, 3, 5, 38).

As a result, it is difficult to enact legislation affecting the distribution of income—whether by changes in land tenure or by other means. And if such legislation is passed, it is nearly impossible to enforce. Taxes are usually low, the system of taxation confused, and compliance minimal. The same problems exist relative to enforcement of labor laws governing working conditions, and laws defining land rental contracts (3).

The concentration of power in a relatively small group has many implications for development and change. For one thing, power at the central state level is likely to be closely related to and connected with that at the regional and local level. That is, the same people, the same interests, are involved. Thus, if a local group outside this power structure formulates pressures for a certain program, it may be confronted by opposition from the local power elite. But it may likewise find this same opposition at the regional and central level because of the common interests involved. Under these circumstances, a people remain either politically lethargic or they revolt. The prospect of an intermediate alternative, pragmatic compromise and evolution, is largely precluded.

In a society with economic and political power more widely dispersed and diffused among a great number of economic interest groups, local opposition may be overcome by appealing to, and gaining support from, power at another level. Civil rights and legislative reapportionment in the United States are examples. In the former case, local and state opposition was countered by a Supreme Court decision followed by support in the legislative and executive branches of the federal government. In the latter, the highest court of the judicial branch was the only power source that could respond to the problem.[3]

An analogy might be drawn between the distribution of income and the distribution of political power. A highly skewed income distribution may result in a lower level of effective demand and thus a smaller total national income. Under the conditions of mass unemployment and under-utilization of resources, a more equal distribution which stimulates demand—given time for the multiplier effect to register its full impact—enlarges the total income pie. The analogy suggests that political power may also be of this nature. That is, a wider distribution may in the long run enhance the power of all.

The length of run and the dynamics of the particular situation are key variables. In a rapidly growing economy the generation of new wealth and power may be sufficient to provide new opportunities for all interest groups. But since this cannot be guaranteed, those who stand to lose in the short run will not voluntarily take this risk. The point is that they may have to accept this risk if power is sufficiently diffused among a wide group of interests. But the more agrarian a system, the more highly this power is likely to be concentrated and the greater is the influence of the associated land tenure system. This influence recedes in importance as industrialization advances and groups other than those favored by the landholding system gain a larger share of the income and power.

INVESTMENTS IN AGRICULTURE
AND SUPPLY CONSEQUENCES

Two aspects of this question need to be distinguished—investments by individual entrepreneurs or private groups and investments by government. The latter will be treated more fully in the next section. However, it cannot be completely separated and isolated from the discussion of private investments.[4]

The basic question is to what extent, if any, particular land tenure arrangements affect investments and thereby the supply re-

---

[3] These examples are used to illustrate a point rather than to cite the United States as an ideal. There is a great deal of power concentration in the United States, but agriculture and landownership are not the focal points of this power. On the one hand there is the so-called military-industrial complex of which President Eisenhower warned the nation when he left office, and which has recently been discussed in a cogent analysis by Galbraith (20). On the other hand, there is the power struggle associated with poverty and racial questions. A major attack on poverty and racial problems must involve a restructuring of power and a much wider participation on the part of relatively excluded groups.

[4] Investments in state-controlled or collective agriculture will also be dealt with in the following section.

sponse from agriculture. Raup has argued that "capital formation in farming is rarely concentrated either in space or in time. It accumulates by an incremental process that is best described as accretionary. A nation's livestock herd is a good example." He goes on to point out that tenure security can contribute to this "by making the use of productive assets the preclusive right of an individual or group. This security of expectation is crucial for biological forms of capital, for slow-maturing enterprises, and for undertakings involving numerous incremental additions made successively over many production cycles." (42)

Parsons has formulated the issue in a slightly different manner, maintaining that "the tenure system of a country influences the productivity of agriculture, both through the incentives which the tenure arrangements offer for the effective participation of workers, managers, investors, etc., and through the capacity of a tenure system to adjust to the requirement of economy, such as: the adoption of new technology, changes in the size of farms, the equalization of the labor earnings between agriculture and other sectors." (36)

The tenure form that seems to come closest to providing the necessary incentive conditions is the owner-operated family farm (26). However, leasing arrangements can be devised that create about the same security of expectations for tenants as an owner-operator system. Unfortunately, such leasing arrangements are seldom found in developing countries (27, 30, 42). As Long has described, the tenant must share heavily with the landlord the fruits of his extra labor, and given time, the landowner finds ways of absorbing virtually all the extra production. "Thus the tenant learns not to smile, lest the landlord raise his rent: as the Eastern proverb has it, 'A smile on the face of a tenant speaks of the stupidity of his landlord.' " (27)

There are, of course, cases of progressive agriculture outside the pattern of family farming (34, 42). Cultural and social factors are extremely significant in determining the success of different tenure arrangements (4). This makes generalization difficult.[5]

In discussing these relationships, a distinction between production for export and for internal markets must be drawn. Although there are exceptions, export crops of the developing countries have generally shown higher rates of increase in production than have crops and livestock grown primarily for the internal market. The crux of the world food problem is found in the slow rate of growth (relative to population increases) in food production for domestic use. In part, this may be a consequence of the colonial experience and the long history of foreign entrepreneurs operating in the export crop field.

---

[5] In the United States, attempts at establishing cooperative farming have generally failed. But also, attempts to establish family farming patterns among the American Indians were unsuccessful.

Most of the developing countries are concerned with balance of payments problems, and export crops are frequently large earners of foreign exchange. Thus the government is interested in and tries to enhance production of export crops. Current foreign loans added to already large international debts increase the need for exports to service these debts. A government's concern and its efforts to encourage expansion of production in the export sector are understandable.

This emphasis on exports, however, may give the statistical impression of high rates of growth in the agricultural sector, but the level of living and income of the majority of farm people may actually be deteriorating. Some Central American countries, like Guatemala and Nicaragua, with rapid growth in the production and export of cotton are nevertheless faced with deteriorating conditions in the countryside. The feature of the land tenure system important here is that production for export is frequently organized in large scale operations or plantations and often financed or run directly by foreign entrepreneurs.

Governments, in their effort to resolve the balance of payments problems (and under great pressure to do so by international lending agencies) sometimes invite foreign companies for the purpose of increasing the production of export crops. For example, in 1966 the government of the Dominican Republic was negotiating with a consortium of United States companies a long-term rental contract for operating a large area of excess sugar cane land. The companies insisted upon a guarantee in the contract that they not be pressured to hire undue amounts of labor and that they be allowed to operate efficiently with modern mechanization. The Dominican economy is largely agricultural, and estimates of unemployment in the country at the time were in excess of 30 percent. Such an arrangement might help solve the balance of payments problem, but it will likely do little to create opportunities for the unemployed and the excluded.

This example emphasizes the need for finding ways to create opportunities—even subsistence opportunities—for the mass of rural people. Where land constitutes the major resource base, ways must be found to use it in such a way that it can serve as the vehicle by which people gain experience and the discipline that comes from productive work.

Most farms, however, large or small, are geared to production for the domestic market. And while production is increasing, it is not growing at a sufficient rate to meet the needs of rapidly growing populations. A number of factors have been identified as being critically important: (1) the cost/price relations in agriculture, (2) production incentives related to land tenure institutions, (3) availability of new production inputs, and (4) services, credit, etc. All are related to the supply side, and all are undoubtedly important (30, 45).

But one also needs to look at the structure of demand. In the developing countries, the extent of the market is not only limited for industrially produced goods, but also for those produced on the farm. Empty stomachs do not shift the demand function to the right. Large increases in farm output may depress prices unless this output is distributed in a way that will generate an equivalent increase in demand.

Where the agricultural population makes up a large percentage of the total, a major part of the increase in demand for food (required to avoid price declines following increases in farm output) must come from the farm population. Where agricultural production is carried on under a system of small owner-operated farms, for example, part of the increased production naturally flows into increased consumption on the farm. But where incomes and consumption of a large majority of the farm population are very low and dependent on a wage or rental system controlled by a landowner class, increases in production may not automatically accrue to the mass of rural people. Under these circumstances, increases in demand are dependent mainly on the growth in urban incomes and employment. If such growth is not sufficiently rapid, then farm prices will decline. Therefore, increases in farm output need to be distributed among the rural population in a way that will generate sufficient demand.

A key variable is the control of the investment decisions in the agricultural sector.[6] Where investment decisions are decentralized with many small investors reaping the benefit of the increased output, the demand generated will more nearly match the supply and thus be less likely to depress prices. If the land tenure arrangements leave most of the investment decisions to large landowners and landlords, many of whom may view investments only in the monetary sense (not in the accretionary, labor-time sense) and whose business connections provide alternative investment opportunities in other sectors, they may well decide to limit investments in agriculture and shift their investments elsewhere (12). This may be the economically rational decision, given the limited demand and the resulting price structure. But a wider sharing of the investment decision could, under these circumstances, have two advantages. First, it would provide a more equal distribution of income and thus generate more demand. Second, it would enlarge the conception of investment to include capital creation on the farm through use of the investors' labor.

Of course governments may have a cheap food policy and thus

---

[6] Conceiving investments in a broad sense is important—not only investments representing purchases in the capital market but also investments of labor time in the capital creation process on the farm. Raup's concept of accretionary processes of capital development in farming is significant here.

control prices received by farmers in order to lower food prices for urban consumers. This is sometimes judged necessary to avoid unrest in the cities. Even if this is not the case, agricultural product prices sufficiently high to make investments more attractive in agriculture than in other sectors may be inconsistent with the requirements of economic development. Land tenure patterns have a direct bearing on these questions, essentially through location and control over investment decisions in the agricultural sector.

What about the size-of-farm issue that has been so widely debated? The above reasoning suggests that small farms may be more advantageous, at least in early stages of the development process. But the size of the operating unit is perhaps less important than the arrangements by which decisions about monetary and labor-time investments on the one hand and rewards for additional effort on the other are integrated.[7] The evidence from various parts of the world supports the hypothesis that productivity per unit of land on small farms is as great or greater than that on large farms[8] (3, 14, 16, 17, 23, 25, 42).

In any event, internal population density and the need for employment opportunities on the land should be more important determinants of farm size than the possibilities inherent in imported machine technology (8, 36).

INVESTMENTS IN OTHER SECTORS OF THE ECONOMY

That investments in agriculture are influenced by the land tenure arrangements is evident. But do these institutions also affect the nature and level of investments in other sectors of the economy?

The fact that landowners who have the ability to evaluate investment alternatives may find the more profitable ones in sectors other than agriculture has been noted. How well such investments serve the overall requirements of development is not always clear. Many of the investment needs are for social overhead, or of a scale requirement in the private sector that calls for pooling of capital which is difficult without well-organized financial markets.

In all cases of developing countries today, there is need for a large scale public investment program which means that government must

---

[7] Cultural factors and social organization also become important at this point—tribal custom, extended family obligation, expenditures on social functions, etc. (4). The above arguments assume economic responsiveness on the part of decision makers.

[8] If output per unit of land is the unit of measurement (the more limited and thus appropriate resource for which to measure output rather than per unit of labor, the more abundant resource in most developing countries), "small farms" compare very favorably with "large farms."

gain access to a substantial pool of investment funds. In those countries where the agricultural sector is large relative to the total economy, agriculture must be a major source of savings. In simple physical terms, agriculture must provide the food with which to feed the people who have been released from the agricultural sector and are now engaged in building such capital structures as roads, schools, factories, canals. Since these investments do not have a quick payoff, agriculture must donate part of this food without an equivalent short-term return. Owen has stated the case: "how can peasants be encouraged to produce a cumulative surplus of food and fiber over and above their own consumption, and how can this surplus largely be channeled to investment activity in the nonfarm sector without requiring an equivalent transfer of productive value to the farm sector." (33)

Even in the United States, Owen estimates that this production squeeze was between $1.5 and $2 billion in 1960. Raup points out that among the industrialized nations: "those countries in which agriculture is well rewarded have made much slower rates of economic growth in the 20th century. France is an outstanding example. England belongs in this class. So do Sweden and the low countries of Europe generally." He also suggests: "capital formation in postwar Germany has again been accomplished in part because of the 'tribute' laid on its agriculture in the form of lower rewards than those available in industrial occupations." (41)

This squeeze on agriculture, according to Owen, is a feature of all developing societies, whether socialist or capitalist. "The difference between the Russian and U.S. approaches to development lies not in the fact that one exacted or exacts a special contribution from the farmers and the other did, or does not. Rather the difference lies in the way in which the squeeze has been applied and in the relative efficiency with which the process has operated in each case." (33)

This concept of the squeeze on agriculture presents a dilemma of somewhat contradictory requirements. Investments in agriculture must be made and agricultural productivity must increase, and at the same time the terms of trade must be kept somewhat unfavorable to agriculture (28). This seems inconsistent with the recommendation of many economists for increasing farm prices to encourage investments. As discussed earlier, the land tenure institutions are significant here in that they determine who controls the investment decisions.

This squeeze on agriculture cannot be applied without a return flow of public investments. In the United States, this return flow of investments included public subsidies for the construction of transportation systems, land grants for the establishment of agricultural colleges, federal financial support for agricultural experiment stations and extension services, building a system of rural credit institutions, direct payments for soil conservation practices, and price support programs. All were part of government policy aimed at achiev-

ing increased agricultural production *and* helping to redress the imbalances in the distribution of income and opportunity which accompany development (13). The realization of these policies was
influenced in an important way by farmers themselves working
through their organizations within the political process (39).

In many of the developing countries the squeeze has been applied to the peasants for generations—indeed for centuries in some
cases. But it has been a one way exploitive process. The return flow
of public investments and redress have been ignored. It is not a simple
matter to rectify the exploitation consequences of several centuries.
Peasants are not stupid and lazy but frequently they are unschooled,
poor, unorganized, and neglected.

Tenure institutions are important because in many cases the
landlord extracts the surplus from the peasants. If landowners are
also very influential in government, and there is no public power to
get it away from them, the decision for investing this surplus rests
with the land-owning class. And investments guided by landowners'
private interests are not necessarily consistent with those required
for developing the country.

An interesting question is posed by the Russian experience. The
large landlords' estates, as well as many of the larger peasant holdings, had been eliminated through the land reapportionment of
1917–1918 together with the class war in the villages in 1918–1920
(32). Yet ten years later, in 1928, the drastic decision was taken to
collectivize Soviet agriculture. Obviously an individualistic farm
sector represented certain political threats to the communist party
leadership. But there was also the underlying economic rationale.
The magnitude of the surplus that had to be squeezed from agriculture in order to support massive industrialization efforts which the
Soviets set as their goal could not be obtained under a system with an
independent peasantry. Commenting on this, Schiller says: "Most
likely it would not have been possible in the Soviet Union under conditions of individual farming to effect a restriction of consumption
to the same extent as was in fact achieved under the conditions of
collective farming." (44)

The situations facing many of the developing countries today
differ greatly from those in Russia in 1928. Population pressures and
continuing rapid increases in the population are new conditions.
In 1928 Russia had a sizeable agricultural surplus (31, 44). The task,
as seen by the officials, was to squeeze this from the peasants and
divert it to the towns and industrial centers. But India, for example,
is today in a much different position. Given its large food imports,
it cannot ignore investments in its agriculture as Russia did for many
years, and it may have little to squeeze from the peasant without facing the prospect of mass starvation.

PREMATURE FARM TO CITY MIGRATION

Rapid rates of population growth characterize most of the developing countries. Technical assistance and the transfer of technology has effectively reduced death rates over the past twenty years, while an equivalent effort to lower birth rates is still in its beginning stages. The developmental policy options available to a country are influenced in an important way by this population question.

A universal phenomenon in the process of development is a declining farm population—first a decline relative to the nonfarm and later an absolute decline. Land tenure institutions play an important role in governing the rate at which this process occurs and in contributing additional capital to the developmental process in the form of investments embodied in young men and women who leave the farm for work in the city (24).

Owen calls this the "expenditure squeeze on agriculture" and identifies its two components as "emigrant capital" and "farm-financed social welfare." (33) If the emigrant capital represents adults who have had little schooling or work experience, their contribution to nonfarm industrial development is open to question. However, the cost of rearing them to adulthood on the farms still represents substantial drains on the farm economy. The farm-financed social welfare, according to Owen, represents a "claim to maintenance at farm-sector expense of any labor that is rendered redundant by the development process in that sector until such time as this labor actually realizes an alternative employment opportunity in the nonfarm sector." (33)

These processes have never functioned in quite the absolute terms indicated by the above statement. But in the United States, for example, the agricultural system did serve as a refuge in the deep depression of the thirties, and there was a movement back to the farm. Even in the milder recessions of the fifties, migration to the cities was slowed down. The agricultural sector in the United States even today continues to hold labor far beyond its productive needs.

However, while United States historical experience has some relevance, present circumstances are too different from those in the developing countries to offer any meaningful parallel. Near subsistence existence in the United States is simply an unacceptable alternative. Educational and skill requirements, both in agricultural and industrial employment, are at a very high level. Such educational and skill levels are difficult to transmit to young people whose parents operate near a subsistence level. While massive public investments to "save" the next generation are obviously required, the overwhelmingly important influence of home and family must also be enlisted to realize this achievement. This requires opportunities for the parents that are substantially above subsistence.

Unfortunately, developing countries do not have the option of bringing large numbers of their poor much above the subsistence level in the near future. One of the great failures of land tenure institutions is their inability to provide opportunities for their large and still growing farm populations. Thus the mass migrations to the cities represent, in part, a premature movement since there are insufficient jobs being created in the nonfarm sector.

Large migrations of rural poor to cities is occurring in most of the developing countries. In the seven Latin American countries studied by CIDA,[9] for the period 1952–1960, 11 million people of a total natural increase of 19 million in rural areas migrated to the cities (3, 47). A World Health Organization release[10] notes that with present trends and world population doubling between now and the year 2000, "the proportion of urbanized world population will also double—in other words, the city population will increase fourfold. The shantytowns of more than 100,000 inhabitants at the fringes of our modern cities concentrate 12 percent of the world population, more than one-third of the world's city population." (46)

Land tenure institutions need to be flexible to hold and absorb more of this labor in productive work in agriculture. Even though opportunities may be meager, they are better than no opportunity at all. As people continue to flock to the cities, they create threats to political stability. Thus, governments make investments and incur expenditures to maintain order. But these expenditures do not add greatly to employment opportunities. Equivalent investments in agriculture could concentrate on directly productive capital and create additional employment (47). As Raup has put it: "Wherever there is surplus agricultural labor and shortage of working capital, the task of the tenure system is to put people to work." (42)

The above areas define some of the major influences which land tenure institutions may have on the development of agriculture in particular and economic development in general. Clearly, however, land tenure is bound up with many other rural institutions that affect the development process. Long has pointed out: "economic underdevelopment is itself largely a consequence of institutional underdevelopment" and "social, economic, and political institutions developed through an ageless past to achieve accommodation to an environment are ill-equipped to serve as vehicles of controlled and creative transformation of the environment to serve human ends." (27, 4) Land tenure arrangements are among the important institutions in this connection.

---

[9] The Inter-American Committee for Agricultural Development. The seven countries are Guatemala, Colombia, Peru, Ecuador, Chile, Argentina, and Brazil.
[10] Cited by Schumacker, full reference not given (46).

Given all these complexities, development is obviously not a simple matter. But all complexities notwithstanding, the need to increase food production to feed growing populations and to earn foreign exchange is urgent. In responding to this need, governments frequently try to obtain this increase by focusing attention on the large farm sector. All the supporting services—information, farm inputs, credit, marketing, etc.—can be provided more easily in dealing with a smaller number of decision-making units. But this simply delays, and does not eliminate, the need for positive steps to provide more viable opportunities for the large rural masses and to give them a more secure stake in the development process as well as a means of developing the experience and skills without which future development may be slowed.

To state the issues as a choice between equity and productivity is an oversimplification. The distributional issues are not confined to equity and justice considerations, they have profound economic development implications. In most developing countries, attention must be given to both distribution and production issues. Reforms that focus on only one may fail to achieve the developmental consequences anticipated (35, 43).

Matching millions of rural people with more viable opportunities on the land is of course an overwhelmingly difficult task. But governments must face up to these issues and the threats posed from various groups within the nation as a result of policy alternatives that might be adopted. In this arena of difficult political choices, the courses of action chosen will be influenced by the extent to which there is active participation in the process by the rural poor (18, 39, 40). And the prospects of achieving effective rural organization are also a function of land tenure institutions.

REFERENCES

1. Abel, Martin E., and Anthony S. Rojko. *World food situation,* Foreign Agricultural Economic Report 35. Washington D.C.: U.S. Department of Agriculture, 1967.
2. Barraclough, Solon L. Agricultural policy and land reform. Paper read at Conference on Key Problems of Economic Policy in Latin America, University of Chicago, November, 1966.
3. Barraclough, Solon L., and Arthur L. Domike. Agrarian structure in seven Latin American countries. *Land Economics,* 42 (November, 1966), 391–424.
4. Brewster, John M. Traditional social structures as barriers to change. In *Agricultural development and economic growth,* ed. Herman M. Southworth and Bruce F. Johnson. Ithaca: Cornell University Press, 1967.
5. Carroll, Thomas F. Land reform an explosive force in Latin America. In *Explosive forces in Latin America,* ed. J. J. TePaske and S. N. Fisher. Columbus: Ohio State University Press, 1964.

6. ———. Reflexiones sobre la distribución del ingreso y la inversión agrícola. *Temas del BID,* Año 1, Agosto, 1964.
7. Castillo, Carlos M. *Growth and integration in Central America.* New York: Frederick A. Praeger, 1966.
8. Christensen, Raymond P. Population growth and agricultural development. *Agri. Econ. Res.,* 18 (October, 1966), 119–28.
9. Conrad, Alfred H., and John R. Meyer. *The economics of slavery and other studies in econometric history.* Chicago: Aldine Publishing Company, 1964.
10. Currie, Lauchlin. The relevancy of development economics to development. Paper read at Workshop on International Development, University of Wisconsin, November 23, 1965.
11. Dorner, Peter. Land tenure, income distribution and productivity interactions. *Land Economics,* 40 (August, 1964), 247–54.
12. ———. Open letter to Chilean landowners. (Spanish) Santiago, Chile: *La Nación,* June 21, 1965, and (English) University of Wisconsin *Land Tenure Center Newsletter,* no. 22, November, 1965–February, 1966.
13. ———. Land tenure reform and agricultural development in Latin America. Presentation to Subcommittee of International Finance of the Committee on Banking and Currency, House of Representatives, 89th Cong., 2d sess., August 29, 1966.
14. ———. *Interpretive synthesis and policy implications of land tenure center and related research,* Land Tenure Center Paper no. 31. Madison: University of Wisconsin, December, 1966.
15. ———. The human side of development. *International Agricultural Development Service Newsletter,* no. 35, September, 1967.
16. Dovring, Folke. Flexibility and security in agrarian reform programs. In *Agrarian reform and economic growth.* Washington D.C.: U.S. Department of Agriculture, 1962.
17. ———. *Land reform and productivity: The Mexican case, a preliminary analysis,* AERR-83, Department of Agricultural Economics, Agricultural Experiment Station, University of Illinois, November, 1966. A revised version published as Land Tenure Center Paper no. 63. Madison: University of Wisconsin, January, 1969.
18. Fraser, Donald M. The farmer—new focus for national growth. *International Agricultural Development Service Newsletter,* no. 35, September, 1967.
19. Galbraith, John Kenneth. *Economic development in perspective.* Cambridge, Massachusetts: Harvard University Press, 1962.
20. ———. *The new industrial state.* Boston: Houghton Mifflin, 1967.
21. Kaldor, Nicholas. *Economic problems of Chile.* (Santiago, Chile: United Nations, Economic Commission for Latin America, 1959. Published also (in Spanish) in *El Trimestre Económico,* Mexico City, April-June, 1959.
22. Kanel, Don. The social setting of land tenure systems. In *Agrarian reform and economic growth.* Washington, D.C.: U.S.D.A., 1962.
23. ———. Size of farm and economic development. *Indian J. Agr. Econ.,* 22 (April-June, 1967), 26–44.
24. Long, Erven J., and Peter Dorner. Excess farm population and the loss of agricultural capital. *Land Economics,* 30 (November, 1954), 363–68.
25. Long, Erven. Economic basis of land reform in underdeveloped economies. *Land Economics,* 37 (May, 1961), 113–23.
26. ———. Problems in foreign policy. *J. Farm Econ.,* 44 (May, 1962), 550–59.
27. ———. Institutional factors limiting progress in the less-developed countries. In *Agricultural sciences for the developing nations,* ed. Albert H.

Moseman, Publication 76, American Association for the Advancement of Science, Washington, D.C., 1964.

28. Mellor, John W. Toward a theory of agricultural development. In *Agricultural development and economic growth,* ed. Herman M. Southworth and Bruce F. Johnson. Ithaca: Cornell University Press, 1967.

29. Moore, Barrington, Jr. *Social origins of dictatorship and democracy.* Boston: Beacon Press, 1966.

30. Mosher, A. T. *Getting agriculture moving.* New York: Frederick A. Praeger, 1966.

31. Nicholls, William H. The place of agriculture in economic development. In *Agriculture in economic development,* ed. Carl Eicher and Lawrence Witt. New York: McGraw-Hill, 1964.

32. Nove, Alec. The decision to collectivize. Paper read at the Conference on the Agrarian Question in Light of Communist and Non-Communist Experience, University of Washington, August 23–26, 1967.

33. Owen, W. F. The double developmental squeeze on agriculture. *Am. Econ. Rev.,* 56 (March, 1966), 43–70.

34. Parsons, Kenneth H. Land reform in the United Arab Republic. *Land Economics,* 35 (November, 1959), 319–26.

35. ———. The place of land reform in a developmental agricultural policy. In *Modern land policy.* Urbana: University of Illinois Press, 1960.

36. ———. The tenure of farms, motivation and productivity. In *Agriculture,* vol. 3, of papers prepared for the U.N. Conference on the Application of Science and Technology for the Benefit of the Less Developed Areas, GPO, January, 1963.

37. ———. Agrarian reform policy as a field of research. In *Agrarian reform and economic growth.* Washington, D.C.: U.S.D.A., 1962.

38. Penn, Raymond J. Public interest in private property (land). *Land Economics,* 37 (May, 1961), 99–104.

39. ———. *The rural community and its relation to farm policies,* Land Tenure Center Paper, no. 32. Madison: University of Wisconsin, April, 1967.

40. Powell, John D. The politics of agrarian reform in Venezuela. Ph.D. dissertation, University of Wisconsin, 1966.

41. Raup, Philip M. Land tenure adjustments in industrial-agricultural economies. In *Modern land policy.* Urbana: University of Illinois Press, 1960.

42. ———. Land reform and agricultural development. In *Agricultural development and economic growth,* ed. Herman M. Southworth and Bruce F. Johnson. Ithaca: Cornell University Press, 1967.

43. Ruttan, Vernon W. Equity and productivity in modern agrarian reform legislation. Paper read at the International Economic Association Conference on the Economic Problems of Agriculture, Rome, Italy, September 1–8, 1965.

44. Schiller, Otto. The communist experiences in dealing with the agrarian question: Their significance for developing countries. Paper read at the Conference on the Agrarian Question in Light of Communist and Non-Communist Experience, University of Washington, August 23–26, 1967.

45. Schultz, T. W. *Transforming traditional agriculture.* New Haven: Yale University Press, 1964.

46. Schumacker, E. F. *Economic development and poverty,* Intermediate Technology Development Group Limited Bulletin no. 1. London: ITDGL, September, 1966.

47. Thiesenhusen, William C., and Marion Brown. Survey of the Alliance

for Progress: Problems of agriculture. Presentation to the Subcommittee on American Republics Affairs of the Committee on Foreign Relations, U.S. Senate, December 22, 1967. Reprinted as Land Tenure Center Reprint 35. Madison: University of Wisconsin.
48. Viner, Jacob. *International trade and economic development.* Glencoe, Ill.: The Free Press, 1950.

DISCUSSION by S. M. SHAH

DORNER EXAMINES the hypothesis that land tenure institutions are of critical importance in determining agricultural development. He first discusses the concept *economic development* and asks: What is the aim of economic development? Should growth (i.e., development) be identified with the rate of increase in output (gross or net) per capita or should economic development mean the development of opportunities and human capacities?

He mentions the interrelationships between political stability and economic development. History provides a number of illustrations of withdrawal of investments by people in countries that become politically unstable or, within a country, from states that are habitually in turmoil. The question here is why economic development should not be measured with the yardstick of growth in output. Overall rates of economic growth conceal the pockets of poverty within a country. The question then is: Is the process of economic development selective and, Why are there imbalances in regional growth?

To discuss such issues will lead one beyond the scope of this particular chapter, but Dorner's concern is that land tenure arrangements are most immediately and directly associated with income distribution. He maintains that the output, i.e., GNP, concept of development does not ordinarily include income distribution consequences of the development process.

Dorner equates skewed distribution of land ownership with skewed income distribution. Substantial numbers of agricultural laborers, poor peasants, and tenants, do nonfarm work. But considering that apart, Dorner still states that a skewed distribution of incomes leads to conspicuous consumption on the part of high income recipients and consequently high rates of savings and investment are not achieved. If peasants can get a *little* more income and a secure expectation that their efforts can yield them more in the future, this can have a significant impact on demand. He thus switches over to secure expectation from income distribution.

The absence of high rates of savings and investment generation may be because the inducements or rewards to investments either in agriculture or outside that sector are insufficient. Conspicuous consumption may then be a result of absence of opportunities of investment.

There is great merit in Dorner's observation that land tenure arrangements are given only passing mention in much of the economic literature on development. Owen has contended that such questions as land tenure, etc., can be approached with a new sense of their relevance to the overall process of economic growth.

Schultz also has observed that attention focused on land reforms hitherto has been mainly social or political. What is required is a study of the economics of land reform. Dorner readily sees the connection between land tenure institutions and economic development when the latter is conceived of as the development of opportunities and human capacities. Yang, in his current work relating to socioeconomic results of the land reform in Taiwan, mentions that one of the aims of land reform is to raise what he calls farmers' "hopefulness towards the future of life." Such factors may be invisible and imponderable but are important. Since land reform is a reform in institutional arrangement, it should not be judged merely with the yardstick of increases in agricultural production. It builds a base—institutional base—for such increases in production later. Like irrigation projects, land reform also has a long gestation period. Its performance should be judged over time.

That tenure arrangements are of critical importance in determining agricultural development no one would dispute. Difficulties are felt, however, when it is put to test with empirical data.

Dorner's sweep, i.e., taking the entire topic and trying to be provocative, is due to the absence of material, absence of data to put observations to scientific test. Those of us working in land reform have been repeatedly asking the question, Has land reform increased agricultural production? We are not able to provide answers. Why this state of affairs? It is because people have discussed land reform in the social and political context rather than in terms of economics. Hence, literature on land reform is full of emotion.

The experience in India might be cited. As a result of work initiated by the National Planning Commission, studies were initiated in different states, in 1955 (most land laws were put into action in 1948) to find "the economic and social effects of land reforms." What a big order!

A 10 percent sample of plots and a 10 percent sample of cultivators in selected villages were taken. Material was collected on changes in agrarian structures, purchase and sale of land, terms of tenancy including effectiveness of rent, and regulations of tenancy, etc. As for effects on agricultural production, these studies threw no new light. But these reports had policy impacts as they revealed ineffective implementation of land laws, evasions, and landlord-tenant collusions, etc. Thus, what started as studies in social and economic effects of land legislations revealed the serious ineffectiveness of their implementations. As a result, loopholes in laws were plugged. Nevertheless, the studies failed to answer the question—Has land reform led to an increase in agricultural production in a causal sense?

Variables are many and the task is difficult. The thought being developed now is to approach the problem in a simpler way—via investments. Has there been more investment in agriculture in rural areas, as a result of land reform? Observations based on the above findings suggest there has been a spurt in investments in the rural areas as a consequence of land reforms, particularly in the Zamindari areas in India. Work at the moment is in a crude stage, but refinements may be developed later. A proper methodology for the study of land reform is needed. It is good to have worldwide experience on this. More interest, not less, is needed in the study of land reforms.

In his second section Dorner cites five policy issues that are influenced directly or indirectly by the land tenure institutions. These are (1) Income distribution and demand consequences, (2) Economic and political power distribution, (3) Investments in agriculture and supply-consequences, (4) Investments in other sections of the economy, and (5) Premature farm to city migration. Unfortunately, Dorner has drawn on the experience of the United States and U.S.S.R. for points 4 and 5 above. Then relevance of such experience to developing economies is projected.

Dorner advances a thesis that economic and political power are positively related to income levels. As an economist, one may analyze what are the factors that give the landlord, for example, economic power. Why are there landlord-tenant collusions in evasion of law that seeks to protect the economic interests of the tenant; why does a tenant (in fact a tenant) declare himself a wage earner although he continues to work on the same terms as before? What compels him to accept a position on the lower rung of the agricultural ladder? Why is minimum wage legislation in agriculture throughout most of the world difficult to enforce?

One needs to take into account the realities of agriculture and ask: Does the legislation stipulate an artificial price for a factor tenant? This is a crucial issue full of policy implications. More debate in the form of economic analysis on such evasions is called for. Within tenure arrangements one needs to inquire what institutional arrangements have hindered economic development. Not all share the belief that people from rural areas or from agriculture flock to cities or to the fringe of modern cities where there is no opportunity at all. For a migrant there are inconveniences and personal difficulties in integrating himself into a new environment. But he does this because he expects new opportunities to develop.

Some remarks are finally offered on investments in agriculture and investments in other sectors of the economy. Land tenure institutions are significant in that they determine who controls investment decisions. Allocation of resources depends not only upon market prices but also on various institutional arrangements which determine how much incentive they offer and to whom. Hence, the system of land tenure has a particularly decisive role to play. For example, a landlord is interested in maintaining the fertility of the soil over time whereas his tenant is interested in getting the maximum out of the soil he rents during the particular year.

The other aspect concerns what incentives tenure arrangements provide for: (1) current investment, and (2) future investment. The landlord buys a piece of land and he makes a future investment; the tenant buys machinery, he makes a current investment. Does the tenure arrangement provide incentives to the landlord to improve his land and buildings? What is necessary for the tenure arrangement to provide a climate favorable to make such investments which may lead to higher forms of production?

Dorner has correctly put it: Is it possible to devise leasing arrangements that create about the same security of expectations for tenants as an owner-operator system? Dorner feels such arrangements are seldom found in the developing countries. But the Bombay Tenancy Act of 1948 confers the title of "Protected Tenant" who has almost the same security as an owner-operator. However, one might again emphasize that providing a legal framework does not take one far, except for its enabling provisions. A climate of economic opportunity must prevail.

Agricultural production is highly decentralized implying decentralized decision making. There are large opportunities for investments in the farm sector—both private and public investments—in developing countries.

DISCUSSION by WILLIAM H. NICHOLLS

THERE IS MUCH in Dorner's paper with which one can agree in principle and, had he wished to do so, he could have found a number of statements quite congruent with his in some of my own earlier writings. As applied to many severely overpopulated and land scarce countries of Asia, there are a number of his generalizations with which one can still agree. With reference to Latin America, however, my recent eighteen months of intimate observation of, and detailed research on, the agriculture of Brazil has forced me to substantially revise my previous appraisal, at least for countries like Brazil where land scarcity and overpopulation are still not yet pressing problems. Out of this experience, I have become (much to my own surprise) quite convinced that, in Brazil at least, land reform ranks very low in the priorities for sound public policy and that indeed it would probably do more harm than good.

Before trying to support this revised view, let me say at the outset that, had Brazilian land settlement been more equalitarian at the outset, Brazil would probably be more developed economically and politically today. It is conceivable that, had Brazil (like Mexico) instituted a land reform fifty or more years ago—before the agriculture of the more advanced countries had undergone its modern technological revolution and before Brazil had entered its recent era of rapid industrial urban development, bringing a comparable modernization of its own agriculture well within the realm of possibility—it might be better off today. Nonetheless, since evolution is much more consistent than revolution with the Brazilian national character—with its remarkable spirit of moderation and accommodation in race relationships and in social and political institutions—even this is by no means certain. In any case, Brazil has been relatively free of the more extreme abuses of landlord-tenant relationships and, despite a history dominated by a traditional and status-ridden agrarian system, has increasingly shown a degree of vertical social mobility that is making its urban *and rural* societies more open and fluid than is commonly recognized.

One can find in Brazil much to support Dorner's concern about premature mass rural-urban migration. The relatively low farm wage rates within fifty to one hundred miles of the city of São Paulo offer a striking example of the lack of adequate nonfarm job opportunities. However, I am unwilling to accept the view that the best solution under Brazilian conditions is to fix "millions of rural people . . . to viable opportunities on the land." The reasons are several. First, for one more generation, Brazil will have agricultural frontiers where farm people can markedly improve their incomes by rural to rural migration. While well-conceived public colonization schemes on these frontiers have much to recommend them, the Brazilian government's past performance in this area gives little reason to expect much from such policies. Second, given Brazil's rapid rate of industrialization during the last two decades and the market potential of its large population, there is reason to hope that nonagricultural job opportunities will continue to expand at a fairly satisfactory pace. Here, much depends upon the extent to which the government's public industrialization policy henceforth gives greater weight to promoting those industries which offer larger employment opportunities, which better serve mass markets, and which provide more adequate supplies of modern agricultural inputs, all at a higher level of efficiency and lower prices. Third, there is much evidence that industrial-urban development, initially within the state of São Paulo but increasingly within the whole south of Brazil, is having very favorable effects on farm labor productivity and agricultural incomes, although cash-wage farm workers have not yet benefited much because of the continuing large in-migration from the less advantaged Northeast. Under these circumstances, it would appear to be more desirable to continue the present public emphasis on industrial development than to divert efforts to land reform or other policies which, in fixing men to the land at the present level of a hoe technology, will create an important barrier to the modernization of agriculture, now clearly under way in every region whose favorable location or improving transportation facilities gives it access to burgeoning urban markets.

Given Brazil's still plentiful land supply, moderate population density, and its increasingly dynamic economy, its need for land reform can hardly be equated with that of India, Korea, or Bolivia. Brazil still does not face a serious problem of feeding its rapidly increasing total and urban populations. During the last fifteen to twenty years, with population increasing at 3 to 3.5 percent (and urban population at 5 to 6 percent) per year, Brazilian agriculture has been able to expand its crop production sufficiently (largely through the use of more land) to supply the major stable foods (beans are the principal exception) at declining relative prices. Only its livestock sector has fallen behind, with rising relative prices reflecting the greater managerial complexities of expanding milk, pork, and poultry and egg production and the extremely high income elasticities of demand for these more expensive foods. While this relatively favorable situation leaves no grounds for complacency, there is no reason for agriculture to become a serious bottleneck in Brazilian economic development if the government at last does its part in supplying the public agricultural services and modern agricultural inputs at remunerative prices for which Brazil's larger farmers are increasingly eager, particularly in the South but to a growing extent even in the Northeast.

Since Brazil's medium-to-large landowners are presently at the forefront of modernizing agriculture, such improved agricultural services must of necessity initially concentrate upon this sector of agriculture, although the beneficial effects on production and efficiency will be increasingly felt by smaller farmers as well. Dorner also recognizes that such "supporting services . . . can be provided more easily in dealing with a smaller number of decision making units," but finds that "this simply delays, but does not eliminate, the need for positive steps to provide more viable opportunities for the large rural masses. . . ." Accepting his addendum as I do, however, does not commit me to the particular policy of agrarian reform—with its inherent difficulties compounded by the weakness and incompetence of Brazilian public administration. Land reform would appear to be far less appropriate than the use of scarce public resources, both financial and administrative, for improved rural education and health and for a more adequate infrastructure in terms of transportation, energy, and further industrial development.

Modernization of Brazilian agriculture does not, of course, imply primary emphasis upon mechanization although certain regions of the South which have substantially mechanized their crop production appear not yet to have carried too far (from the standpoint of efficiency) the substitution of machinery for labor, even at present low farm-wage rates. At the same time, by causing large landowners to operate their property as a single unit with cash-wage labor instead of using sharecroppers and *moradores,* mechanization has frequently not only reduced agricultural employment but also the status and average incomes of farm workers in the South, as compared with that found in the more traditional and labor intensive agriculture of the Northeast. In any case, quite apart from mechanization (the efficient use of which requires larger land holdings), there are many modern agricultural inputs which can benefit the small owner-operator and sharecropper as well as the larger farmer, although the latter is most likely to serve in the local agricultural community as the innovator whose successful use of new agricultural inputs leads to their more generalized adoption.

While such an argument turns on the availability of such progressive and profit motivated large landholders, no part of Brazil where market opportunities exist is lacking such landholders, all of the folklore about the dominance of the parasitic *latifundiario* to the contrary notwithstanding. Nor should too much yet be made of Brazil's very low crop yields, given its relative abundance of land. It should be noted that the index of crop yields in the United States was virtually constant during 1910–1939. As the relationships between the prices of farm products, land, and yield-increasing agricultural inputs become more favorable to the use of land-saving inputs, Brazilian farmers will certainly move rapidly in this direction if they also have improved technical orientation about the effective and efficient use of these new inputs. Much of the present agricultural problem of Brazil exists because the best of its farmers, already far ahead of the ability of the government to supply such technical orientation, are having to deal with increasingly complex production decisions on a haphazard and often ineffective empirical basis.

Thus, to defend Brazil's larger farmers is, in my opinion, the result of the necessity of starting where its agrarian structure now stands rather than starting from a more equalitarian structure which both Dorner and I would have preferred to find. At the same time—thanks in considerable part to Brazil's rapidly improving highway network and its growing industrial-urban development—Brazil's larger farmers are not nearly as bad as commonly depicted while (particularly given the public neglect of agricultural services) most of its family farms hardly inspire great enthusiasm or homage. Under these circumstances, there are tenant families who, even when free land is available close by, choose to stay as croppers on large properties—apparently because the latter gives them greater social amenities; greater security of processing facilities, markets, and credit; and often (through cash-wage labor for the landlord's account) supplementary employment to round out their annual crop incomes. Another striking phenomenon is the extent to which small landowners, with enough family workers to meet most of their labor requirements, choose instead to hire their labor at the cost of a substantial reduction in their relatively low family incomes. Such phenomena reflect how unfavorable is the cultural environment for a viable family-farm structure in Brazil.

To be sure, particularly in the two southernmost states of Rio Grande do Sul and Santa Catarina, one can find areas characterized by many family farms whose operators are usually the descendants of German and Italian immigrants of 1850–1880. These family farms have furnished the southern cities with a more than proportionate number of successful migrants and the southwestern agricultural frontiers with many successful (now often large) farmers. Even so, for those who have remained behind, several generations of large families have taken a severe toll in the size of landholding and in economic well-being, indicating the ephemeral benefits of small landholdings (even in a more favorable cultural environment) when rural education and public agricultural services remain largely neglected. Their experience suggests that, without concomitant public services, land reform is likely to be very ineffective; while, with adequate public services and continued industrial-urban development, land reform can easily become a major impediment to agricultural modernization and general economic development.

By now I should have made clear my own position that, to a large extent, the issue in Brazilian agriculture is indeed a choice between equity and productivity and that, if this is an oversimplification, it is not very much of one. But, Dorner answers, attention must be given to distribution as well as to production, not only for reasons of equity but also because a less skewed income distribution will itself contribute to increased production and accelerated economic development. While admitting this, I question whether—given Brazil's plentiful land supply and increasingly dynamic economy—the solution to the equity problem any longer lies *within* the agricultural sector.

Dorner's argument to the contrary runs as follows. Given a very skewed distribution of land ownership and a relatively slow rate of growth in nonfarm employment, most rural workers have only a very meager and insecure income which is constantly pressed down by abundant labor supplies. The concentration of agricultural wealth leads to land tenure institutions which produce a highly skewed income distribution within the agricultural sector. The rural masses are desperately poor and poor people are poor customers. If the rich landholders saved and invested more of their high incomes instead of engaging in conspicuous consumption, there might be sufficient economic development to justify their position of wealth. Even if they do invest, however, they may invest too little in agriculture, particularly since general developmental objectives require keeping the terms of trade unfavorable to that sector. Furthermore, economic power carries with it political power, which the rich landholders use to prevent paying their share of the funds needed for supporting the outlays for social overhead, so badly lacking to the rural poor, or for financing industrial urban development. Thus, economic underdevelopment is a consequence of institutional underdevelopment, which takes its most serious form in the structure and land tenure arrangements of the agricultural sector.

During most of Brazilian history, Dorner's statement is a rather accurate picture of what actually happened. However, it becomes a caricature of the state of São Paulo since 1900 and of most of southern Brazil since 1950, and is beginning to be much less accurate than was once true even for the Northeast as urbanization and the elimination of age-old barriers to communication are proceeding apace. São Paulo's phenomenal industrial-urban development was built upon the fabulous wealth which a large-scale, well-managed, and highly capitalized coffee agriculture created. Not only were agricultural savings large (in spite of a modicum but not extreme amount of conspicuous consumption) but they found their way into investment first in further agricultural development but increasingly in industrial-urban development as well. If a more equitable income distribution was slow to come in the rural sector (primarily because of the almost inexhaustible supply of labor flowing in from the rest of the country), many enterprising rural workers were ultimately able to achieve considerable wealth as landowners or to join the rapidly growing urban middle classes. While this industrial-urban development was stimulating further agricultural development into an ever-widening periphery of neighboring states, it was also increasingly undermining the political power of the landed classes in favor of a new industrial-commercial urban elite. In the process, spreading from the center, public investments in higwhays, education, and other social overhead have at last begun to grow; more effective collection of taxes on rural properties and income is finally being achieved; and other public policies have been increasingly successful in capturing agricultural surpluses for diversion to industrial development well beyond those already coming on a voluntary basis.

By now, therefore, land tenure is not a major policy need in the south of Brazil, even though the cash-wage worker, rural even more than urban, has thus far borne the brunt of the developmental squeeze. Curiously enough, the more traditional land tenure system of the Northeast, so often condemned by agrarian reformists, has actually offered greater protection to tenant families who—deriving most of their income in kind and paying lower land rents than one would expect under the circumstances—have a built-in hedge against inflation which the cash-wage farm workers of the South lack. While it was clearly the intent of Brazilian public policy since 1950 to squeeze the incomes of large landowners and other farm operators as well, this objective was largely frustrated by the revival of coffee price-support policies and—because too little of the captured developmental resources was returned to agriculture for purposes of raising the productivity of the domestic food sector—the recent turn in the terms of trade in favor of (particularly livestock) food producers. As an offsetting factor, however, the more progressive farmers—with their rapidly increasing dependence on purchased modern agricultural inputs—have faced a growing cost-price squeeze, which has reduced their savings and their incentive to invest any savings in agricultural improvements, while confirming the wisdom of the less progressive farmers' preference for sticking to less risky traditional techniques which keep agricultural productivity low.

Thus, there is an urgent need for current Brazilian public policy to give greater attention to agriculture, both directly in the form of greater price and credit incentives and much improved technical assistance and indirectly through industrialization policies which better serve agriculture's requirements for more nonfarm employment and cheaper manufactured production goods. By such policies, the increasing dynamism of the Brazilian economy and continued general economic growth can be preserved, with land tenure institutions adjusting to changing economic conditions in an evolutionary way— a way much more congruent with present and prospective realities and the achievement of a modern and efficient agricultural economy than a diversionary and disruptive land reform policy would be, at this stage of Brazilian economic history.

3

FACTOR MARKETS

LAWRENCE WITT

THE ROLE of factor market institutions in agricultural development in the developing nations is linked with factors and institutions that assist in the intensification of agriculture, rather than with those that facilitate an expansion in land area. This intensification derives mainly from the increased use of nonfarm produced inputs, for reasons that will be developed shortly.

The institutions and factors will be discussed under the following categories: (1) The creation of new inputs, (2) The development of supportive infrastructure, (3) The operation of the agricultural labor market, and (4) Institutions and policies to facilitate the intensification of agriculture.

These categories will be related to the process of agricultural development. Space does not permit much exploration of the patterns of social relationships which these institutions provide, stimulate, or control; nor does this chapter go very far in suggesting the pattern of human relationships that these institutions should stimulate.[1] Instead, the assignment is to describe the kinds of institutions that exist, how they contribute to development, and some strengths and weaknesses.

Credit institutions, part of the infrastructure, can facilitate and lack of credit can inhibit the use of new inputs, but Jones deals with credit institutions subsequently.

Finally, the specific literature on factor market institutions is more limited than controversial. Thus, to incorporate controversy, as requested, some contemporary views on agricultural development are presented here. The limited work on factor markets in develop-

---

[1] The author is indebted to Al Schmid for pressing him some distance in this direction, following his reading of a draft. The author also appreciates the suggestions of Carl Eicher and Refugio Rochin.

ing countries should not be surprising, since, in commenting on factor market research in the United States since 1950, Schuh writes:

> The need for research on agricultural factor markets became increasingly important as agriculture evolved from an almost complete dependence on resources available either within the farm family or produced on the farm itself, to an increasing dependence on inputs produced in the nonfarm sector. (21)

Purchased inputs have only recently become of some importance in developing nations.

FRAMEWORK OF ANALYSIS

Agricultural leaders in developing countries have been prone to emphasize a particular item as the strategic factor or missing link. They sought to stimulate agricultural development by land settlement, or by land reform, or by creating an extension service, or through irrigation, or by agricultural mechanization, etc. Typically, until recently, leadership did not try to use a number of these tools jointly, perhaps influenced also by the low priority they attached to agricultural development. Fortunately, such oversimplifications are less prevalent today, although by no means absent.

Agricultural advisers from the United States, or other developed nations, often have erred in assuming the presence of a number of agricultural institutions similar to those at home. Thus, they concentrated on developing or improving a few institutions in which they had competence, with limited attention to the availability of other inputs, complementary and infrastructure institutions, and so on. Yet the absence of this complex of institutions often causes slow rates of growth in agriculture.

More recently, domestic and international leadership recognize the need for a complex of interrelated activities. This awareness led to the development of a number of lists or packages of necessary conditions, as suggested in the United States AID-MIT seminar (10).

Such lists can be long to include sociopolitical as well as economic factors; they can include environmental facilitators as well as essential elements; they can be comprehensive to apply to all countries or they can concentrate on the needed additions in one or a few closely related countries. For my thinking in recent years the following list has been used as a first approximation. Subheadings are required when applying this to a specific country.

1. Sufficient law and order and personal security to provide a basis for normal agricultural investment decisions.

2. A fund of adapted research knowledge which can enhance the productivity of agriculture.
3. A communication system which transmits this knowledge to the farm decision maker.
4. The availability at the proper place and time of the inputs necessary to apply this knowledge.
5. Credit at reasonable rates compared with the productivity of the added inputs.
6. A rural situation which provides sufficient incentives so that the decision maker who takes the risk of an innovation benefits from a favorable result.
7. Adequate markets for the products at reasonable prices.

Note the use of such normative language as "sufficient," "reasonable," and "adequate." The viewpoint of the farm decision maker is determinant in deciding whether the interest rate is reasonable, the markets adequate, and the incentives sufficient.

Current efforts to increase the rate of agricultural development lead to a desire to identify practical, not too complex, meaningful activities. Hsieh and Ruttan note: "A new consensus seems to be emerging that intensive investment in research and development . . . represents the missing link. . . ." (13) The testimony of Schultz and Hardin to Congress in 1966 on the need for new research institutions and a vastly increased flow of adaptive research supports this view; the Ford-Rockefeller activity in creating new tropical agricultural research institutions reflects this view. Continuing, Hsieh and Ruttan warn that:

> There is danger that these insights may be contributing to a new set of oversimplifications . . . evidence presented in this paper emphasizes the essential complementarity between (a) increased investment in research and development leading to higher rates of return on purchased inputs, (b) increased investment in land and water development, and (c) improved institutional and organizational systems for providing technical inputs and services to farmers.

Thus, a complex of conditions stimulates agricultural development.

ROLE OF FACTOR MARKET INSTITUTIONS IN A DEVELOPMENT PLAN

What influence should factor market institutions make upon the economic development of agriculture? Clearly the normative answer is that they should stimulate and facilitate expansion (efficiently, it is hoped). During the early period of agricultural development, expansion in land area usually is central to the expansion of agricultural production.[2] As the majority of the productive land is occupied, the important current problem for most countries becomes: How can the existing agricultural land, labor, and capital be used to increase the volume of production? Clearly this means intensification, in the sense of more product per unit of land, as much and preferably more product per unit of labor, and more capital per acre and per man. In most cases, capital within agriculture will increase, and much of it will become indistinguishable from land; but also, capital devoted to producing inputs for agriculture will increase in the nonfarm economy. The larger volume of purchased inputs will carry a larger value equivalent of imbedded capital. Some will incorporate adapted research and human capital; hence many of these will be new inputs, at least for many farmers. For such reasons, factor markets in the main should stimulate and facilitate intensification.

Some inputs used in intensification will be derived from other parts of the agricultural sector, such as improved seeds, livestock, and feed. Farm labor can increase as population grows, or be used more fully during off seasons. Their regular tasks may be restructured to make labor more productive, though Schultz argues that existing resources are efficiently organized within the present knowledge framework (22).

Two prominent characteristics emphasize the role of factor market institutions which provide nonfarm produced inputs:

1. The combination of rapid population growth and rapid urbanization and industrialization implies an explosive rate of growth in the flow of products from farm to city (24). To provide this increased flow of food with a smaller proportion of the total manpower requires intensification, almost certainly with a substantial expansion in the use of nonfarm produced inputs.[3] Thus, an important part of the question becomes: How can the institutions in the factor market be created, changed, or stimulated to increase the use of mainly nonfarm produced inputs?
2. The paucity of factor market institutions which provide nonfarm inputs is more than evident in the developing countries.

Ruttan emphasizes this need when he writes:

> It seems incredible in an economy in which Coca-Cola can be purchased in almost every sari-sari store in the most remote barrio that agricultural chemicals such as Cyano-gas (for rat poison) are only in-

---

[2] In some developing countries significant increases in production continue to depend upon an expansion in land area (6).
[3] Urbanization also requires a substantial increase in transportation and marketing facilities, since a larger share of the total produce must be moved from farm to city.

termittently available in the municipal center near the nation's leading agricultural college. (20)

This situation is repeated time and again in other parts of the developing world; however, even when such inputs are locally available, the response in farmer purchase and use is often disappointing. Demand for such inputs needs to be created, before a substantial improvement can be expected in the factor market institutions that distribute many of the nonfarm inputs. Obviously the two are interacting. With this, attention is turned to the institutions relevant for the four categories of inputs identified in the opening paragraph.

INSTITUTIONS DEVELOPING NEW INPUTS

What are the relevant institutions in this area? This list includes a variety of government research organizations in the developing countries. Many are organized with a fairly straightforward, single-minded research mission, separated in function and distant from extension, teaching, or the production of inputs. In others, research is a subsidiary function, carried on by a public action agency.

Research activities by private agencies are significant only in a few countries but have some importance in many additional countries. Some public minded businessmen support research because they believe privately supported research can be more effective than (in their view) existing public institutions. More often, private research is associated with large scale agriculture or processing firms (United Fruit, pineapples in Hawaii, tobacco companies in Sudan and Nigeria, sugar cane and rubber in several countries). Only occasionally but increasingly, private research attempts to produce a saleable product (input to agriculture). Foundation operated research is placed in a separate category.

Public research institutions dot the landscape of the developing countries. National, state, even local, they usually are small in size, low in quality, and have a limited scope. In numbers, they are too many, considering the present level of research investment. Few are well financed, well staffed, with relevant and imaginative research programs. More commonly the program is routine, repetitive, and unduly narrow; the results are inadequately analyzed, unpublished, and not carried to completion by testing in actual farming.

For many analysts of development, the functioning of the research and related communicating institutions is central to the entire agricultural development process. They argue that realistic, adapted research which creates the knowledge base for new inputs, new input complexes, and new flows of income over time is far more productive than marginal increments in capital equipment, irrigation water, or improvements in prices or reduced marketing costs. This view is widely accepted. But this is broader than the view that it constitutes *the* central feature.

In practical development operations, increased emphasis on research is not fully operative, partly because of lags in adjusting from earlier priorities for other instruments of development, partly the inevitable slowness of the research process, and partly the difficulties in implementing programs to utilize knowledge. As Glenn Johnson has pointed out (15), knowledge eventually must be reflected in the inputs. Only then can it affect the production function.

The existing agriculture requires certain kinds of studies, e.g., the response of domestically consumed commodities over a wide range of fertilizer applications. Yet, research administrators are pressured by political leaders and their own socioeconomic environment for research to create the base for a new export crop which diversifies the economy, and increases the earnings of foreign exchange. Often these become long range commitments, yet never actually attain their economic objectives despite high quality technical research. One can argue that such research is related to the needs of the country, as seen by one reference group. Yet looking back after ten or fifteen years, the research on new products often was not productive and did not contribute to agricultural development. The supply and demand for agricultural research never intersected. For example, the excellent research station at Campinas, Brazil developed projects on cotton in the early twenties, but none on coffee until sometime in the forties. Brazil lost position in the world coffee markets but gained position in world cotton markets at a time when the bottom fell out of the coffee market. Here, one can argue the validity of cotton over coffee research, at least, after the fact. However, other research on potential export crops, still not produced in the state, clearly represents a frittering away of research resources on low priority projects, no matter what reference group is considered. Similar examples in other Latin American countries could be cited.

In a related connection, Eicher points out for Nigeria (3) that several export crops provide substantial economic potential, especially if export taxes are made less onerous. But:

> Turning to domestic food production, virtually token efforts have been devoted to research on domestic food crops; *there are no available research findings for any crop which will increase yields by as much as 25 per cent.*

Eicher endorses this strategy of emphasizing research on exports, since no internal food problem exists;[4] but one should hasten to add that he is considering research on actual exports, not on aspired export

---

[4] Excluding the food problems in Biafra.

products. One is tempted to compare the known production potentials with those suggested by Johnston (16) for Japan and Taiwan at comparable periods in their agricultural history, but this draws attention too far into the discussion of products rather than factors.

Thus, much agricultural research effort is devoted to minor products and possible exotic exports and too little to domestic food and current exports in many developing countries (and is not absent in the developed nations). Herdt and Mellor (12) in an analysis of rice response to fertilizer, suggest that biological and physical conditions do not explain the differences in returns, and recommend that research to raise and extend the production function has a good chance for success.

Substantial international funds are now devoted to strengthening agricultural institutions, although this emphasis by the United States is relatively new. The colonial powers of the past created these institutions in various parts of the world, and they persist in various stages of excellence in present-day Indonesia, Malaysia, Nigeria, Ghana, and elsewhere. For Latin America, the United States rubber development program in 1940, the complementary crops program of the USDA in 1942, and the War II activities of the Coordinator of Inter-American Affairs gave some attention to agricultural institutional development. Later, under Point IV, agriculture received substantial emphasis. Still, in 1966, Schultz, referring to Latin America said, "Not a single first-rate agricultural research center was developed by this program." (23) Perhaps the record is different in Asia and Africa. But in fact, much of the United States Government effort has strengthened teaching institutions, a point of view with substantial merit, but also a difficult way to restructure the research institutions, if this is what is needed.

The approach of the Rockefeller Foundation, now joined by the Ford Foundation with modifications, reflects a view that much research is needed, built from the beginning around the idea of creating productive new inputs. In Mexico, Chile, Philippines, Colombia, and Nigeria, new research institutions have been created through international funding, utilizing a variety of nationals, and dedicated to providing inputs useful in a number of countries. The international character of the new institution was evident from the beginning for the last three countries, but the institution in Mexico, originating with a national focus, became internationally significant only as the new dwarf wheats provided dramatic improvements in wheat yields for Pakistan and India. Such improved crop varieties have created new hope that adequate world food supplies can be produced.

Clearly, within the established areas of work, those institutions have been strikingly successful in creating productive new inputs (improved varieties, highly responsive to applications of fertilizer and water). Could the same scientists have made similar breakthroughs with similar continuity of effort, working in one or another national research institution? Certainly part of the success is due to the long time staff and continuity of research effort, not readily obtained in the periodically buffetted ICA-AID programs, nor in most of the purely national research institutions staffed by national scientists.

The international private commercial sector also conducts research on new inputs. The first effort may come when a disease like Sigatoka threatens to destroy the production of a major article of international commerce (bananas), and as a variety of testing, spray programs, and other techniques are studied in an effort to maintain production. Or, the research may start in an effort to test United States developed inputs in another environment (Dow-agricultural chemicals) leading perhaps to adaptive research to make the product more useful and acceptable in another country. Or, the incentive may be to produce an internal raw material (tobacco) for a new industry. The research projects developing from such activities tend to be rather specialized. Still, in view of the existing limitations of other research institutions, may this particular institutional complex provide additional leverage?

Thus, new inputs for agriculture may be provided by domestic or international, public or private, institutions. In recent years international public and private institutions have increased in importance and in accomplishment. The allocation of research resources within and among the several research institutions is substantially less than ideal. True, the estimation of the likely productivity of research expenditures is a difficult task, fraught with uncertainties; nonetheless, substantial improvements could be made in the allocation. The argument for adaptive research appears valid, that is, for investment in research which carries a possible innovation to the point where it is a profitable and readily applied innovation for the farmer. But the basic innovation must come first. The creation of this combination of applied research and new inputs which embody a meaningful new stream of income, represents a major challenge to the research institutions in the developing world. Existing institutions must become more effective to meet the development.

THE SUPPORTIVE INFRASTRUCTURE INSTITUTIONS

Input creation is not enough; it must be used if it is to contribute to agricultural development. The arguments for adaptive research claim that efforts to induce improvements in farming fail because little information in the pipeline between research and application can really be applied. But also, when new productive factors are created they make an impact only as such inputs become available at the time and place when needed. What institutions are required? What is their character?

Clearly, marketing institutions need to move sprays, fertilizers, new seed varieties, insecticides, and pesticides from import ports, factories, or seed houses to locations close to farmers. Such institutions are increasing in number and effectiveness. In some countries new inputs are making a real impact upon the intensification of agricultural production. In others, institution building still requires a policy decision on the degree of public and private activity, and the extent to which the function is part of a multipurpose institution or a specialized institution. A few examples of alternative approaches are cited below.

The provision of inputs as a function of the Caja Agraria in Colombia (a semipublic credit agency) did make these inputs widely available through the rural sector. However, the associated educational program on the functions of new inputs was not adequately implemented. In contrast, a comprehensive blending of credit, extension, sale of inputs, and purchase of output program in the Taiwan Farmers' Associations did meet with substantial success, even though the extension agents were appendages and were used for other functions when the need arose (27). This was, and is, a package program.

Direct operation of input marketing by the Ministry of Agriculture, through extension, has not been a resounding success. But the explanation may lie in the administration of the extension program, such as low salary levels, quality of personnel, the lack of adequate local transportation, concepts of function, etc., rather than with the specific organizational location of the marketing function.

The development of special-purpose private institutions to manufacture and wholesale new nonfarm inputs undoubtedly is easier than the creation of distributing institutions in the rural sector, particularly if communication to farmers is a significant part of the task. The initial small sales volume is easier to resolve if there is reason to expect volume to grow rapidly. For a small market, the addition of a line of products to existing distribution channels would be preferred, but with the risk that local managers will not invest sufficient time in the learning-teaching function, and will concentrate upon regular activities for most of their volume.

Specially created public institutions to distribute inputs can be subsidized while the learning process is proceeding, provided responsible officials are prepared to live with financial losses for the necessary time interval. But, in future governmental reorganizations, likely, most single-purpose institutions will be reorganized into multipurpose organizations, unless fairly early success is attained.

Thus, in the real developing world, distribution through multipurpose institutions has more likelihood of survival in the short run, whether public or private, if the demand for new inputs is limited.

Special effort will be necessary, however, to insure adequate attention to this process.

On public versus private efforts, there is some question whether indigenous entrepreneurship with capital exists in the near rural environment. The Pakistan experience (7), when water pumps were made a function of the private sector, demonstrates that both entrepreneurship and the ability to repair, quickly became available. The Nigerian poultry experience, although related to the product (1), also indicates that entrepreneurship is available, can marshall capital, can be drawn into government sponsored training programs, and can be given a significant technical ability.

One needs also to recall that much agricultural development, some of it utilizing new inputs, did occur in the preorganized development period. For example, the small farmers in West Africa expanded the production of cocoa, peanuts, and other exports rapidly between 1900 and 1940, without an extensive network of development institutions. Labor was switched from leisure to clearing the land under the stimulation of a profitable export market. Transportation and marketing improvements were the major changes, once the idea of producing cocoa had been imported (3). There were few institutional changes.

Probably the major infrastructure institutions in most of the tropical world are those dealing with the distribution of water. Two types of institutions are required. The first is the complex of engineers and construction activity that designs and builds the dam and develops the primary canals. A major one-shot investment is made over a period of years. Typically, a second separate institution has responsibility for the construction of the secondary canals and operation of the total structure.

In Turkey, the first institution commands high prestige and substantial funds. Consequently, water behind some recently completed dams cannot be distributed to farmers; the distributive system may not even be on the drawing boards. Pump irrigation usually does not require such massive capital investments; it too requires a distribution system, but of a different kind from the large-scale irrigation project. The institutions relevant to each water utilization operation will now be examined.

The distribution of impounded water to farmers represents a moderately sophisticated series of activities. Farmers, along the canals, need to know when the water will be available. A sufficient head of water must be maintained, the water must be available at proper intervals to maintain crop growth, and excessive water and evaporation which leads to salt accumulation should be avoided. With rice, a continuous supply of water is required but wastage should be avoided. There seems to be no reason for an overflow of water into wasteland or drainage areas. A frequent complaint is that the farmers closer to the source take most of the water, so that farmers near the end of the canal face great uncertainty in water supplies, despite overall adequacy. More important, to use the larger and more certain water effectively, other changes are needed. For example, the Technical Subcommittee on Water and Land, part of the Panel on World Food Supply, writes:

> In many developing countries, the bringing of costly irrigation water has failed to increase crop production and in some cases, has actually decreased it, because of failure to recognize that water is but *one* of the essential inputs for successful agriculture. After the lack of adequate water is eliminated by irrigation, many other factors may then limit yields. For example, . . . unless the supply of plant nutrients is soon increased, yields are liable to fall back to previous levels or to decline below them as the hitherto unused reserves of nutrients in the soil are exhausted. . . . (19)

Thus, the distributor of water should allocate the water equitably, and communicate information on using the water effectively. Yet neither task is well performed. Why not?

One possible improvement is to develop appropriate charges for water. Actual charges vary greatly. In some countries no charges are assessed; the water is a stimulus to agriculture, paid for out of tax funds. Farmers are not encouraged by water charges to use any economizing function; nor does the cost of water operate to induce an intensification in order to pay the bills. Not surprisingly, the expansion in productivity often is less than programmed by the agricultural technicians. In other cases, a flat charge for water is assessed; again no economizing function is encouraged, but higher costs may support a shift to higher value crops.

The Gezira scheme in Sudan operates a sophisticated distribution system. In essence, the farmer, the water distribution institution, and local government are joint tenants. The water agency distributes inputs at no added cost and provides information. Payment is made on cotton, even though water is available and used for other crops. The farmer receives the entire value of the crops other than cotton. For cotton the distribution of returns is by formula, as follows (14):

Sudan Government	42 percent
Tenants	40 percent
Tenants Reserve Fund	2 percent*
Sudan Gezira Board	10 percent
Local Government	2 percent
Social Development Fund	2 percent

* This reserve for contingency goes to the tenant when the reserve reaches £S 25 per feddan.

This project distributes water to about 5 million feddan (1 feddan = 1.038 acres) and is generally conceded to be successful (18). Even so, there are problems. First, the 40 feddans originally allocated were too large for common practices, so that subleasing occurred. In later extensions the size was reduced. The share payment transfers some uncertainty to the water agency. Some smuggling of cotton reduces payments. Since 100 percent of some other crops is worth more than 40 percent of the cotton, farmers shift more land from cotton than would be warranted by gross output. More important, yields have remained virtually constant at a large bale per acre, despite (or because of) the provision of seed, fertilizer, pest control, financing, transport, ginning, baling, and marketing by the Gezira Board.[5]

Turning now to the institutions relevant in pump irrigation, Gotsch, after indicating that fertilizer and plant protection in West Pakistan increased substantially, goes on:

> The spearhead of the development activity, however, was in the water sector. A new technology for producing water, the tubewell, had been introduced. . . . Coupled with the example provided by several Government tubewell projects, these . . . wells were instrumental in initiating the diffusion of a technology that was to result in the installation of some 28,500 wells in the Punjab by 1964–65, an increase of 20 per cent over historical canal water supplies. (9)

Falcon and Gotsch (7) indicate that after considerable frustration at the slow rate of adoption of this new technology, a role in providing inputs was permitted for the private sector with appropriate facilitating commitments. An infrastructure of stores, repair shops, trained mechanics, and associated technical information developed rapidly. Capital to underwrite the costs of the wells and the infrastructure appeared. Tubewells and pumps made dramatic contributions to agricultural production. Gotsch indicates that the adoption of this new technology was extremely profitable with internal rates of return between 50 and 150 percent.

In the Comilla area the same basic irrigation experience occurred. But in this case cooperative efforts among farmers, the training of mechanics by the Development Training Center, and the development of a repair shop at the Center became the institutional vehicles. The extension and educational activity spearheaded by the Comilla Center was a vital factor insuring that crops and practices were adopted to use the water effectively (25).

Thus, supportive infrastructure institutions can have a substantial positive impact. Private entrepreneurship does respond to proper stimuli, and public institutions can be created to provide the necessary pattern of relationships. Yet some substantial operating institutions created some time ago do not provide sufficient support for further dynamic development in agriculture. Further analysis of the func-

---

[5] The author is indebted to Ahmed Abdulla Osman of the Sudan for some of these insights. For further discussion of policies in irrigation development, Thornton provides detailed economic analysis comparing such projects in Sudan and India (26).

tioning of such institutions may be a useful research investment and help make them more dynamic for future assistance programs.

FACTOR MARKET INSTITUTIONS FOR LABOR

Traditional agriculture applies much farm labor to agricultural land. Some characteristics of the institutional structure of this market seem important.

First, the so-called land tenure institutions are also human factor market institutions. They tie a certain amount of labor to a certain extension of land often defining part of the wage rate at the same time. Such arrangements probably reduce uncertainty for both parties. Equity is likely to be relatively unsatisfied. But the paternalism that is part of the system can also put the landowner in an unsatisfactory situation with respect to progress or growth. Within agriculture, the landowner escapes by trying to change the rules; the farm worker moves to town or to the frontier.

Second, seasonal labor requirements are met through a variety of streams of labor time: (a) the wives and children of the plantation workers are paid extra to participate during busy periods; (b) workers are drawn from adjacent villages and farms to increase the labor supply during certain times of the year; (c) similarly, longer distance migration is stimulated when labor peaks are particularly strong; (d) in developing countries most of the wage rates attendant to the above adjustments are too low to encourage very much mechanization of harvesting, or more broadly, substitution of capital for labor. Although the labor market may be relatively efficient in short-term resource allocation, it does little to create human capital, to educate the children, and to contribute to growth.

Third, the attraction to the city of a part of the rural labor force represents the most dynamic force in the labor market. Another force is the inflationary pressure so frequently associated with development plans and other activities of the national government and banking system. General inflation and the outmigration of farm people do bring upward pressures upon rural wage rates, but not equally to each set of class and tenure groups.

To many farm workers city life is attractive, but only in part because of higher wage rates. Higher wages may not offset the higher costs of living. And, in fact, migration to the city occurs even though no job is in sight. The results are seen in packing-box slums, street-side sleeping, and large masses of urban underemployed. One gains the impression that labor factor markets function very unevenly between the farm and the city.

Somewhat intuitively Harbison in 1967 argued that moderniza-tion is a generator of urban unemployment because of the heavy emphasis on labor saving technology in industry, commerce, and government and that the "traditional sector . . . must therefore absorb the great bulk of the labor force." Further, this problem has led to the formulation of several models of migration by Harris and Todaro (11), utilizing the concept of probability in finding an urban job as a determinant of rural to urban migration.

Eicher et al. (4), applying this concept in Africa, suggests that the improvement of rural and small town employment opportunities is the most effective way to slow down rural-urban migration.

The rapid rise in population in the last decade or so will increase the labor force rapidly during the seventies. Past debates about the existence or nonexistence of substantial unemployment with given technology and resources (17), give way to other problems. The creation of employment opportunities in both rural and urban sectors already is a significant problem and undoubtedly will put great pressure upon existing labor market institutions—institutions which do not now function very effectively.

INSTITUTIONS AND POLICIES
TO INTENSIFY AGRICULTURE

One prominent institutional characteristic is the multiplicity of public or semi-public extension operations. While the Ministry of Agriculture carries general responsibility for extension, its own efforts, especially in Latin America, are split between a livestock and a general crops service. Certain major crops may have their own service, such as coffee in Colombia. Credit agencies may do extension work, such as the Caja Agraria in Colombia or the supervised credit agencies in Brazil. Valley development agencies have special programs for a limited geographical area. Private input marketing firms, to the extent that they exist, also dispense information. Depending upon the circumstances, this may be described as an undesirable duplication of effort and dispersal of resources, or it may be viewed as a desirable development of a pluralistic society.

Related to this, the special area programs, extending the TVA example, encompass a wide range of activities stretching from engineering design, construction, through extension, and including research. One consequence is that the existing institutions are not strengthened and given vital new missions. Moreover, such agencies often carry out programs that are imperfectly coordinated with national goals. Most such regional entities operate at or near the fringe of settlement, thus seldom contribute to the intensification of agriculture.

A third characteristic is the paucity of private communication of technical information through feed and fertilizer dealers, the sellers of farm equipment, etc. One of their problems is to identify and locate in a small town intelligent and technically trained individuals who can absorb and extend new technical information and who are willing to commit themselves to residency in areas where limited social amenities exist.

Fourth, the technical advances (other than new varieties) that are in the pipeline and will contribute to an intensification of agriculture seem rather limited. Some argue that the old saw about the United States farmer who "is not now farming as well as he knows how," does not apply in the developing world. Schultz (22) makes this point by generalizing from Tax's study in Guatemala and Hopper's work in India. The four experiences cited by Millikan and Hapgood (18) in Taiwan, Sudan-Gezira, Peru-Vicos, and East Pakistan-Comilla seem to suggest, however, not only that there was something to extend, but also that continued and subsequent development occurred as innovations were identified and fed into the communication pipeline. More intensive work in Comilla by Stevens (25) indicates that the low-lift water pump played a significant but not exclusive role. Stevens underscores the need for associated education and technical change requirements:

> one major approach has been to focus on technical change and the appropriate capital inputs, with relatively minor consideration being given to possible associated educational and institutional change requirements. The unconscious intention perhaps is to keep costs in these latter areas to a minimum. Dramatic, disappointing, results of this approach exist . . . where newly completed irrigation facilities are only partly used. In many cases, the cause is lack of the right amount of appropriately timed effort in the area of education and institutional change.

Finally, economic policies to stimulate the intensification of agriculture are necessary parts of the institutional background. The pattern of taxation may include tariffs on inputs such as fertilizer, quantitative restrictions to protect foreign exchange, the assessment of turnover taxes several times as ownership is transferred from importer or manufacturer to wholesaler, to local stores, and to the farmer, all of which increase the input cost. Import substitution industries which produce farm implements and machinery have high costs and tariff protection. The concept of low cost inputs often is lost in the maze of revenue producing and industrial stimulation institutions and policies. Political pressures from the urban minority interested in low cost food may lead to national policies to hold down commodity prices. In consequence many input-output price ratios do not stimulate the adoption of known intensification techniques; with narrow price spreads they simply do not pay off. Of course, other institutional characteristics, such as the traditional division of product enforced by land tenure rules, further discourage intensification. Also, internal capital rationing stemming from uncertainty is a common characteristic. Spending money to make money does not have a good reputation in many agricultural areas; rather an increase in farm level self-sufficiency has provided greater evidence of viability in many areas in the past. Thus, policies, institutional arrangements, and technologies to reduce farm level uncertainty provide potentials for the increasing use of nonfarm produced inputs and agricultural intensification. Will farmers respond?

That the adoption of innovations depends more on social than economic incentives is argued by Fliegel, Kilvin, and Sekhon (8). They compare Punjabi farmers with two groups of Pennsylvania farmers and indicate that social approval may be more important than financial returns as an incentive. While not denying that economic incentives are necessary:

> We conclude that while the Punjabi respondents are by no means subsistence farmers, they are a long way from being commercial farmers in the American sense of the term. It follows that it is going to take much more than financial incentives to obtain widespread and rapid adoption of improved practices. . . . Unlike the Pennsylvania dairy farmers, the Punjabi respondents attach greater importance to social approval and less to financial return.

These findings conflict with Schultz's rather single emphasis on economic incentives (22). Erasmos, himself an anthropologist, is relevant at this point:

> society must continually adjust to its technological changes, but it does not lag far behind them waiting for the students of society to find a short cut to utopia . . . a better case might be made for technological . . . rather than social . . . lag, that is, the technology is not able to fill the current felt needs. (5)

But when appropriate technology is available, adoption rates are high. During 1968, Eckert (2) studied the fertilizer practices among growers of dwarf wheat in Pakistan. While preliminary and based on a small sample, the farmers' decisions on proportion of land devoted to new varieties and the use of fertilizer indicate a notunfamiliar pattern.

> Throughout this survey, farmers showed that while they are eager to try a promising innovation they were also cautious enough to avoid a complete commitment based solely on the word of others. . . . Regardless of size or the year in which they first planted dwarf wheats, they approximated one-third of the wheat land under dwarf varieties for their initial experience. The percentage doubles in the second year and nears 100 per cent . . . thereafter.

Thus, these highly profitable innovations, at least in irrigated areas, are being adopted, earlier by larger farmers, but with judicious speed. Fertilizer applications lag behind recommendations but are increasing as experience is gathered and as the willingness and ability to borrow to buy fertilizer increases.

Yotopoulos, trained in economics, draws on his detailed case study of farming:

> These two alternative hypotheses (inefficient and poor, or efficient but poor) are tested for the region of Epirus. It is the most underdeveloped region of Greece with poor agriculture. . . . The empirical evidence . . . lends support to the poor but efficient hypothesis. The tests performed reveal that an admirable harmony between marginal productivities and opportunity costs graces the peasant agriculture. (28)

Another set of economic policies relates to the private nonfarm sector. These range from government subsidies to heavy taxes and the creation of uncertainty. A consistent policy probably has more importance than the specific allocation of activities between the public and private sector. Few firms will make major investments in producing and distributing agricultural inputs if continued uncertainty exists as to whether the Ministry of Agriculture will soon take over such functions, or price authorities drastically modify the relative pattern of prices and costs.

A review of institutions and policies to facilitate agricultural intensification identifies a number of serious gaps. Too few such institutions exist, their quality leaves much to be desired, some (tax patterns) have negative effects, and the entire set of policies and institutions has not been welded together into a comprehensive, integrated program to promote the intensification of agriculture. Though the issue is not settled, there is strong evidence that farmers will respond when technology, relative prices, and institutional patterns provide incentives.

CONCLUSION

Can the evidence and experience marshalled in this paper support the hypothesis that factor market institutions are critical for agricultural development? How essential are such institutions? Or, are particular types of institutions essential while others are not?

First, many institutions are closely related to a particular factor. It is the factor, water or improved seed for example, that contributes to the expansion of agricultural production. Some institutional arrangements are necessary in order to make the factor available, but even a poorly functioning distribution system will provide a quantity of the factor and hence an increase in production. Thus, some sort of institution inevitably is associated with the availability of the factor; if the institution functions well the factor can make a larger contribution.

Second, the factor market institutions need to be examined at the same time as the factor. A decision to produce or to import a supply of a factor is a necessary but not a sufficient condition. The marketing and communicating institutions relevant to that factor need to be examined and perhaps strengthened or even created. Specific country situations will determine whether institution building efforts are required, and the possible characteristics of this activity.

Third, experience suggests that certain existing institutions (water distribution and labor market) need to be studied carefully to determine their areas of strength and weakness, particularly as to how they may contribute more dynamically to the intensification of agriculture. This analysis suggests that a number of changes will be desirable.

Fourth, the experience reviewed in this paper confirms that agriculture development is a complex process. A combination of effort is required. The creation or improvement of factor market institutions often needs to be a part of this combination of efforts. There continues to be debate as to whether social forces may be sufficiently strong to limit the effect of economic institutions and price incentives, but the evidence is increasing that strong profit incentives override social limitations.

Fifth, since development is a complex process requiring a combination of efforts, certain specifications of relationships will be more effective than others. Thus, a comparative study of institutions should help identify whether certain multifunction institutions are better than others, or whether certain combinations of single function institutions are more effective than other combinations, or even compared with effective multifunction institutions. Research on these patterns of relationships can help identify the appropriate management and administration of agricultural sector plans.

REFERENCES

1. Billings, Martin H. The economics of commercial egg production in eastern Nigeria. Ph.D. dissertation, Michigan State University, 1967.
2. Eckert, Jerry B. Fertilizer practices among growers of dwarf wheat in Pakistan's Punjab. Discussion paper, Lahore, September, 1968.
3. Eicher, C. K. The dynamics of long-term agricultural development in Nigeria. *J. Farm Econ.*, 49 (December, 1967), 1158–70.
4. Eicher, C. K. et al. Employment generation in African agriculture. Draft paper prepared for African Bureau, U.S.A.I.D., March 17, 1970.
5. Erasmos, Charles. *Man takes control: Cultural development and American aid.* Minneapolis: University of Minnesota Press, 1961.
6. ERS. Changes in agriculture in 26 developing nations, 1948 to 1963. Foreign Agriculture Report no. 27, Washington, D.C.: USDA, 1965.
7. Falcon, W., and Carl Gotsch. Agricultural development in Pakistan: Lessons from the second-plan period. Report no. 6, read at the Bellagio Conference of the Development Advisory Service, June, 1966.
8. Fliegel, F. C., Joseph Kivlin, and Gurmett S. Sekhon. A cross-national

comparison of farmers' perceptions of innovations as related to adoption behavior. *Rural Sociology,* 1969.

9. Gotsch, Carl. Technological change and private investment in agriculture: A case study of the Pakistan Punjab. Ph.D. dissertation, Harvard University, Cambridge, Mass., 1966.

10. Hapgood, David, ed. Policies for promoting agricultural development. Report of a Conference on Productivity and Innovation in Agriculture in the Underdeveloped Countries, Center for International Studies, Massachusetts Institute of Technology, Cambridge, Mass., 1965.

11. Harris, J. R., and M. P. Todaro. A two sector model of migration with urban unemployment in developing economies. Cambridge, Mass.: MIT Working Paper no. 33, December, 1968.

12. Herdt, Robert W., and John W. Mellor. The contrasting response of rice to nitrogen: India and the United States, *J. Farm Econ.,* 46 (February, 1964, 150–60).

13. Hsieh, S. C., and V. W. Ruttan. Environmental, technological and institutional factors in the growth of rice production: Philippines, Thailand, and Taiwan. *Food Research Institute Studies,* 11, no. 3, (1967), 307–8.

14. International Bank for Reconstruction and Development. Sudan: Gezira and Managil Schemes, Annex A IBRD-1215 R, September, 1963.

15. Johnson, G. L. A note on non-conventional inputs and conventional production functions. In *Agriculture in economic development,* ed. Carl Eicher and Lawrence Witt. New York: McGraw-Hill, 1964, pp. 120–24.

16. Johnston, Bruce F. Agricultural development and economic transformation: A comparative study of the Japanese experience. Food Research Institute Studies, Stanford University, vol. 3, no. 3, November, 1962, pp. 223–76.

17. Kao, Charles H. C., Kurt R. Anschel, and Carl K. Eicher. Disguised unemployment in agriculture: A survey. In C. K. Eicher and L. Witt, *Agriculture in economic development.* New York: McGraw-Hill, 1964, pp. 129–44.

18. Millikan, Max F., and David Hapgood. *No easy harvest.* Boston: Little, Brown and Co., 1967.

19. President's Science Advisory Committee. The world food problem, water and land, chap. 7. In *Report of the Panel on the World Food Supply,* vol. 2, The White House, May, 1967, pp. 454–55.

20. Ruttan, Vernon W. Notes of agricultural product and factor markets in Southeast Asia. Paper read at ADC-University of Kentucky Seminar on Adapting Agricultural Cooperatives and Quasi-Cooperatives to the Market Structures and Conditions of Underdeveloped Areas, Lexington, Kentucky, April 26–30, 1967, p. 11.

21. Schuh, G. Edward. The agricultural input markets—A neglected area of agricultural policy and economic research. Proceedings, Western Farm Economics Association, 1963, p. 44.

22. Schultz, T. W. *Transforming traditional agriculture.* New Haven: Yale University Press, 1964.

23. ———. Increasing world food supplies: The economic requirements. Proceedings National Academy of Sciences, vol. 56, no. 2, August, 1966, pp. 322–27.

24. Stevens, R. D. Elasticity of food consumption associated with changes in income in developing countries. USDA, ERS, FAER No. 23. Washington, 1965.

25. ———. Institutional change and agricultural development. Agricultural Economics Report no. 64, Department of Agricultural Economics, Michigan State University, April, 1967.
26. Thornton, D. S. Contrasting policies in irrigation development. Development Studies no. 1, University of Reading, September, 1966.
27. Witt, Lawrence W. Personal visit in 1958 supplemented by a letter from Dale Adams dated October, 1967.
28. Yotopoulos, Pan A. Allocative efficiency and economic development: A cross section analysis of Epirus farming. Center of Planning and Economic Research, Athens, 1966.

DISCUSSION by ERVEN J. LONG

BASICALLY, this chapter explores issues rather than attempting to resolve them (or ignore them). It claims no more for its principal inferences than the examined evidence merits—and on most of these issues the evidence is fragmentary, inconclusive, and often contradictory. The conclusions are not startling; however, they may very well be sound.

The lack of adequate, systematized evidence on the major issues addressed by the chapter is simply a fact of the case. Therefore, good scholarship which attempts to relate and weigh the evidence probably must, as in this case, counterpose one bit of evidence or one line of argument against the other. In such a setting, individual, anecdotal observations probably weigh far more heavily than they should—as do the personal attitudes, professional biases, etc., of the observers. Therefore, the kind of deliberate effort at intellectual honesty characterizing this paper is far more to be cherished than are the world-shaking, window-rattling conclusions which can be derived from oversimplified assumptions (or overdrawn observations) by anyone who combines a modicum of skill in elementary logic with a flair for rhetoric and a lack of modesty before the problem.

Rather than criticize the paper, a few general questions that relate to policy implications will be posed.

The initial question is: Should the proper functioning of factor markets in developing countries be considered a truly important ingredient of United States foreign assistance policy? Please do not too rapidly rush to judgment on this question! Obviously, factor markets are important or they would not be on this agenda. But so are many other things important. Everything in the universe is related in some way to everything else, and in some way to the success of the human enterprise. But the capabilities of public policy are extremely limited; it can pull some levers, perhaps, but not all.

Especially limiting is the fact that results of United States policy and activity must be spun out of actions undertaken primarily by other peoples, their governments, and their institutions.

Not only because of budgetary restrictions—devastatingly important as they are—but also for other reasons the United States can influence importantly only relatively few processes in typical situations. They must be chosen with care; they must be strategic to United States objectives. Collectively, they must bid fair to set the developing country on its path to growth, else the whole point is missing.

Do the problems posed by the proper functioning of the factor markets of the developing countries pose *important* issues for United States policy? Do they provide the strategic handholds by which the United States and other countries' representatives in these countries can attack the basic developmentary problems?

If not, these discussions are at least healthy opportunities for academic reminders to ourselves and each other that we are, after all, trained as economists—not merely as mechanics or philosophers. If, on the other hand, factor markets do provide strategic operational as well as analytic handholds, then one should press some further questions. They occur in such numbers and complexity as to create what Immanuel Kant referred to as a "big, buzzing, booming confusion." Let us ask only one.

Are the strategic elements in the mix of factor-market problems meaningfully embraced within the individual developing countries? Is it meaningfully addressed by the presently accepted country-by-country programming approach—which only dances at the edges of economic interrelations among countries? Such economic interplay as is considered is on the product side. Stated differently, the question is: Is the malfunctioning or inadequacy of the *factor* markets primarily a within-country phenomenon, or primarily a deep, structural maladjustment between the advanced countries on the one side and the less advanced on the other. Though of course it is both, it could be argued that either policy or analysis addressed almost exclusively to within-country issues (if the factor markets *are* central to policy) is so inadequate as to be almost inconsequential. Just as it is now accepted that low income pockets within our country can only be effectively treated as a problem of inadequate integration into our total national growth processes, so is the problem of the developing country effectively treated as that of historic nonparticipation and nonintegration.

In Heady and Timmons' succinct formulation, the developed countries have overinvested and the developing countries have underinvested in agriculture. With this the author thoroughly agrees. And, the techniques which have been invoked the last fifteen years or so to accommodate to this deep structural flaw through subsidized commodity transfers could scarcely have been better designed to aggravate it.

If even partly right, the line of reasoning of the last few paragraphs is extremely sobering in its implications. For one thing, with the sole exception of capital markets, almost nothing systematic has been done through the many bilateral and multilateral agencies involved to work directly on the problem of international factor markets. And even capital markets are limited only to essentially raw finance—not capital processed into those forms (e.g., research inputs), specifically needed by developing countries.

Furthermore, if one approaches it from a factor market, structural worldwide imbalances viewpoint, essential nonmobility (as between countries) of certain key factors (land, labor) puts great stress on those which are mobile. Among these mobile factors, one would list especially the enormous powers of new science and technology—powers which, *if* properly oriented, are not necessarily selective toward large farm complexes. Far too often, discussion of research to create new technology is in terms of organization of activities *within* individual developing countries, while the real punch appears to be coming from research which is organized as an international system to bring advanced science to bear on needs of the developing countries—science developed by such countries as the United States which have been able to afford it. The Rockefeller corn-wheat programs can be cited. Similar bridges are being built from our scientific capabilities by the small Agency for International Development central research program.

If, again, the factor market maladjustment in the world context is a strategic handhold, it is extremely important to formulate major problem objectives properly. If the problem is that of getting agriculture to perform its proper role in the respective developing countries, then entirely different solutions are required than if the problem is that of the currently popular formulation—can the world feed itself. Consider that India and the Congo are about the same size and have roughly the same resources, and India is *almost* feeding twenty times as many people as inhabit the Congo. Their respective development must be of different character if the problem is to mobilize the world's food-producing resources to postpone an inevitable famine than if it is to effect an optimally efficient world investment for development process, in which each country's agricultural sector should play its proper economic role. Scholars, it is hoped, will worry about these issues. Policy does not follow scholarship perfectly—nor is there often much perfect scholarship to follow. But the relationship is much closer than might be expected. Dangerous times do lie ahead, and these analytical issues are really dark and deep. If economists try to tackle agricultural development problems through factor market channels, they should be warned by an old East Indian proverb: "If you wish to hunt for tigers, be sure before you start that you really want to meet one."

DISCUSSION by HOWARD W. OTTOSON

As ONE REVIEWS this chapter, one is haunted by the question: "Have we adequately examined factor market institutions with respect to United States agriculture?" The answer probably is "no."

Witt's emphasis on factor systems—the package approach—is well placed. One is aware, in thinking of the past twenty years, of the emphasis on single factors by developing countries—often with great political values attached, but also with great costs. This emphasis is reminiscent of the United States experience during the latter part of the nineteenth century and much of the present one. In the developing countries one sees initiation of large land distribution projects, large reservoirs, national airlines, and steel mills. Likewise, emphasis on mechanization has been manifested sometimes in the introduction of large-scale power sources and large-scale machinery, with great cost and resource inefficiency associated with them.

The basic policy problem in intensifying agriculture is how to get the "biggest bang for the buck." This objective can violate, or at least complicate, the package approach in development. However, where capital is scarce, difficult choices may have to be made between input alternatives; the marginal productivity between various types of inputs may vary greatly. Thus, an attempt may be made to maximize the portion of scarce capital going into highly productive, fast return inputs, at the same time deliberately keeping investments in other parts of the production system at minimum levels until new capital is generated. Witt might have elaborated this point in his paper.

Witt's comments on research as a creator of new agricultural inputs in developing countries still have implications for our foreign programs. Despite a history of more than twenty years of foreign assistance, the United States has not yet effectively committed itself policywise to the development of adaptive research capability in the developing countries. Congress did, in 1966, take a couple of first steps toward this end, but has not supported the gesture with funds. Up to this point, the resources available in our agricultural research complex—the USDA-Land Grant System—have not been tapped substantially for the development of research programs abroad. The record of foundations is much more impressive.

Half the problem with respect to labor markets probably resides in the last three paragraphs of Witt's section on labor. One is impressed with the dilemma in Colombia, for example, as one looks at large-scale, extensive ranching, or large-scale intensive enterprises, on the one hand, and compares these with the sector of agriculture represented by millions of campesinos, on the other hand.

The problem is obviously bigger than the labor market. For

example, how does one inject knowledge, and selected nonland inputs, into the campesino sector? What kinds of inputs should be injected? What kinds of products will result? How is part of the product captured for reinvestment? This is a matter of breaking the cultural and economic circle, and trying to generate some surplus on which more intensification can feed.

Effective action on the labor supply side is needed also. Of course, I refer to birth control. Again thinking in terms of Colombia, one may readily intrigue himself with the thought that the campesinos in the mountains around Medellin will never break out of their economic circle until the rate of population increase is cut by one-half, or two-thirds, or three-fourths.

A book could be written on Witt's last section, and specifically on the effects of economic policies on the factor market in agriculture in developing countries. Thinking again in terms of Colombia, as well as Argentina, to which my brief experience is limited, the impression is created that when one has done everything else correctly with respect to credit, the factor markets, the development of research programs, and the development of education, Argentina and Colombia will not move ahead until they develop rational, integrated price, tax, and trade policies which will affect the agricultural industry. To some extent, agriculture has been the forgotten man in the formulation of the general economic policies in both these countries.

The research implications of Witt's papers are obvious. Thus, what can we tell country X about the effect of factor markets, given the social milieu, on economic development? What are the relative merits of alternative institutional devices? One can define a respectable task, for example, in analyzing the alternative ways of organizing a system for the injection of fertilizer into the agricultural economy of country X. How much of our own experience is transferable? Not much, I suspect. How then, do we assist country X in providing the information that is necessary for making choices in building institutions with respect to the factor market? The need for research, on location, is obvious.

4

PRODUCT MARKETS

HAROLD F. BREIMYER

SOME ELEMENTS in the role of product markets in agricultural development can be generalized from nation to nation. Unfortunately, a great many cannot. The temptation is scarcely resistible to pose more by way of generalization than can be justified. Literature on the subject frequently does so.

Yet one generalized starting point seems almost unchallengeable: economic development universally involves attaining more specialization in economic enterprise than prevails in primitive economies.

Specialization is often thought of in terms of Adam Smith's pin making. It is more complicated than that. Belshaw calls it "differentiation of role." (3) It includes both technical process and division of administrative functions. What is important is that specialization involves not only separate functional units as viewed horizontally, but a hierarchical structure vertically; and the whole constitutes a single organism of mutually interdependent parts. In such a system a specialized individual is part of a specialized group that has a distinctive role in the next larger entity, and so on. Because the system is characterized less by the refinement of units than by mutual interdependence, Boulding among others has applied the term, "ecosystem." (4)

Within the composite system, interchange of goods and services must take place. The capacity to develop institutions for interchange that are satisfactory enough to endure may be the most crucial test to be applied to an existing or potential economy.

If a higher degree of specialization and, along with it, a need for institutions of interchange is a universal characteristic of economic

The major assistance William J. Staub provided in the writing of this chapter is gratefully acknowledged.

development, it may be the only one. Definitely, a market exchange system is not an invariable requirement.[1] That is, the interchange of commodities and services need not be directed by a market system utilizing price. Other mechanisms are possible; historically, others have been employed more often than have markets.[2] There was specialization in the medieval manor and on the plantation of the ante-bellum United States South. In both cases interchange was basically either conventional or authoritarian.

DECLINE OF MARKETS IN ADVANCED ECONOMIES

Advanced economies of the world are currently turning away from the classical forms of exchange markets based on commodity price. Market transactions are giving way to vertical integration. Industrial integration often is accomplished by the conglomerate business firm that combines many products and processes. Administrative decision replaces market exchange, even though shadow prices may be devised as an aid in management.

Moreover, final sale to consumers is governed less by price alone than it once was. On the one hand, various forms of nonprice competition typically accompany price in regulating the distribution of commodities and on the other, schemes seem to be on the increase for getting food to parts of the population either outside a market price system or by stratification of the market. Examples in the United States are direct distribution, school lunch, food stamps, and other supplementary food programs.

To be sure, two-price marketing of food did not originate with developed nations. On the contrary, it has long been practiced in various developing nations. Yet attitudes sometimes expressed compound the irony: spokesmen for developed nations may counsel developing nations to turn to uniform pricing, even as their own countries expand their concessionary mechanism for distributing food.

A DUAL MISSION

A market system, or any alternate, has two tasks: (1) distribute products to consumers in a way that meets at least minimum performance standards, (2) give directional control to the production of products and services, including market services. The admonition

---

[1] Throughout this chapter *interchange* and *exchange,* otherwise almost synonymous, will be given separate meanings. Interchange will be the generic term, and exchange will be confined to its conventional meaning of a market exchange system based on price.

[2] Polanyi has emphasized the absence of a prevailing system of price-making markets in economies prior to the last few centuries (17).

that a marketing system must not only "get the job done" but contribute to further development includes both tasks, neither of which is subordinate to the other.

This is not to suggest that a single system must work reciprocally, performing both tasks. Admittedly, in the classical market exchange model, price serves as the single instrument, guiding both distribution of product and allocation of resources. This was its most salient and most beneficent feature.

In both developed and developing countries separate systems can be devised for the two missions. For example, government action can regulate production while a product moves freely by price alone; or government programs can distribute some of the product (as in food programs in the United States) even though price alone guides production.

Authors tend to fall into two camps as to which aspect of the marketing mission they emphasize. Abbott, for instance, writes much about shortcomings in various developing nations in getting incentives back to farmers (1, 2). Schultz has long been concerned with the form and adequacy of a system of incentives to farmers (20). Slater and Riley, writing about markets in the Recife area of Brazil, have much to say about reduced food costs as a means of improving welfare of consumers and generating demand for other goods and services (22).

ANOTHER DUALITY—PHYSICAL INFRASTRUCTURE AND INSTITUTIONS

In a similar vein, any system of interchange, including market exchange, invariably embraces both the necessary physical facilities, including a network of transport, and the supporting institutional structure.[3] This pairing of requirements also finds individual writers tending to show partiality. Some stress the inadequacy of storage, wholesale market facilities, highways, and other infrastructure. Others defend the crucial role of institutions, reporting various instances of institutional shortcomings. They also proclaim a psychological handicap in their homiletics. Human beings, they say, have a psychic preference for dealing with material things rather than comparatively ephemeral institutions.

Collins and Holton, for example, declare that development plans typically "call for improved distribution facilities . . . [when] more often the really critical need is a change in the organization and operation of the distributive sector. . . ." Further, "materials are notably more malleable than men. . . ." (7)

---

[3] Market institutions are considered here to encompass all the practices and arrangements under which marketing is done, ranging from entrepreneurship to restrictive or supporting laws. Some authors would include custom, convention, even taboos and folklore.

The contest is easily resolved by once again separating what can be generalized from that which cannot. Both infrastructure and well-designed institutions are essential to any good system of interchange. In a given case, the greater deficiency and more pressing need may be for a certain infrastructure. But if institutions are deficient, their improvement may take priority. Not infrequently the two will be inseparate and equal: new public commercial warehouses, to be fully useful, will likely require (1) an inspection service to assure integrity, and (2) lending practices by banks that accept warehouse receipts as collateral. All these become empirical questions, resolvable only in terms of specified place and time. To try to calibrate globally is interesting intellectual exercise but without practical value. The actual situation at any place and time is what counts.

PICKING AND FITTING THE PUZZLE'S PIECES

Rather as all roads, high and low, seem to lead to London, the argument thus far funnels to the familiar dilemma that setting up options is easy but picking and choosing from among them is perilous. How indeed are markets to be improved in a given circumstance?

To what extent is the distributive and coordinational mechanism to be a system of markets versus vertically integrated private control that compromises the role of price, versus some form of cooperation, versus central direction by government?

As though to complicate the choice even further, the interchange system for farm products does not exist *in vacuo*. It is embedded in the political and social system of any community or nation. For example, Polanyi argues, as expressed in Shaffer's paraphrase, that "the liberal state was a creation of the self-adjusting market and the key to the institutional system of the nineteenth century lay in the laws governing the market economy." (21)

Such a statement brings joltingly to mind the circumstances that prevail in many communities of developing nations. The all too common situation and its implications is described by Myrdal in powerful language:

> In a stagnant community, with low levels of living and education, which has inherited a rigid and inegalitarian social and economic structure, the difficulties of building up institutions for self-government, collective bargaining, and cooperation are immense. The fundamentally different problem facing the state in under-developed countries is that it will have to plan to build up such institutions. (16)

The system of distribution and coordination to be sought depends heavily on the general conditions that prevail in the nation as well as those that are aspired to. The more highly specialized the system of production, the more dependent it is on complementary supporting services which therefore need to be relatively advanced and efficient. On the other hand, unless the social and political structure is reasonably advanced the interchange system in agriculture must be kept fairly simple.

A market exchange economy, for example, probably can work well only if the population is relatively literate, distribution of wealth is not too unequal, traditions of the citizens are conducive to responsible individual performance within large organizations, and central government is capable and enterprising.[4]

When a *campesino* takes his produce to a village market and himself sells it to a local buyer, the transaction needs only simple supporting services other than police protection against brigands. If he instead ships corn to a distant market, perhaps for storage pending sale later, he relies on a complicated institutional system. He depends not only on the integrity of each transaction, but on the efficiency of a price-making mechanism. The latter can seldom be assured unless central government provides basic services, including restraining syndicates or monopolies from obstructing competitive trading.

Usually, the ambience for market institutions is to be appraised not in absolute terms but as a matter of degree. If a system approximating market exchange is to be established, it must be sufficiently competitive that no great injustice occurs at any stage. There must be reasonably unrestricted entry and exit. Devices of nonprice competition probably will be accepted but they cannot be so elaborate as to interfere seriously with entry, exit, and other attributes of an efficient market system, nor dare they add too much to cost. Perhaps the minimum requirement is that tests of effective or workable competition be met.[5]

If those tests cannot be met, the only recourse is to keep the interchange system simple, even at the cost of realizing less than maximum possible economic development; or utilize the central government to perform a tight regulatory function or involve itself directly in the market.

THE CHICKEN AND THE EGG

The above remarks directed to the need for consistency and mutual support among market and other social and economic in-

---

[4] These do not run the gamut of conditions necessary for a modern market exchange economy. A contrast between a primitive and a wholly industrialized economy can be enlightening. In the former, a model of an "economy of immutable resources of heterogeneous endowment" where "demand schedules are practically non-existent," it is "doubtful that any system approaching a free market economy would be permitted." (Cf. 6, p. 681)

[5] A contemporary reference to this principle is Sosnick (23).

stitutions are not intended to prescribe fixed patterns. There is no one unique combination of institutions for a market-exchange system —nor for vertically integrated production and marketing or any other system that may be devised. But there are combinations that carry certain burdens of nonviolability. The example of public storage warehouses is illustrative.

In the same vein, in any program for development, one operational question invariably arises: since it is not possible to move forward on all fronts simultaneously, which ones are to be chosen for priority? This dilemma also has generated a fund of literature. In most situations it is necessary to move ahead first on certain carefully chosen fronts—the concept of leading thrusts. Moreover, a survey of the existing situation may reveal some glaring deficiencies that call for priority of attention. But finally one returns to the principle that development must eventually involve many aspects of an economy.[6]

Further, this simple axiom needs emphasis if only because it happens so often that individuals and organizations that offer advice on how to inaugurate or speed development reveal a kind of professional favoritism. This is true of both native officials and technical aid specialists of outside countries—including those from the United States. Soil scientists want to add nitrogen to soils; conservationists seek to build dams; retail trade specialists offer to cover the place with supermarkets; and conventional farm marketing men hurry to establish a market news service and build a grain storage elevator. Indulging one's own competency is one of the human hazards of counsel for development.

Moreover, the consequences of unbalanced measures may not be innocent. In marketing, a common mistake with regard to physical facilities is to advocate constructing new facilities that are costly of capital and labor-saving in an economy where labor is surplus and capital scarce. "Wasteful" employment in marketing adds nothing to cost in the absence of any power either to add to quantity of servicing or to influence price—in those circumstances there is no *a priori* cause to reduce it. Recommendations for institutional change may be in error if they call for cooperatives where either leadership or discipline of group action is absent, or for private agencies that easily would become monopolistic. Instances are legion of "good advice for the wrong place," which is indistinguishable from outright bad advice.

For illustration rather than any rigid cataloging, the remainder of this discussion is divided into marketing in the subsistence sector, commercial sector, and export sector.

---

[6] The notion of internally balanced composites of institutions, put into Ruttan's nomenclature, denies growth stage theories and comes close to dynamic dualism (19).

THE SUBSISTENCE SECTOR

The subsistence sector may be best defined by the high percentage of its production that is consumed by the producing family outside of market exchange. Characteristically it is also a sector of small land holdings, illiteracy, and rudimentary social structure.

Obviously, a handicap to efficient marketing is the rather small volume of marketable output. Moreover, the marketed product may be variable as to season and quality.

Two mistakes could easily be made: (1) write off the sector entirely, (2) assume that few market services are needed. The former is a mistake for political reasons if not economic ones. Often, this is the sector that is properly the object of technical aid. The latter is in error because market services can be fairly numerous while kept simple.

By no means should improvement in production for self-sufficiency be discouraged. Benefits can frequently be obtained by increasing indigenous production for local consumption.[7]

With regard to subsistence sector markets, a necessary distinction is made between local markets (of the same village, or neighbor villages) and distant urban markets. There are thousands of village markets, yet they remain largely outside the expertise of economists. Often they employ labor in a way that seems wasteful; yet until alternative employment becomes available there is no reason to think that the practice is socially undesirable or that it adds to the cost of marketing. In the words of Holton, "the phenomenon of the unemployed taking refuge in trade may be a satisfactory substitute for a comprehensive unemployment insurance program." (10) Similarly, Lawson observed in Ghana that "the long chain of distribution which utilizes thousands of small-scale traders is in fact a rational use of existing economic resources." (14) Can these markets benefit from conventional market services? For staple products, probably. The simplest kind of price reporting, such as by blackboards, may be helpful. However, classification schemes (grades and standards) other than the simplest ones probably have limited application.

According to some authors, local markets are sometimes marked by restrictive trade practices such as guild rules or exclusiveness of access to stall space. Those practices are just as damaging to markets in a primitive setting as in central exchanges of New York or London.

More difficult to analyze and prescribe for are the markets for surpluses that go to distant urban centers, or are exported. In this portion of marketing, plus that from smaller commercial farms,

---

[7] This can amount to converting subsistence agriculture to small scale commercial agriculture. Johnston and Mellor comment on this kind of development in some countries (12).

markets are likely to be deficient in various respects including freedom from exploitation. This is where the moneylender may dominate local marketing, the itinerant trucker may take advantage of uninformed sellers, and infrastructure is deficient. Yet the volume of trade may not make a sound market system profitable.

As will be inferred, in circumstances such as these, neither improved marketing institutions nor better physical facilities (including roads) are likely to spring up of their own accord. Moreover, action by government may not prove worth the cost in the short run. But the commercial sale of surplus products by the subsistence sector may be vital to the survival of the economy of that sector. Furthermore, there must rest a hope that the sector itself will develop and become commercial; and so government investment in contemporary improvements in marketing may have a longer-run developmental aspect. Furthermore, it may be politically and sociologically unavoidable. In developing and developed nations alike, some subsidization from centers of wealth to backward or impoverished areas is inescapable. Cost-benefit concepts, as usually formulated, may be inapplicable.

The call is not for elaborate services but for essential ones at minimal levels of sophistication. This may mean constructing crude access roads, providing simple kinds of market information, or encouraging the beginning of credit unions or production credit. Better sources of credit could free farmers from practices such as precommitting their cash crops to moneylenders. For some storable commodities a price support and storage program may be desirable; and if it is begun, precaution must be taken to ensure that it reaches the subsistence sector.

DOMESTIC COMMERCIAL SECTOR

For commercial agriculture the repertory of activities and services developed in the United States and similar nations can be drawn on as a sort of shopping list. Never can any or all be prescribed *a priori* without careful analysis. Further, easy analogy with familiar conditions in the United States can be a trap: local problems may be surprisingly complex.

The sector is itself highly variable, and the label "domestic commercial" takes some liberties. Farm units may range from tiny to huge, and their organizational structure may take a variety of forms. Moreover, there may be considerable production for export. However, a contrast can be sketched with the large scale export agriculture described below.

Even though circumstances are not uniform, as a rule simplified versions of such traditional services as market information, grading and standardization, and certain kinds of trade practice regulation are well suited. With regard to infrastructure, the decision to build or not to build a road is at least clear cut. Other infrastructure can be more clouded. Almost always, storage and processing facilities are needed. Regrettably, too often in those facilities there is an economy of scale that leads to monopoly. In smaller countries the quantity of products marketed may not be large enough to support a sufficient number of firms to assure active competition. The choices are to retain smaller, more numerous facilities at some loss of operating efficiency; form farmer or consumer cooperatives; apply government regulation over market practices; or conduct a parallel government action to serve as a yardstick.[8]

Rather frequently the problem of adequate markets arises when a developing nation opens up new land areas. Too often, colonists have been helped to settle on new land without adequate provision having been made for the physical or institutional requirements for good marketing. This is unwise action, manifestly.

LARGE SCALE EXPORT SECTOR

A number of developing nations have an export sector that is almost a world apart. It features large holdings operated with hired labor and professional management. Owners may live in the capital city, or they may be investors from other nations. The marketing process is highly advanced. The producing firms may be nearly self-sufficient in providing marketing services, either independently or through commodity organizations. Even government service may be highly client oriented, confined to that sector.

The export sector of various nations often includes a marketing institution that is virtually unique to that sector, namely, the marketing board. The board will usually have a sizeable industry representation as part of its membership and leadership.

Even more singularly an export institution is the arrangement for participating in an international commodity agreement. Agreements are in force for several major products. Adjusting to the terms of an agreement may put a strain on the commodity organization,

---

[8] In an excellent study, Haag and Rioseco describe the market system that was brought about for the commercial agriculture of the Yaqui Valley of Mexico. Of the 9,000 farmers in the valley, 5,400 were ejidatarios, 1,200 were colonos, and more than 2,200 were private landowners. Virtually all the crops produced were marketed. Government support in the form of buying agencies, plus providing production credit, was a pervasive influence on the agriculture of the valley. The government agencies set minimum prices. A government bank provided production credit to the farmer, and it had the right to designate either a government buying agency or a private wholesaler as the market to which the borrower must deliver his product.

Reportedly, the wheat and corn cultivators netted about 95 percent of the stated purchase prices for their products. In scarcely more than a decade the acreage planted to cash crops was doubled (9).

marketing board, or government agency that provides storage or credit services to the industry. Almost certainly, in some years part of the available supply cannot be exported. The surplus must be stored. Not only are facilities and finance required, but a question arises as to equity of treatment of individual producers. Further, steps to restrain production in the future may be necessary. Commodity agreements may simplify some aspects of foreign trade, but they make life more complicated domestically.

Governmental service to the export sector may include engaging in market promotion abroad and in political negotiation as well. Almost always, farm products sold in export are given tight inspection for quality. Some developing nations are more circumspect in protecting the worldwide reputation of their export products than are developed ones!

INCENTIVE PRICING—FOR PRODUCTION AND CONSUMPTION

This discussion has thus far omitted one subject that is always prominent in policy-making for developing nations, namely, a price policy. Implicitly assumed herein has been the idea that if a market exchange system can be helped to function efficiently, there is a good chance that the price returned to producers will be high enough to have incentive effect.

It is sometimes argued that in order to get fastest acceleration in production, there must also be a subsidy—a bonus to make further output more attractive. This is clearly one more issue that cannot be resolved in general terms. Doubtless a subsidy incentive will sometimes be necessary.

Yet a few things can be said. One is that most developing nations do not have the fiscal resources to enable them to offer large incentive payments to producers. A second is that expanded production that rests on subsidy is seldom the policy goal. If national welfare is to be enhanced, *un*subsidized expansion in output is sought.

A question may be raised as to whether generous subsidy is in fact essential for expanded output. This is not to disinter the issue of whether a backward sloping supply curve exists. Doubtless such a curve is to be found in some cultures. But the evidence is that it does not predominate. What is more pertinent is whether a certain delicate balance between economic pressure and economic incentive is after all the most stimulative setting for development—and particularly so if the means toward expansion of output are provided through technological progress. This was the pattern of most of the increase in agricultural output in the United States. The periods of fastest rise in gross output were periods of steady or declining prices of farm products.[9]

But if all this is true, a premium is placed on facilitative uses of resources of government, as through making new technical knowledge available, and through removing bottlenecks in the marketing process wherever they may be found to exist.

Still a further conundrum is posed. It concerns incentives to consumption. These could achieve the maximum welfare benefit from farm production, and enhance demand and prices as well. Even in developed countries a fraction of the consuming population lacks enough purchasing power to be strong buyers of food. Conditions in some developing countries are much worse. Wise policy may call for establishing multiple pricing of basic food products. Among other merits, such a policy best converts physical need for food into demand for farm products at the farm; it narrows the discrepancy between "physical demand" and "money demand."

THE ROLE OF GOVERNMENT

The above analyses have been sprinkled liberally with suggestions as to where the arm of government might be used advantageously. In most cases, the arena of service is the same as in the United States and other advanced countries. It includes providing information and grading services, credit, certification of public storage warehouses, promotion, storage and price support, regulation of trade practices, and multiple pricing of food to consumers. Mentioned less often in foregoing pages were measures to sponsor self-help actions by farmers, such as forming cooperatives, not because they lack potential value but because favorable conditions often are not present.

But a point or two indicates a more aggressive role for government. The most notable and perhaps most controversial is direct government intervention for so-called yardstick purposes. The agency so engaged might be wholly governmental or mixed. The rationale is that in some smaller national economies private firms cannot be kept competitive. The market just is not big enough to support enough firms for competition. There is a choice of deliberately retaining a small scale and decentralized marketing system or of relying on countervailing activity by government. A number of developing nations now conduct a modest government activity along with the private system. Presumably the private firms and government agencies keep each other honest.

---

[9] More and more evidence gives reason to distrust the dogma promulgated by developed nations as to the interplay of price incentive and resource adjustment in development. Boulding and Singh, with a slight suggestion of tongue-in-cheek, remark on "curiously perverse reaction to adversity" and within a "general theory of social dynamics" they "distinguish at least four reactions" to disappointment (5).

Yet this picture of alternatives may be too simple. Blends and combinations of private and governmental institutions have been devised in some nations. Even though they appear strange to United States eyes, they may be a rational invention for the circumstances. These can be industry-government combinations, or they can be of other makeup.

ALTERNATIVES TO A MARKET SYSTEM

Although discussion at the outset of this chapter takes note of systems of "interchange" and poses the question of choice among them, most of the later detail relates to a market exchange system.

Because a socialist system of total direction by central government is assumed to be unacceptable in most or all developing nations, the most relevant alternative is that of integration in private hands. In its most extreme form it would embrace all production from the farm to retail distribution. Integrated firms of considerable size and scope are now found in some developing and many developed nations. They often are financed by capital from outside the country.

To do justice to this subject is not possible here. An integrated economy would operate in a manner vastly different from a market exchange economy. One outcome would be the combining of persons and organizations having common interests into bargaining fronts. Also, inasmuch as most vertically integrated firms are also large horizontally, in most developing nations competition among them would usually not be found.

The form that would finally emerge probably would resemble cartelization. Checks and balances would be applied not so much through market buying and selling as through contests leading to bargained arrangements among various groups, notably the "farmers" and wage labor and perhaps retailers. Quite likely the government would involve itself in the dual capacity of providing surveillance of bargaining techniques and representing interests of consumers.

In a developing economy of limited size, the hard fact is that it is difficult to establish a viable market exchange system impelled by competitive forces alone. One can be sympathetic with Cook's injunction that developing nations may have to "learn to live with monopoly as one price of self-sufficiency." (8)[10] On the other hand, in those instances where there is little hope of preserving even a minimum acceptable degree of competition, the best alternative might be, as Collins and Holton suggest, to treat the private firm as a public utility (7).

---

[10] Cook is a good source of observations on cartelization, integration, and restraint upon growth in lieu of satisfactory institutional structure (8).

DEVELOPMENT OF THE INSTRUMENT OF GOVERNMENT

It is generally acknowledged that the capacity of government to perform marketing services effectively varies widely by country. It leads to Cook's further observation that "the quality of government must be taken into account in deciding the form of government intervention." (8) Another conclusion is that as an evolving modern market system in a developing economy necessarily relies on central government in some manner, a part of economic development must be the development of capacity for responsible performance by government. In fact, among all institutions for marketing, that of an effective and stable government may be the most important.

Nor is good government an act of God. It too can be cultivated. Further, as Raup insists, there are choices as to forms of "administrative structure" in government (18). Improvement of the capacity of government may well be one of the underappreciated and undersupported elements in the mix that is known as "planning for development" of a nation that wants to improve its economic and social station.

MAKING HASTE SLOWLY—AND INTEGRALLY

Another theme sensed throughout this chapter is that progress will usually come at a measured pace rather than at breakneck speed. There will be exceptions. Kriesberg is one among several who point out the arithmetic of how fast marketings can increase when a subsistence sector catches fire (13). The result can be to force grain or other products on the market at a rate that exceeds the capacity of facilities and market institutions to handle it. Wharton calls this unsettling experience the "Pandora's box" of the "Green Revolution." (24)

Although planning and prodding ought to speed progress, undertaking herculean action on a few selected fronts while neglecting all else would usually be a mistake. To add physical facilities that soak up scarce capital funds while displacing workers from employment faster than industrial expansion can reemploy them reflects doubtful wisdom. As another illustration, coating a country with asphalt highways overnight may do some good; but other aids to marketing would often yield a higher return to the marginal investment dollar.

Most developing nations now present a patchwork quilt of forms of agriculture and agricultural markets, as the primeval coexists with the ultramodern (11). The three sectors used for illustration in this chapter (subsistence, domestic commercial, and export) may each persist for many years, and justify separate enhancement. More than that, the powers of government may have to intercede to prevent one sector from impinging on, and harming, another.[11]

When all is said and done, generalizations are suspect and particularizations hard to come by. Improvements in a system of product markets can contribute greatly to the development of a nation. More than that, they are crucial to it. Yet they are only one part of an overall scheme for development, one link in a chain. The game of fighting for priority of attention is a bad game.

And it may not be denigrating of economists' expertise to accept the words of Martin: "Decisions to accomplish . . . goals [in marketing] will call more for ingenuity in organization and human relations than for elaborate economic analysis. (15)

CONCLUSION

The thread that runs through this chapter is a reluctance to form universal judgments as to desirable policies for product markets in developing countries. On the one hand, if a nation is to pursue a higher degree of specialization, including geographical division of enterprise, it must have a viable system of markets of some kind. On the other hand, a highly sophisticated marketing system requires a network of supporting activities that often is hard to bring about in a developing economy. Particularly does a self-regulating market exchange system rest on cultural and political maturity in the nation as a whole.

Frequently the best policy calls for interchange systems of mixed makeup, containing roles for both government and private organizations. Boards and commissions of joint composition may be needed as well.

Moreover, if a market structure capable of supporting a more advanced production system is not forthcoming, technological gains in production may have to be restrained. Although precisely coordinated advances in all sectors are not mandated, neither can a marked imbalance be lived with for an indefinite period of time.

On the whole, the point of view presented here includes a large dose of pragmatism in preference to conforming to a single doctrine of development. But this does not depreciate critical analysis as a base for planning and stimulating the agricultural development of a nation that seeks to enhance the conditions of life for its people. On the contrary, more ingenious analysis is made essential, and if the techniques and tools are less stereotyped they are also less constrained.

---

[11] Boulding and Singh forthrightly defend not only retaining but consciously supporting two contrasting sub-economies, a combination they call "technological dualism." Developmental tactics would be "capital-intensive for the basic producer goods" and "labor-intensive for a variety of consumer goods and light engineering industries." (5)

REFERENCES

1. Abbott, John. *Marketing problems and improvement programs,* FAO Marketing Guide 1. Rome: FAO, 1958.
2. ———. The role of marketing in the development of backward agricultural economies. *J. Farm Econ.,* 44 (May, 1962), 349–62.
3. Belshaw, Cyril S. *Traditional exchange and modern markets.* Englewood Cliffs, New Jersey: Prentice-Hall, 1965.
4. Boulding, Kenneth E. *The organizational revolution.* Chicago: Quadrangle, 1968.
5. Boulding, Kenneth E., and Pritam Singh. The role of the price structure in economic development. *Am. Econ. Rev.,* 52 (May, 1962), 28–38.
6. Breimyer, Harold F. The three economies of agriculture. *J. Farm Econ.,* 44 (August, 1962), 679–99.
7. Collins, Norman R., and Richard H. Holton. Programming changes in marketing in planned economic development. *Kyklos,* 16 (August, 1963), 123–37.
8. Cook, Hugh L. Market structures and economic development in the Philippines. *J. Farm Econ.,* 41 (December, 1959), 1316–22.
9. Haag, Herman M., and German Rioseco. *Marketing of grains and other farm products in the Yaqui Valley, Sonora, Mexico.* Carbondale, Illinois: Southern Illinois University School of Agriculture, Publication no. 21, August, 1965.
10. Holton, Richard H. Marketing structure and economic development. *Quarterly J. Econ.,* 4 (August, 1953), 344–61.
11. Hopper, W. David. Discussion: The role of agriculture in the world economy. *J. Farm Econ.,* 43 (May, 1961), 345–47.
12. Johnston, Bruce F., and John W. Mellor. The role of agriculture in economic development. *Am. Econ. Rev.,* 51 (September, 1961), 566–93.
13. Kriesberg, Martin. Miracle seeds and market economies. *Columbia J. World Business,* 4 (March-April, 1969), 53–62.
14. Lawson, R. M. The market for foods in Ghana. In *Readings in the applied economics of Africa, vol. 1: Microeconomics.* Edith Whethan and Jean Currie, eds., Cambridge: Cambridge University Press, 1967, pp. 173–92.
15. Martin, Lee R. Some marketing problems in Pakistan and India. *J. Farm Econ.,* 41 (December, 1959), 1323–26.
16. Myrdal, Gunnar. *Beyond the welfare state.* New Haven: Yale University Press, 1960.
17. Polanyi, K. *The great transformation.* Boston: Beacon Press, 1944.
18. Raup, Philip M. Some interrelations between public administration and agricultural development. In *Public policy,* pp. 29–58. Cambridge: John Fitzgerald Kennedy School of Government, Harvard Univ., 1967.
19. Ruttan, Vernon W. *Growth stage theories, dual economy models and agricultural development policy.* Guelph, Ontario, Canada: Department of Agricultural Economics, University of Guelph, Publication no. AE-1968/2, 1968.
20. Schultz, Theodore W. Economic growth from traditional agriculture. In *Agricultural sciences for the developing nations,* Albert H. Moseman, ed., Washington, D.C.: American Association for the Advancement of Science, Publication 76, 1964, pp. 185–205.
21. Shaffer, James D. On institutional obsolescence and innovation—background for professional dialogue on public policy. *Am. J. Agr. Econ.,* 51 (May, 1969), 245–67.

22. Slater, Charles C., and Harold M. Riley. *Market processes in the Recife Area of Northeast Brazil.* East Lansing: Michigan State University, Latin American Market Planning Center, 1968.
23. Sosnick, Stephen H. Toward a concrete concept of effective competition. *Am. J. Agr. Econ.,* 50 (November, 1968), 827–53.
24. Wharton, Clifton R., Jr. The green revolution: Cornucopia or Pandora's box? *Foreign Affairs,* 47 (April, 1969), 464–76.

DISCUSSION by ROBERT D. STEVENS[1]

WHILE in general agreement with the major points on the topics which are covered in Breimyer's analysis, I am left unsatisfied and disappointed. The judgments relating to product marketing institutions are generally wise, if cautious. But the main question of how changes in product markets can make major contributions to agricultural development is not dealt with directly. More effective overall strategies are required in the area of product market institutions in order to rapidly transform the agricultural sector. Breimyer's suggestions focus primarily on the usual specific marketing activities without adding up to a comprehensive strategy.

With respect to details of Breimyer's paper, of particular interest are his more novel points stressing: (1) the importance of developing the instrument of government, and (2) the use of a conceptual separation between the general interchange system and the more limited market exchange system. Associated with this are the insightful distinctions between the distributional system and the directional control system for marketing. However, the overall conclusion of the paper asking for "a large dose of pragmatism" and "more ingenious analysis," while unarguably sound, does not carry us much further than we were some time ago.

One important missing element in the chapter relates to government price stabilization policies for food. Recent experience in a number of countries, including particularly Pakistan, has suggested that public food grain price stabilization policies which reduce price uncertainty may have had very high returns in increasing incentives and the production of major commodities.[2]

I turn now to further exploration of the main question examined in the Breimyer paper; what are the contributions that changes in

---
[1] The author appreciates the comments of Lawrence W. Witt and Harold M. Riley on an earlier draft.
[2] Gustav F. Papanek, *Pakistan's Development* (Cambridge: Harvard University Press, 1967), pp. 128 and 154, and Mujibur R. Bhuiyah, "Improved Planning and Changing Strategies for Agricultural Development in East Pakistan" (Ph.D. diss., Michigan State University, 1968), pp. 136–40.

markets and market institutions can make to accelerate development at various phases in the agricultural transformation. Two important additional dimensions to this discussion are offered here.

The first dimension can be highlighted by the hypothesis that high returns to institutional change in product markets will only be obtained after appreciable momentum is underway in increasing agricultural production. Different views are held on this hypothesis. Rostow, in his national marketing strategy, argues that agricultural marketing can play a leading role in economic growth. He states that four major jobs must be done to make a national market in low income countries. They are: (1) a build-up of agricultural productivity, (2) a revolution in the marketing of agricultural products in the cities, (3) a shift of industry to the production of simple agricultural equipment and consumer goods for the mass market, and (4) a revolution in marketing methods for such cheap manufactured goods, especially in rural areas.[3] Thus, Rostow sees the revolution in the marketing of agricultural products as a basic part of the strategy for accelerating agricultural development. Research by Slater et al., discussed below, supports this thesis. They use a pragmatic systems analysis approach to changes in institutions affecting marketing.

A different view subscribed to by Mellor and others is illustrated by a recent paper by Ruttan who concluded in 1967:

> My own inclination in view of the empirical evidence from Southeast Asia, just cited, is to treat the structure approach to product market reform as dead-end.

However he adds:

> In view of the explosive growth of demand for resources in the product market during the early stages of economic growth suggested by Stevens' analysis[4] I would argue for a positive approach to the problems of technical efficiency and resource use in the product market. . . . I would hypothesize, for example, that investments in roads would do more to narrow differences in farm-retail margins among regions of the Philippines than any policies or programs designed to correct defects in market structures associated with the behavior of marketing firms or institutions. . . . It is entirely possible that the attempts to achieve technical efficiency in the marketing sector may be constrained by structural defects. In this event policies designed to deal with the structural defects can be instituted as part of the total process of modernization of the marketing sector rather than as intervention in a traditional marketing sector which by and large appears to function fairly effectively.[5]

---

[3] W. W. Rostow, *View from the Seventh Floor* (New York: Harper and Row, 1964), pp. 135–39.

[4] R. D. Stevens, *Elasticity of Food Consumption Associated with Changes in Income in Developing Countries.* USDA, ERS, FAER no. 23, Washington, D.C., 1965.

[5] Vernon W. Ruttan "Notes on Agricultural Product and Factor Markets in Southeast Asia" (Paper read at ADC–University of Kentucky Seminar on "Adapting Agricultural Cooperatives and Quasi-Cooperatives to the Market Structures and Conditions of Under-developed Areas," April, 1967).

The second important dimension focuses on the new kinds of marketing technology that exist in developed countries which might be applied usefully in the developing countries. Here not only machines and buildings are being considered, but business management practices, and sales promotion procedures are also. The likelihood of transferring our marketing technology wholesale is not great for many reasons. Breimyer noted that the adaptation of marketing changes to the local economic environment is particularly necessary in view of the relatively high cost of capital and the low cost of labor in developing countries. The issue focuses on what new marketing technologies or institutions may appreciably reduce the costs of marketing in these rather different economic environments.

One example of the applicability of modern marketing technology in low income countries comes from the study of market processes in the Recife area of Northeast Brazil. A conclusion of this study is that in large urban centers, food marketing reforms appear practical and likely to reduce prices and expand sales. "For example, discount supermarkets are getting started in Recife and are expanding as rapidly as their investment capital will allow. The discount supermarkets are affecting the price structure . . . and have been attempting vertical coordination to reduce the number of transactions and to cut costs of acquiring major food items. They have used their market power to cut distribution costs for rice and eggs for example, and are contemplating similar actions on other items."[6]

A final potentially tragic marketing issue relates to the technical and institutional changes required in marketing for the effective conversion of major increases in agricultural production into real income. In those areas where major spurts in agricultural production are now underway, there is considerable concern that these large increases in agricultural products will not be absorbed into the marketing system and converted into useful products.[7] Are there marketing and processing strategies which can contribute in a major way to rapid solving of this impending problem? The irony of large quantities of "surplus" food rotting in countries where most people remain half-starved may soon face us. For the solution of this problem our discipline has primary responsibility.

---

[6] Charles C. Slater and Harold M. Riley, "Market Processes in the Recife Area of Northeast Brazil" (East Lansing, Mich.: Michigan State University, October, 1968).

[7] T. W. Schultz, "Production Opportunities in Asian Agriculture: An Economist's Agenda" (Paper read at the "Symposium on Development and Change in Traditional Agriculture: Focus on South Asia," Michigan State University, June, 1968).

DISCUSSION by WILLIAM C. MERRILL
and LEHMAN B. FLETCHER

AT THE SECTOR LEVEL, feeding a growing nonfarm population is one of the functions of agricultural development which has received theoretical and empirical emphasis. Thus, while reliance upon a price-coordinated, market exchange system may not be a generalizable requirement for development, the increased demand for marketing services concomitant with economic progress surely is. Specialization, urbanization, changing technology, and rising incomes all lead to a growing interchange of agricultural products and substantial increases in the demand for marketing services. An increase in the supply of marketing services and a decrease in the real cost per unit at which they are supplied are required, or at least desirable, if the pace of development is to be maintained. This functional role—the provision of desired marketing services with reasonable efficiency—is one of the tasks of marketing systems emphasized by Breimyer.

Marketing functions are performed in both major sets of exchange relationships that connect agriculture to other sectors of the economy. One set includes those activities connected with the movement, handling, storage, processing, and distribution of food and fiber commodities from the time they leave the farm until they reach the final consumer. The other involves the movement of agricultural inputs from the manufacturer to the farmer. The markets for inputs and outputs are closely related. Credit and technical assistance extended by food marketing or processing firms, for example, can facilitate access by farmers to new inputs. Introduction of new inputs and technology may increase the flow of farm products through the food marketing system and eventually require new investments in marketing activities. The ability of marketing agencies to obtain favorable prices for farm products and to keep marketing charges low relative to the final value of the product affects the profitability and demand for new inputs and technology. Agricultural development involves changes in both systems of agricultural markets.

A good deal of discussion in recent years has been concerned with the importance of marketing in agricultural development. Some experts argue that marketing improvement programs should receive high priority in development plans because "marketing margins are high while farm prices are low." Contrary to Breimyer, our experience has been that those experts most innocent of knowledge or experience in the marketing field are most likely to hold this view. The implication is that there are more possibilities for reducing marketing costs than for reducing production costs. While this is undoubtedly true in some cases, improvements in the marketing system may in fact increase marketing margins in other cases. A change in the marketing system that provides consumers with products during seasons when the products were not formerly available or results in exporting products not previously exported, for example, may represent a market improvement even though marketing margins are higher. Similarly, providing consumers with higher quality products frequently involves increased marketing costs and yet still may be classified as an improvement in the marketing system. Programs to introduce improved packaging of farm products, for example, may increase both marketing costs and product quality.

In some cases, the key to reducing marketing margins may well be to concentrate on cultivation and harvesting techniques which result in a better quality and more standardized product being available at the farm gate. Marketing margins for many products will undoubtedly remain high as long as marketing firms must deal with large numbers of very small farmers who continue to mix both high and low quality products in the lots which they offer for sale.

PROBLEMS IN MARKET PERFORMANCE

Even casual inspection of the wholesale and retail markets and typical handling and storage facilities in Latin America, for example, leads one to the conclusion that food losses due to spoilage, rodents, and insects are substantial. Substitute "excessive" for "substantial" and you have a "problem." An alternative approach to creating a "problem" is to use countries such as the United States as your standard of comparison in order to determine what losses "should be" or "can be" reduced to.

Similarly, anyone familiar with food marketing systems is aware that there are several layers of "buyers," "wholesalers," and "retailers" between the farmer and the consumer. This can easily become a "problem" if you substitute the words "too many" for "several" in the previous sentence.

EFFICIENCY IN MARKETING

How does one determine how many middlemen are "too many?" The engineer studying a marketing system may have no problem in answering this question. If the job of moving food from the farmer to the consumer can be done with fewer people there is room for improving the "efficiency" of the food marketing system. Such a response implies: (1) that anyone who earns any income from food marketing is a middleman, and (2) that "efficiency" is to be measured in terms of the number of units of food moved from farmer to consumer say, per man hour. In practice, the engineer seldom defines what a middleman is. He merely accepts the popular contention that there are too many of them and agrees that more "efficient" means of food handling will eliminate some of them. The engineer may use several different measures of efficiency depending on the "problem" being studied, but his basic definition of "efficiency" is almost always in terms of output per unit of input with both output and input being measured in physical units. The engineer typically uses the marketing system of a country such as the United States as his "standard of comparison" by which to judge the "efficiency" of a marketing system in a developing country. He is thereby almost inevitably led to conclude that the "efficiency" of such a marketing system can be improved if the middlemen will simply adopt handling procedures and construct processing facilities such as those used in his "model" country. He is usually unconcerned with the employment alternatives for displaced middlemen and unmindful of the requirements of his technology for changes in production practices and market outlets.

The economist studying a food marketing system usually views the middleman as someone who buys and sells. The worker who moves the food products from one place to another is important because he affects costs, but he is not a "middleman" in the economist's sense of the word. The economist is especially interested in the "middleman" because he is the "decision maker." The decisions of the middlemen determine how well the food marketing sector performs. Attention is usually focused on factors related to the level of food prices and the rate of investment in the food marketing industry such as: (1) the profit rates earned by middlemen, (2) the level of costs, and (3) the progressiveness of middlemen in introducing new handling and merchandising techniques.

The economist is faced with several dilemmas when he attempts to measure the performance of the market and to determine if market performances can be improved. First, reliable data on costs and profit rates at the various marketing levels are extremely scarce in developing countries. Second, even if data are available, there is the problem of selecting appropriate benchmarks or standards against which to measure market performance.

The lack of data is probably not as serious a problem as the lack of benchmarks. There seems to be little if any disagreement on the type of data needed. Furthermore, the amount of data available has expanded considerably in recent years. The more troublesome problems are: (1) what to do with the data once it is available, and (2) how to interpret the results.

The standard theory of perfect competition is frequently held up as an ideal source of benchmarks. According to the theory, if the market is "efficient" then costs must be minimized and profits must be equal to zero—at least in the long run. This assumes, of course, that costs include all opportunity costs. In practice, the definition of the long run and the measurement of opportunity costs is left to the individual economist's discretion. Given the basic data, the good economist, like a good lawyer, usually has little difficulty in proving what he wants to prove. Thus, there is a tendency for economists to conclude that marketing margins are "excessive" and the profits of middlemen "too large." The tendency is not likely to be reversed unless more middlemen begin hiring more economists!

If profits are in fact "too large," then theoretically one would expect this dimension of market performance to be improved if the market structure were altered so as to increase competition. One way to do this would be to increase the number of middlemen. Yet economists typically tend to agree that already there are "too many" middlemen. They usually feel that marketing costs could be reduced if there were fewer "buyers" and "sellers," less loading and unloading of food products, and more large volume transactions. At first glance, the implication is that fewer competitors will mean more competition. This is certainly a possibility, but the call for fewer middlemen is probably a reflection of the belief that most middlemen are operating short of the point of lowest average total cost rather than a concern over the degree of competition in the market. The hope is that lower average costs will lead to higher farm prices and lower retail prices, rather than higher profits for middlemen. There is, of course, no assurance that the hope will be fulfilled. Even so, lower average costs are usually considered desirable even if the middlemen are the only ones who benefit from them.

The economist interested in determining the most "efficient" way to market food has to first determine how to minimize the marketing costs and then determine how to eliminate the pure economic profit of middlemen. The job is a difficult one due to the large number of variables involved. Furthermore, there is no assurance that "efficiency" in this sense is feasible.

Given the difficulties of measuring pure economic profits, let alone devising a way to assure they will be eliminated, economists tend to concentrate on cost minimization. Thus, when economists talk about improving the "efficiency" of a food marketing system, they are usually talking about lowering the cost of moving a unit of food from the farmer to the consumer and assuming that everyone will benefit in the process. The present level of costs provides the "standard" to be improved upon. Unlike the engineer, the economist initially has no "model" system with which to compare the present marketing system. Furthermore, the model that he eventually derives is usually a nebulous one based on a multitude of cost estimates and assumptions. The currently fashionable version of this exercise is termed "systems analysis." Given the difficulties involved in developing a minimum cost marketing system model, explaining it to the decision makers and justifying the data and assumptions used, it is not surprising that economists frequently accept the marketing system of a developed economy as their "model" system and simply recommend that the existing system be made more like the "model" system.

SUPERMARKETS AND MARKETING REFORM

There was a time when many people believed that a substantial expansion of the supermarket system of food retailing was "the answer" to the marketing problems in Latin America and elsewhere. Supermarkets would increase the efficiency of the food marketing system. Increased efficiency mixed with generous amounts of competition would undoubtedly lead to lower food prices. The high retail price of food was certainly a "problem" and one which many people viewed as a "marketing problem." Some saw this "marketing problem" as too many middlemen between the farmer and the consumer. Others felt that it was due primarily to "improper" handling of food products in the marketing system.

Whether "too many" middlemen or "improper food handling" was considered to be the primary problem, there seemed little doubt but that supermarkets were the answer. Supermarkets could deal directly with the farmer and thereby "eliminate" the middlemen. Furthermore, supermarkets would undoubtedly handle farm products properly. Few asked how much it would cost to save food formerly lost or how much of the food formerly "lost" in the market place would now be "lost" on the farm if supermarkets failed to purchase low quality food products.

Persons interested in financing supermarkets, operating supermarkets, or selling equipment and supplies to supermarkets could certainly see the advantages of supermarkets quite clearly. Public officials under pressure to increase farm prices and lower consumer prices had little choice but to view the middleman as the villain. If the middleman could be eliminated, the price and supply "problems" would be solved. Thus, both private businessmen and government officials had reason to believe that the supermarket system of food retailing could be of great benefit to any nation. Mutual agreement by the private and public sectors that supermarkets were the "solution" to the big problems of "low efficiency" and "high food prices" led naturally to the question: How can we increase the number of supermarkets?

The answer seemed obvious to many. "Rely on private investment and foreign know-how with the government providing any tax incentives or legal changes needed to assure the financial success of such ventures." This seems a reasonable answer if all parties are agreed that the benefits of an extensive supermarket system exceed the costs of establishing the system. Both businessmen and public officials tended to agree that such is the case—even though very little information is available on the benefits and costs.

The existence of more information on the costs and benefits would not have changed substantially the rate of increase in the number of supermarkets in developing countries. However, the rate of growth has been less than the apparently desired rate for two reasons: (1) the preconditions required to allow supermarkets to earn profits equivalent to those that could be obtained elsewhere have not always existed, (2) even where the preconditions have existed, businessmen and government officials have not always been able to agree on how the benefits and costs are to be distributed.

Businessmen themselves can do very little to provide the preconditions required to induce investors to build supermarkets. If electricity, water, or adequate transportation facilities are not available in a certain section of a city, there is not likely to be a supermarket or even a superette located in that section until the government provides such facilities. If per capita income in another section is so low that people spend most of their food money on bread, rice, and beans, there is simply no need for a supermarket with 3,000 different items on its shelves.

MARKET PRICING AND CONTROLS

A market can be described in terms of its institutional structure. Part of this structure represents rules made outside the market which set limits on the behavior of individuals participating in the market. Many of these rules result from governmental policies and interventions at the local, regional, and national levels. Market institutional arrangements include not only control of sales conditions through sanitary regulation, inspection, and licensing, but also programs and policies that affect costs, price structures, and general competitive conditions. In Latin America, the organizational system for providing marketing services is not separable from the role of market prices in coordination and control, the second market function identified by Breimyer. Production (including production of marketing services) is unavoidably linked to pricing.

Existing food marketing systems in most developing countries do not always offer farmers an incentive to produce more or to market more of what they produce. A great deal of research has been devoted to ways to change the "rules of the game" in order to change the performance of the food marketing sector. Much of this research has been concerned with the role of prices in agricultural development. The centuries old belief in the unproductive nature of marketing is still widespread. This belief coupled with the general opinion that marketing margins are "excessive" frequently leads to government efforts to fix food prices. Many middlemen in developing countries have some monopoly power because of such things as: (1) the lack of a complete transportation system, (2) the shortage of storage facilities for some products or the concentrated control of storage facilities for others, (3) the possession of better market information than the farmer can obtain, (4) the difficulties of independent merchants in importing products, and (5) the relatively small size of the markets being supplied. Whether or not such factors allow middlemen to earn "excessive" profits depends on one's definition of "excessive." Whether or not marketing margins are actually excessive, the fact that people believe they are excessive often leads to price policies intended to reduce the margins. The effects of price control programs on the food marketing system will depend upon the form and magnitude of the programs. Such programs by themselves seldom serve to eliminate the sources of market power and in some cases may even serve to increase (or at least maintain) the market power of certain groups of wholesalers.

Government agencies frequently feel they can accomplish a wide variety of goals, in addition to reducing marketing margins, through price controls. A few of the common goals are to: (1) keep retail food prices low, (2) keep farm prices stable, (3) reduce food imports, (4) increase agricultural production, (5) maintain "fair" farm prices, and (6) promote regional development. Price controls alone can seldom accomplish all of these things at the same time. In practice, some of the goals are considered to be politically more important than others. In many cases, the legal structure or financial resources of the government may limit the forms price controls may take. Frequently, price control programs create at least as many problems as they solve. A "successful" price support program for wheat, for example, may create a "surplus" of wheat and a "deficit" in corn production.

Occasionally governments try to directly eliminate the "excessive" profits of middlemen by taking over part or all of the buying and selling of a farm product. This "solution" to the "problem" of excessive margins seems to have especially strong appeal in the case of storable products. If the government can operate its buying and selling operation on a smaller mark-up than the private sector, then it may be able to raise the farm price, lower the retail price, or do both without losing money. Otherwise the government's wholesale operation will result in either lower farm prices and higher retail prices or government losses.

Many governments buy and sell part of the domestic production of some food grains as part of their price control programs. Such programs may tend to perpetuate inefficiencies in the private marketing channels by creating uncertainty about the profitability of new investments in marketing facilities. A grain dealer considering an investment in new storage facilities may decide to construct a standard warehouse rather than bulk facilities, for example, because the warehouse can be used for other purposes if the government decides to expand its grain buying programs.

Government price policies are often designed to provide both "fair prices" for farmers and "low prices" for consumers. The resulting "squeeze" on marketing margins frequently leads to changes in the structure of the food marketing sector. The form and extent of the changes depends upon such things as: (1) the technological factors related to the marketing of food products whose prices are controlled, (2) import policies, (3) the form and extent of the price controls, and (4) the ability of the government to enforce its price controls.

THE PROBLEM OF PRIORITIES

Breimyer recognizes there is no general solution to the pervasive problem of priorities for projects to improve the organization and efficiency of marketing systems. He counsels pragmatism, deliberateness, and inclusiveness but neglects to explain how the proper mixture of these qualities can be determined.

There is a wide variety of factors that must be taken into account when assigning priorities to marketing projects. A few of the more important factors are: (1) the scale and organization of production, and the nature of the marketing and utilization system for the product, (2) the existence of other programs that might create marketing problems, and (3) the availablity of personnel and financial resources to carry out the project.

Timing is also an important consideration. In some cases, prospects for increased production of a product may not justify a high priority for programs to improve the efficiency of the marketing system. In other cases, production and marketing programs may need to be carried out simultaneously and to receive equal priority. Where new technology is already resulting in increased output, the long run success of the production program is likely to depend upon giving high priority to storage, processing, and marketing facilities for handling the increased production and preventing precipitous declines in the farm price of the product.

5

PLANNING INSTITUTIONS

C. J. MARTIN

To PLACE planning institutions in agriculture in their right perspective, the general outline of planning, including its purposes and methods, should be described. A volume of some 700 pages has been prepared and published by the Johns Hopkins Press which deals mainly with the implementation of planning.[1] Some highlights of the experiences gained in the course of the research for that book will be presented here, together with other information specifically related to agriculture.

THE PURPOSE OF PLANNING

Planning means different things to different people and there probably are as many views on planning as there are planners. For the purposes of this discussion, planning is considered to be an organized, conscious, and continuous attempt to select the best alternative to achieve specific goals. In this definition the importance of each of the three adjectives and "continuous" in particular should be emphasized. Economic growth and institutional change are the specific goals development planning should try to achieve. Economic growth can be achieved by other types of planning, such as anticyclical,

The views expressed here are those of the author and not necessarily those of the World Bank Group.
[1] Albert Waterston, *Development Planning: Lessons of Experience* (Baltimore: Johns Hopkins Press, 1965).

but in development planning there should be a conscious effort to change existing structures which inhibit development and growth.

Although the formulation of plans is of great interest and importance, this aspect is not covered since the methodology is well known. One could comment, however, that if all the information required for such studies were readily available in developing countries, such countries would be statistically far advanced. There is some correlation between the stage of economic development of a country and the economic information available in it. To ask for accurate knowledge on many aspects of an economy assumes a standard which few countries have yet achieved.

PROBLEMS OF AGRICULTURAL PLANNING

In formulating an overall plan, agriculture often has been taken for granted. A number of plans prepared in the decades of the forties and fifties devoted attention mainly to infrastructure and industry, partly because one can more easily measure the effect on these sectors of policy decisions and of possible investment. The agricultural sector consists of a large number of small farmers and therefore is not so easy to plan because the natural hazards of drought, flood, and pestilence can seriously affect the targets set by planners. Only recently has emphasis been placed on the importance of planning agricultural development, with the resultant uncovering of problems, many of which are discussed elsewhere in this volume.

Agriculture in developing countries usually consists of individual farmers, each interested in producing subsistence crops for his family, often together with supplementary cash crops. The small community in which he lives is wedded to a traditional way of life and forms a part of the wider rural, social, and economic environment. This environment is not usually conducive to change. Increases in production may be recorded from time to time, but these are more likely to be fluctuations resulting from changes in climatic conditions rather than representing a trend of steadily increasing output.

Usually men have decided to become industrialists in order to form new companies or to try to develop new industries in developing countries. They have left the agricultural sector to experiment in this new sector. But the farmer has been born in the agricultural sector. He has to make an effort to move but no effort to stay. Since most people prefer what they know and are not overenamored with change, most farmers in the agricultural sector prefer to behave in the manner similar to their neighbors, while the more energetic ones sometimes move into another sector. But since change does take place, it would seem to occur when farmers: (1) progressively substitute rational production decisions based on the market for decisions previously based on custom and tradition, and (2) use an increasing proportion of purchased inputs in substitution for family labor and homemade inputs and equipment. At the same time, farmers may not be as tradition bound as development economists and administrators sometimes believe. There are plenty of examples of the peasant farmers behaving like truly economic men of classical economics, when given the opportunity.

AIMS OF AGRICULTURAL PLANNING

The main aim of agricultural planning is to produce new policy measures in order to promote and facilitate changes in the direction of the targets laid down in the overall development plan, i.e., to produce a program of development. What are these elements? They include: (1) statement of agricultural development objectives consistent with the overall plan, (2) realistic targets for the development of agriculture over the period of the plan, (3) statements of measures to be taken and changes proposed to achieve these targets, (4) a list of special projects in the public sector required to be implemented to enable these targets to be met, (5) a long-range program in which the annual and medium-term plans form a consistent part, (6) organizational changes required to promote and facilitate implementation of the plan, and (7) a measure of the external and other financial requirements for the plan.

In early stages of planning, plans often consist of individual uncoordinated projects or sometimes only pious wishes and rarely have agricultural plans been complete and consistent. In saying this, one must remember, however, such perfection is difficult to achieve because in a mixed economy with agriculture in private hands, output targets can sometimes mean little but exhortation. The main form of encouragement in such cases is the establishing of basic policies that will provide incentives to the farmer. Within this framework much is still to be learned.

In agriculture, the requirements for data may well be greater than in many of the other sectors. Data collection poses serious problems because of the need to have available long series by many various geographical areas; but before undertaking planning, one should at least have records of climatic conditions, soil types, the effects of irrigation on soil, the importance of fertilizer inputs, and knowledge of the relevant methods of farming. All these physical aspects should be available for study before planning the sector. Planning in the absence of such factors can result in such agricultural activities as the so-called "Groundnuts Scheme" in Tanganyika in the late forties where the planners went ahead without a great deal of this knowledge. In addition to these physical aspects, one has to take into account such aspects as the personal attitude of the farmers, need for credit facilities, availability of markets, and problems of transport.

A basic question which demands attention is whether small farmers will accept a more highly organized cooperative form of farming since it requires changes in mental and social attitudes as well as in economic behavior. Concomitant questions include source of labor, method of purchasing and transporting fertilizers, financing of tractors, and the incentives required to persuade farmers to grow different and more economical crops.

A great deal of research has been done on these subjects individually, but little effort has been made to produce a synthesis of general value from the work of the different specialists. The magnitude of the problems involved can be seen in the study of the water and power resources of West Pakistan, an effort financed by the World Bank and on which teams of consultants were engaged for long periods collecting, analyzing, and interpreting important data. The report on this study was published in 1968.[2]

THE PLACE OF PLANNING INSTITUTIONS IN AGRICULTURE

What planning institutions should be established to allow the implementation of an agricultural program to proceed effectively?

Indications of the method used to prepare an agricultural sector plan have been given above and questions raised mainly of requirements. In the process of implementation, what has to be done if the policies and plans are to be turned into actual programs and projects? There are some general observations which can be made which apply to an economy as a whole, as well as to individual sectors. For example, planning is as good as the government which initiates and undertakes it. Good planning is difficult, if not impossible, with a weak and ineffective government.

Reflection will show the truth of this remark. Unstable governments rarely provide good information or the administrative organization to allow the execution of plans and projects. There must exist the will to implement a plan and the ability to carry out the policies which such a will requires. One sometimes hears governments making proposals which include new economic policies but their actions demonstrate that they are more interested in such areas as foreign affairs.

---

[2] World Bank Study Group headed by Pieter Lieftinck, *Water and Power Resources of West Pakistan: A Study in Sector Planning*, 3 vols. (Baltimore: Johns Hopkins Press, 1968).

After the firm expression of a government's intention to plan comes detailed implementation. To carry out the policies proposed requires the establishment of planning institutions. In a parliamentary system the policy decisions are usually made by a cabinet committee composed of ministers, often with the Prime Minister in the chair, and by the President in a presidential system. Such a committee consists of the whole cabinet or the heads of those ministries which are responsible for implementing the policy recommendations. This observation may sound a little trite but there have been cases where a committee of disinterested ministers with no portfolio responsibility was considered best, since such ministers would not be biased. The dangers and limitations of such an arrangement do not have to be explained.

Below the cabinet committee there is a central planning agency responsible for the overall formulation and review of implementation of the plan. Such an agency has the responsibility for insuring that progress in the various sectors is relatively uniform and in line with the plan targets. That is, if one sector advances more rapidly than the others, the overall plan and the annual development program are changed and adapted so that the main aims and targets of the plan can be achieved. The agency is also responsible for the preparation of the annual development program as well as the longer term plan. Since the annual development program is linked with the annual budget, this unit works closely with the Ministry of Finance.

Where such an organization is sited may be a subject for many hours discussion. In some countries, wherever it were placed it would work relatively successfully because of the will of the government. In others, it might never work at all, even if placed in the Office of the Prime Minister. Fundamentally, it should be placed where the economic policy control is exercised. Such a central planning agency would work closely with the Ministry and Department of Agriculture in any discussions of agricultural matters. In the Ministry of Agriculture a programming unit would be established which would be responsible for preparing the sector program and for coordinating those various projects which individual sections of the ministry or other bodies associated with the ministry have been considering. Its most important functions should include the preparation of a long-term sector program, the agricultural section of the annual development program, and the preparation of projects.

While preparation of a longer-term general plan, other than a perspective plan, is difficult to make, individual sectors programs covering ten or fifteen years can be provided. To prepare good projects takes some time and even longer is required to produce those which will fit into a coordinated sector program. The same programming unit also will be responsible for seeing that the projects are executed and for following up on project implementation.

PROGRAMMING UNITS

The central planning agency prepares the overall plan, and the operational ministry prepares the programs and projects. The work is done in the ministry usually by the programming unit, an organization that should be similar to that of the central planning agency. It sets standards and criteria for the preparation and execution of projects. It formulates the agricultural development plan, the annual agricultural program, and coordinates its activities with the Central Planning Agency and the Ministry of Finance. It prepares alternative development policies for consideration by the policymakers, after it has consulted with interested groups, both within the ministry and in other ministries. It sets the standards for the operating units to follow in reporting progress and it collates the reports on progress and evaluates them. It also is responsible for the technical assistance program.

Task groups may be formed if and as required. They could be formed to deal with such matters as: (1) resources, (2) coordination, and (3) implementation. These groups should operate with the farm specialists; the planners should deal with the targets and the farm management specialists with the methods of production. Specification of an ideal plan of operation is not possible since organizations depend upon individual circumstances, but there should be as much association with local committees and groups as possible in order to obtain rural cooperation in new ventures.

An example can be cited from the history of Pakistan's planning. Early in the period of the Third Five-Year Plan (1965–70) the drought conditions and changing circumstances for obtaining PL480 foodgrains changed the Government of Pakistan's policy with regard to future agricultural production. The government decided upon a self-sufficiency program for foodgrains and set up programs to implement this policy. The Council of Ministers having agreed on the broad policy issues, the Planning Commission and appropriate ministries began to organize the implementation of the program. The need for fertilizers, new seeds, irrigation water, and other inputs became apparent during the examination of the requirements of a self-sufficiency program. The need for the inputs then raised questions concerning the possible supply of electricity for irrigation pumping, transport for the movement of fertilizers and crops, credit facilities, and storage. The programming units began to work on the projects which needed to be implemented, and possible incentives were examined to discover which should be put into operation to persuade the farmer to increase production of foodgrains.

CONCLUSIONS

Agriculture is a complex sector in any economy. Planning is difficult because knowledge usually is slight. The farmers are scattered over wide areas and are often illiterate and tradition bound. Changes made in agriculture require concomitant changes in other sectors too. A number of inputs have to be transported and the crops have to be moved and sold, putting a strain on transport facilities. Extension services must be created or expanded and credit facilities need to be provided. Where rain is scarce or uncertain, dams and irrigation systems need to be constructed. To achieve success, planning institutions are required at all levels: at the highest level, to obtain policy agreement; at the senior official level to achieve coordination of the programs of different sectors to make sure that no bottlenecks occur. The cooperation of private industry and of farmers is essential to ensure that government plans will have the support and assistance of the public.

Each organization requires a competent staff capable of cooperation and yet energetic enough to achieve the completion of the program. But policy determination is basic; the government must decide what changes are required and what the public will accept. It must agree on policies to provide incentives. When these policies have been adopted, the government is firmly committed; the chain of planning institutions will try to guarantee the success of the plan. Without either, agricultural planning will be difficult to accomplish, i.e., without the planning institutions, little will be done to implement the projects which may have been formulated, even if the government's desire has been strongly expressed.

DISCUSSION by ARNOLD PAULSEN

I FIND MYSELF in agreement with Martin's characterization that planning should be defined as "an organized, conscious, and continuous attempt to select the best alternative to achieve specific goals." The planning institutions which are ineffective and especially in need of the reforms I discuss below fulfill this characterization less well, of course. From Martin's statements, such as ". . . success requires planning institutions at all levels," and "Good planning is difficult, if not impossible, with a weak and ineffective government," I find backing for my position that effective planning is and should be associated with all control functions and decision making. Thus, this discussion will not criticize but will elaborate briefly on the nature of planning activity, the reform of planning institutions, and the substance of the planning process.

THE NATURE OF PLANNING

Planning worth its salt is associated with decision making. Development planning should influence the rationality of investment decisions. Economic planning should suggest and evaluate alternatives which affect the economy and thereby accomplish the goals of a country. Planning is a staff function to decision makers and through them to the people.

Planning may be informal, partial, verbal, private, and short sighted, or sophisticated, comprehensive, long run, written, and published, but it is inseparable from control. If associated with control (i.e., influences public or private investment decisions), it is planning which influences economic development regardless of how primitive or decentralized. If separated from control, planning is not effective toward any goal regardless of how sophisticated or close to the prime minister's office. The arrangement under which planning takes place persistently should always be called a planning institution. Reform of planning institutions should upgrade planning presently in operation. It is hard to imagine any control situation with complete absence of planning for the use of power. Thus, it is not creation of planning where none exists that we need, but reform of existing planning institutions.

Planning is political and technical. It is highly political because it is oriented to accomplishing goals, multiple goals, of the people and their decision makers who are politicians. Only one-half the planning equation is identification and evaluation of technical possibilities.

The goals of economic planning have unique but shifting weights for each decision maker using each planning institution. No development plan acceptable to all important decision makers can be written for some regions, nations, and cities. Many development plans accomplishing an unacceptable combination of goals have been written and not executed. Planning institution personnel desire to have comprehensive national or agricultural development plans adopted after they have been painstakingly developed. This is usually impossible or useless. A comprehensive plan cannot be completely acceptable to a large group of politicians. There are thus only two outcomes from efforts to have large voluminous plans adopted legally: (1)

the plan is adopted because it has not been widely read or discussed and probably will not be, therefore the decision maker is not
required to abide by it and has no intention of following it closely;
(2) the plan is not adopted because it is widely read and taken seriously and must thus be torn apart, revised, and after revision can
only be adopted piecemeal. One is well advised to talk of the *influence*
of development plans on development decisions.

The influence of planning on decision making is limited just as
the power or control of any decision maker is less than absolute. The
amount of influence depends on the strength of the economic planning relationship. The planner and the planning institution will be
used and have influence only if they are worth more to the decision
maker than the relationship costs. The decision maker must be able
to accomplish more of his goals during his term in office with the
planners than without them. Therefore the planners must put to the
best possible use both the decision maker's time and his limited staff.
Thus the more productive a planning institution is to a decision
maker and his goals, the more influence it will have.

Planning institutions should have no major decision-making
authority. Planners should not try to change the major value orientations of the decision makers. For example, no planner in Iran in the
mid-sixties would have been able to dissuade the Shah from providing
an extravaganza at his coronation. Anyone who tried probably would
have been dismissed. To try to change major public value positions
or to misarticulate the decision maker's significant values is probably
at all times harmful to the decision maker-planner relationship. The
essential qualifications of a planning staff are loyalty to a decision
maker and accurate value perception.

REFORM METHODS FOR TWO TYPES
OF PLANNING INSTITUTIONS

Institutionalized planning may imply a large or small staff and
formal or informal organization. The most classical is the large
formal planning institution with specialized formally organized advisors. Some planning bodies are so large they become bureaucratic,
stable, even rigid, self-perpetuating—in short, an institution. The
large formal planning institution becomes anthropomorphic, i.e.,
takes on a personality of its own, which endures beyond the tenure
of the employees. (For example, in Iran—social eliteness, exalted self-
importance, self-contemplation, and condescension to the rest of government. In Greece—econometrically sophisticated, occupied with
models and theory, and oriented to worldwide publications, but not
acting as a local consultative service.)

The most effective reform of some large and formal planning

institution which has become irrelevant probably would be dispersal. Like the dispersal sales of purebred breeders, the herd would no longer be identifiable as an institution but the blood line could still be working in the country. Usually the central planning institution gathers and develops a large, well-educated staff, with some empirical understanding of the economy, and the ability to appraise development opportunities. Such skill and knowledge is scarce and is needed for national development, but it may not be most effectively employed in some planning institutions. The staff may serve their country better if dispersed and thereby more closely associated with the decision making of specific ministers or director generals. Effective policy and investment for development requires planning at all levels of the bureaucracy and in all provinces. Those few skilled people who have a broad understanding of the nation as well as of the philosophy and approach of planning will sometimes be allocated to a higher valued use if scattered throughout the ministries. An effective long run strategy for operating large formal institutions of central planning might be to gather and train staff centrally for several years and then disperse them. Thus, the country might create and then allocate human resources for planning among the action agencies.

Another common planning institution is the small and informal group of "cronies" surrounding politically powerful men. This form of planning institution will not be identifiable on the organization chart and thus may not be recognized as a very influential development planning institution. Men in authority are surrounded by loyal confidants with whom important decisions are discussed. If these confidants are technically incompetent and economically illiterate, a reform of the planning institution is needed.

The reform of small, informal, but incompetent planning institutions requires delicate measures. Capable people, technically knowledgeable, can be introduced and made available to decision makers. But the actual reform will require a shift in relationships. The capable planner-adviser must replace the loyal but less capable confidant. This cannot be done by executive order. The new adviser will supplant the old one only if he is more useful and more pleasant to the decision maker.

THE PROCESS OF PLANNING

The goals development planning must serve are multiple: (1) economic development, (2) security of the state and individuals, and (3) equity of opportunity and distribution of income.

The development planning of any sector such as agriculture must compete with and supplement the development of at least four others: (1) manufacturing, (2) public services, (3) business, and (4) household.

Just as the opportunity cost for accomplishing the economic development goal for a country is to be found in achieving less security and equity, the obvious opportunity cost for public attention and investments for agriculture is in the other sectors. A less obvious opportunity cost for economic development of agriculture is less progress toward security and equity goals in both agriculture and the other sectors. The economic development of agriculture is a significant goal but only one of several. The effort within agriculture toward economic development must be effective to compete constantly for the use of scarce resources in other sectors and toward other goals.

The process of economic development is activated by investments. The diversion of resources from providing currently consumable goods and services is not easy in a poor country and investment must promise to raise the capacity to provide goods and services very significantly in the future to be acceptable. Investment only works sometimes. Sometimes it fails and the population loses consumption both now and in the future. Planning actually is also an investment activity. If planning does not raise the productivity of investments it is a cost, a burden on the other productive activities, and reduces current goods and services without raising them in the future. Writing this book has been an investment activity. The only socially valuable product which can justify the investment is for the book to raise the effectiveness of rural development activities throughout the world. Obviously, there are uncertainties in this and all other investment activities. Part of the planning task is to help decision makers make decisions under uncertainty.

Planning for economic development in agriculture involves identifying cost-effective development opportunities and mobilizing the appropriate resources to exploit them. One could dwell long on evaluation procedures, planning consistency, or proper time discount rates. But the really important task of planning is discovering good development opportunities. The identification of development opportunities is a creative act, often an interdisciplinary hybridizaton, or the result of cross cultural insight. It comes often from review of the current situation by teams of analysts from several disciplines who can recognize unseen potential. Evaluation can eliminate poor alternatives but seldom creates good ones.

There are only four ways to invest and the task of planning is to balance the actions within and between each of the four. The most effective investment program for economic development of agriculture must be made for each local situation, but it would contain all of these four classes of investment in some mixture:

1. physical capital—roads, irrigation works, grain silos, plows, tractors, houses, pigs, barns, fertilizer
2. human capital—engineers, teachers, craftsmen, healthy laborers, politicians, general education, managers, an informed public

3. improved technology—death control, birth control, morbidity control, transportation, better seeds, farming methods
4. altering institutions—credit, land tenure, tax structure, markets, planning, political enfranchisement

The relationship between these four categories of investments and economic development of agriculture is more complex than purely additive. The effect of investing in one means is not independent in its effect on economic development of what one has invested in another category or sub-category.

The effectiveness of specific investments on economic development of agriculture is dependent on current local situations of a region, a group of farmers, or a specific crop. Successful investment patterns or investment effectiveness estimates borrowed from other countries can be misleading.

Each investment usually affects *security* and *equity* as well as *economic development*. The effect of an investment may be to raise all goals, but usually will raise one and lower another. How much each will be affected is a local judgment and highly uncertain.

The creativity required in identifying and evaluating alternatives is what makes planning fascinating. The goal complexity, the uncertainty, and the significance of planning requires that it be associated with political leaders. Those with political power are the only ones authorized and capable of weighing different goals and accepting risks in making important decisions. The reforming of planning institutions is largely a matter of increasing the contact between decision makers and technically and economically competent advisors.

REFERENCES

1. Weitz, Raanan, ed. *Rural planning in developing countries.* Cleveland: Press of Western Reserve University, 1966.
2. Rand Corporation, *Program Budgeting,* Washington, D.C.: U.S. Government Printing Office, 1965.

DISCUSSION by G. EDWARD SCHUH

RATHER THAN FOCUSING on the chapter by Mr. Martin, this discussion deals with five factors which reduce the effectiveness of planning institutions.

Lack of political power on the part of technocrats. Unless the people who plan have some political power or some way of getting their plans into the decision-making process, their efforts go for naught. The problem in most developing countries is that the technocrats who have the responsibility for making plans have little esteem in the eyes of most politicians. Hence, the possibility for getting the fruits of their work in the decision-making process is small.

Brazil, for example, has innumerable plans. These are seldom put into action in large part because the planners as such are not in the political process nor do they have access to it. It is interesting to note that one of the few technocrats to have political power in Brazil is now in self-imposed exile after his political rights were taken away.

Lack of competent people. The lack of technical training among the people working in planning institutions is a serious problem. The reasons for this are twofold: first, many of the positions are filled by political appointees, even when competent people are available; second, and perhaps more important, training institutions of high quality to provide the necessary skilled people are lacking. It is pertinent to note that in all of Latin America only about a half dozen persons in agricultural economics hold the Ph.D. degree. As late as 1960 only some half dozen persons held the M.S. degree in agricultural economics in all of Brazil—a country with 80 million people and a geographic expanse larger than the continental United States. The graduate program in the Institute of Rural Economics at Vicosa has since produced approximately sixty M.S. graduates, but this is "a drop in the bucket" compared to the needs of the country.

In this respect one must take issue in part with Erven Long's comments in Chapter 3. True, more research of the kind he described is needed. However, what is *much more important* is the development of talents and institutions in the various countries so they can solve their own problems.

Many persons have to recognize that what the United States is doing is essentially a stopgap effort. Any kind of self-sustaining growth in many of these countries will come only when the indigenous capacity to solve the country's problems has been developed. Outsiders create political difficulties, and will be able to work only for short periods of time. For example, the large number of North Americans introduced into the various ministries in Brazil after the revolution of 1964 has led to considerable anti-Americanism. American personnel are now being reduced in number because of this, and of course the country will still be without the necessary skilled manpower. Had the same resources been used to train Brazilians for this work, the country by this time would have a cadre of technicians available.

Brazil puts a great many resources into research and extension, but the payoff from this is not high. It would appear that this is, at least in part, a question of institutional arrangements and institutional organization.

One can argue that these are not proper problems for economists or agricultural economists. But the fact is that large amounts of resources do go through these sectors and more needs to be known about them.

Lack of data. Effective economic planning requires accurate data. Plans can be no better than the data on which they are based. Yet most developing countries just do not have such data.

To cite an example: Brazil currently has two "official" estimates of the size of their cattle herd, and these estimates differ by 100 percent. If one evaluates the productivity of the livestock sector using one set of estimates, the results would indicate that development resources should be used to strengthen this sector. If he uses the other set, the conclusion is that the livestock sector is doing quite well.

In other cases the problem is the total lack of data. For example, Brazil lacks data on wage rates in the various sectors, the level of unemployment, and the like. Effective planning cannot take place until these basic data are generated.

Lack of information or research on how the economy actually works. This usually comes under the rubric of positive economics. In the case of Brazil very little economic research has been undertaken to date, and even less agricultural research has been done. Hence, the stock of knowledge about how the system actually works is sparce. Because of this, one has little basis for knowing the impact of policy proposals on the pertinent variables.

In this field little can be generalized from other countries. Institutional differences make the basic parameters differ from one country to another. For example, considerable knowledge on the rate of return to investments in United States education has been accumulated. It would seem quite clear that the rate of return would be different in a country like Brazil, where complementary resources are different and where systems of remuneration differ. Similarly this is true for the relevant income elasticities of demand for various products and for the response to price incentives. When programs of minimum prices are suggested for Brazilian agriculture, no one really knows what their impact will be since so little is known about the relevant factor and product markets. Until more is known, the best planning will be fraught with dangers.

Use of inappropriate targets by the planners. The first aspect of this is the failure to identify the targets of the plan with the targets of the power groups of the society. The result is that little or no support is obtained for the plan once it is developed. This point is closely related to the first factor above.

Equally important, however, is the fact that planning targets tend to be too ambitious. When sights are set too high, the cost of the proposed programs become self-defeating, and consequently no part of the plan is ever implemented. The plan goes into someone's files, and that's the last ever heard of it.

What is generally needed is not *a* plan, but a planning *process.* In this, the analysis would be oriented toward how to take the *next step* and not toward where one would like to be once the country were fully developed. It is interesting to note that the Tennessee Valley Authority had no plan. They had a planning process to set goals and examine means for each year's work.

This list of factors that reduce the effectiveness of planning agencies is by no means complete. Nor should it be assumed that planning institutions have no roles. However, until some of these gaps are filled, planning is going to be pretty much of an exercise, with little chance of facilitating a more rapid rate of economic development.

REFERENCES

1. Gittinger, J. Price. *The literature of agriculture planning.* Planning Methods, Series No. 4. Washington, D.C.: National Planning Association, 1966.
2. Waterston, Albert. *Development planning: Lessons of experience.* Baltimore: Johns Hopkins Press, 1965.

6

GRADUATE AND UNDERGRADUATE

TEACHING INSTITUTIONS

D. W. THOMAS and J. H. ATKINSON

WHEN THE HISTORY of the twentieth century is written, a major truth will stand out. This is that the last half of the century constituted a period in which the dominant concern of man was the variability in the level of well-being of the peoples of the world. It will be noted as a period devoted to the identification and implementation of means capable of increasing the rate of economic development and social progress. During this half of the twentieth century there has been and will continue to be a deep concern about this issue.

This is true of all nations regardless of their stage of development or their political values and beliefs. Since the termination of World War II, most nations have concerned themselves with economic growth and development. Affluent societies have accepted irrevocable commitments to assist in the development of the less privileged nations. Their concern has waxed and waned with other national and international issues, but the mainstream of societal behavior has been one of continuous dedication to the development of nations.

Experiences to date have been a fascinating mixture of successes and failures of widely varying magnitude. This is completely understandable when considered in the light of the complex realities of bringing about rapid change in economic, technical, social, and cultural behavior in nations bounded by centuries of tradition. Out of these sometimes disheartening, sometimes exhilarating, but always costly experiences have come lessons of inestimable value to man as he continues the massive struggle to improve his lot.

Among the multitude of significant lessons has been one of recognition that industrialization does not constitute the panacea for poor nations seeking genuine economic development. Many nations also have learned that the agricultural sector cannot be ignored but rather must be given careful consideration in development programs and policies. Fundamental relationships among agriculture and other economic sectors in providing orderly, positive, and rapid economic change have been identified. To an increasing extent, these relationships are being recognized and accepted by those seriously concerned with developmental change.

Man continues to struggle with the fundamental truth that single-factor approaches to development have little to offer. The world has experimented with numerous programs in which principal reliance for developmental change has been placed on altering a single variable or a few related variables. There exist many examples of development programs weighted heavily by activities designed simply to increase an economy's physical facilities. In many other cases, direct transfer of technology from developed to developing areas has been expected to bring about sustained economic growth. Parallel examples can be cited where "importation" of institutional forms characteristic of affluent societies has constituted the major hope for progress. There have been trends emphasizing increased investment in technical research of a limited character and range as the mainspring to development. Educational investment, too, has had its moments of glory as the "magic" developmental variable. Out of these and similar experiences, scholars tend to learn, forget, and then relearn that the stimulation of economic growth depends not upon changing a single factor but rather upon bringing about appropriate change in a wide spectrum of relevant variables.

The interdependencies of institutions frequently mentioned by authors of other chapters of this book help stress the sterility of considering higher education out of context of other educational endeavors and without reference to the economic development process itself. In fact, the remarks which follow turn directly on the premise that the stage of development of a society, its noneducational development needs and total educational demands, have an important bearing on policy questions dealing specifically with the amount, kind, and form of investment in college level instruction. This is true in the general case. It is no less true in the case of agricultural education at the graduate and undergraduate levels.

GENERAL AGREEMENT ON EDUCATIONAL INVESTMENT

Developmental experiences of many nations have firmly established the importance of educational investment in human resources.

Denison[1] and others have provided empirical evidence that a significant fraction of output growth in the United States economy is attributable not to increases in physical inputs but to improvements in the quality of the human agent of production. Others have shown that an important part of increased agricultural output in modern societies is attributable to educational investments in human resources and in scientific knowledge base. Similar studies in the developing nations indicate significant associations between human resource investment and agricultural productivity.

From such scientific inquiry as well as from theory and general observation have grown several widely accepted generalizations. One is that educational investments tend to be characterized by high rates of return. Another is that the rate of economic development achieved by a society is some function of the rate of investment in human resource development. A third is that one basic reason for low rates of economic growth in the developing nations is their historic failure to make adequate investments in education.

Few would seriously question the validity of these generalizations. Yet, specific issues associated with educational investment in human resources continue to be hotly debated by those with either academic or operational concern with economic development.[2] The generalizations are accepted; the specific applications are clouded by controversy. This is true not only of education for rural development but also of primary, secondary, technical, university, and graduate level education.

CONCEPTUAL FRAMEWORK

SOCIETAL OBJECTIVES

The overriding public educational policy issue is one of societal objectives: What does a nation expect to achieve by investing in the education of its people? One cannot say much of any great value about agricultural education or any other form of education or any other social investment until this question is clarified. The point is that a society has many alternative ends which may be achieved, at least in part, through educational programs. For example, a society can place great emphasis on the rapid attainment of a technically modern economy requiring huge masses of technological and scientific human skills. Alternatively, principal emphasis may be placed on the evolution of an electorate sophisticated enough to participate meaningfully in a democratic society. In other situations, the goals of the

[1] E. F. Denison, *The Sources of Economic Growth*, CED (Washington, D.C., 1962).
[2] J. W. Hareson and C. S. Brenibeck, *Education and the Development of Nations* (New York: Holt, Rinehart and Winston, 1966).

society, rightly or wrongly, may be directed primarily toward the maintenance of the economic, social, and political status quo. These are but three examples of a host of possibilities. The alternatives, in all possible combinations, are infinite. It follows that the "right answer" to a nation's human resource investment decisions depends, in an important way, upon the relative weights a society attaches to the several elements constituting its national objective.

Most contemporary nations appear to be characterized by sets of national goals which weight heavily the attainment of economic growth. This is not true of all nations, nor is economic growth ever the unique societal goal. However, for purposes of this chapter, the attainment of higher rates of economic growth is assumed among the more significant goals of nations.

WHO SHALL PAY THE BILL?

A second major issue associated with a nation's investment in its human resources is who shall pay the educational bill. There are two possibilities. One, the direct users of human talents can pay for the education or training required to make specific talents available to them. The alternative is for the society as a whole to assume responsibility for education and provide the necessary investment funds. Those in the agricultural field take this for granted but in certain areas of technical education there does seem to be sufficient economic incentive for the private sector to undertake directly some meaningful part of the whole. Here, too, this will differ widely with the nature of the industry involved. In the industrial sector, there are examples of the industry itself taking responsibility for providing technical education. Except for relatively basic skills there appear to be few examples of this in agriculture. The reason is clear. The private costs of providing technical education exceed expected returns. Given the structure of agriculture in most of the world, it would be wishful thinking to expect much college level agricultural education to be provided by the private sector. Rather, such investments in agricultural education as are called for will be provided largely by the public sector.

EDUCATION VERSUS OTHER PUBLIC INVESTMENT ALTERNATIVES

The third principal issue associated with investment in human resources in the developing nations is one of the allocation of scarce public resources between education and a set of other public investment requirements of the economy. Here, several things must be clearly recognized if wise decisions relative to educational investments of all types, including agricultural education, are to be made. One of these is the irrefutable fact that developing nations do not have unlimited public investment resources at their command. Rather they are faced with extremely limited resources relative to the investment requirements of economic development. Most such nations are characterized by limited economic surpluses. This situation is aggravated by an inability and/or unwillingness to tax themselves in order to expand available public capital. On the other hand, economic development in the traditional societies tends to require rather massive injections of other forms of social overhead capital—transportation, communications, research, public services, utilities, physical resource development, and the like.

A most difficult allocative decision is posed. Alternative courses of action are: (1) to invest all available public resources in human resource development, (2) to invest all available public resources in other forms of social overhead, or (3) to invest in some combination of the two. Logic suggests that neither extreme would often turn out to be optimal. Between the extremes there probably exist ranges in which these alternative forms of investment are complementary and others in which they are competitive. It follows that these nations would find it to their advantage to allocate scarce resources somewhere between the extremes. At the minimum, the complementary ranges should be exhausted. Within the competitive range, the optimal situation turns out to be where the decline in developmental impact associated with refraining from investing in education is offset by the positive effects on development associated with increased investment in other forms of social capital.

Conceptually, the issue and its resolution are straightforward. As a practical matter, they are extremely complex. However, if developing societies are to enjoy maximum benefits from the use of public resources, they must face this fundamental problem. They must, somehow, arrive at an allocation of resources between education and other developmental needs which approximates the optimum. For present purposes, it is sufficient to note that resources available for educational purposes of all kinds—primary, secondary, technical, university, graduate, and adult—are not unlimited; education must compete with other uses; it will share public resources with these other uses to the extent that it contributes to the attainment of the goals of the nation.

WHAT KINDS AND LEVELS OF EDUCATION?

Developing societies face still another closely related allocative decision with respect to human resource development. Given the resources which a society desires to make available for educational purposes, these resources must be allocated among the various forms of education. In the general case this is a most complicated and difficult question. Agricultural education is a no less difficult case; if anything, it is more complicated. University level education is but one of several types of education required for genuine agricultural development. Stated differently, the human skills which may be developed best through formal university education constitute but one of several sets of human skills required for the takeoff and sustained growth of agriculture. University education competes on the rural scene with demands for primary, secondary, and formal and informal technical education.

Here, again, developing societies must choose from among a set of alternative courses of action. Investment of all available resources in university level agricultural education probably would seldom be warranted. That investment of all available resources in other educational pursuits would be optimal is equally doubtful. Most likely there exists some range of complementarity between investments in university and in other forms of agricultural education. It is equally probable that at some point they become competitive.

The particular educational "mix" which will make maximum contribution to the development of agriculture has a single valued solution for a given nation at a given point in time. This solution will depend upon a number of factors. In the first instance, it will depend upon the society's concept of the purposes and objectives of education. It will depend upon the stage of technological and economic development of production, processing, and distribution in agriculture. It will depend upon the quantity and kind of human talents already existing as a result of historical investments in people.

Again, the concept is clear and rather straightforward. The solution of this problem as it exists in reality is highly complex and difficult to achieve. The point, again, is that those responsible for educational investments in the developing nations must clearly recognize the nature of the fundamental relationships involved. They must constantly strive to achieve an allocation of scarce educational resources which will make maximum contribution to the attainment of the level of agricultural development desired by the society.

The hard choices that the developing societies must make with respect to educational investment, unfortunately, do not terminate here. This follows from the fact that university education, itself, is not homogeneous. Rather, it is constituted of many possible curricula each capable of providing the individual with a particular set of abilities. Thus, choices must be made between educational investments in institutions and curricula designed to provide one set of abilities and those designed to provide other sets.

Here, recognition of the nature of the relationship between the level of investment in specific types of university education and the value of such to society is important. It is reasonable to expect this relationship to be one of decreasing marginal returns. With unlimited resources, investment would be rational in a particular type to the point where the marginal value of the returns to such investments were equal to the marginal costs of providing such. But life is not so simple. Resources available for university education always tend to be limited. Alternative forms have value. Given this, developing nations must somehow allocate available resources among alternative types of university level agricultural education in a manner such that the trade offs at the margin are equated.

THE TECHNOLOGY OF EDUCATION

Another fundamental issue of considerable importance to educational investment in the developing nations deals with the "technology" of education. It is a matter to which developing nations have given far too little consideration. The issue is this. A given level of "education" can be achieved with a variety of organizational structures and combinations of human and capital inputs. For example, it is possible to train an agricultural scientist of excellence by employing the archaic "disciple" system. It is possible to train an equally good agricultural scientist by employing modern educational methods. It is possible to impart to a rural population a given quantity of technical skills in a variety of ways—informal youth and adult education as a part of educational programs in the traditional academic forms of primary and secondary education, in specialized technical schools organized in a variety of fashions, and the like. The same is true of all other educational endeavors.

The cost of providing a specified amount of education will differ widely from one system to another. There is some least-cost educational system for achievement of a desired end. Developing nations have extremely limited sources with which to meet the multitudinous exigencies of progress. These nations must examine, with great care, alternative technical means of meeting their educational requirements. They simply cannot afford to do otherwise. To the extent they can achieve "least-cost education," they will get significantly greater "mileage" from the limited bundle of resources at their command. One of the most promising avenues to rapid development in the disadvantaged nations may rest in the imaginative discovery and implementation of a bona fide "technological revolution" in their educational systems. Neither traditional, indigenous systems of education nor those imported from the developed nations may constitute the least-cost way of accomplishing the massive task required. Efforts to identify and experiment with other systems, not only in technical education but in all education, should be encouraged.[3]

In the points made above, more questions are raised than answered. This is by design. A recipe specifying the nature and extent of investment that a nation ought to make in university level agricultural education cannot be written. The same is true of all educational endeavor. Recipes are of no, or even negative, value in situations where "right answers" depend upon a complex of variables, the magnitude of which must be defined endogenously by the society in question. Despite this, nations dedicated to the achievement of national development goals must face, in some fashion, the fundamental issues outlined in this chapter. By the same token, outside entities desiring to contribute, through education, to progress in the developing world must do so in a manner consistent with decisions reached in this kind of analytical framework.

NATURE OF CONTRIBUTIONS OF GRADUATE AND UNDERGRADUATE EDUCATIONAL INSTITUTIONS

At this point, attention is turned to a brief examination of the specific contributions that undergraduate and graduate educational institutions make or have the opportunity of making to agricultural development. In discussing these contributions, the factors are treated which determine the value which a society attaches to investment in these particular pieces of developmental machinery. To do so, one must indicate the obvious as well as point out those things which, while less obvious, may be crucial to the developmental process.

Educators and most noneducators find no difficulty in specifying the unique contributions of higher educational institutions to development. Simply, these turn out to be *trained people* and *useful knowledge*. But this response is hardly adequate to in-depth understanding of the role of these institutions in development; nor is it complete. It begs a number of significant issues dealing with the numbers and kinds of trained people essential to economic development and social change. Equally, the phrase "useful knowledge" tells little of real value when faced with the pragmatic questions and issues of development. In the substantive content of these two generalizations one finds the determinants of the value of such educational and research services to developing societies; the value of these services determines the quantity of scarce public resources that a

---

[3] United States financing of research in the "technology" of education in developing countries might well be justified by the application of such research results to our own educational dilemma.

developing society will be willing to invest in these institutional forms.

The public investment in undergraduate agricultural education institutions required depends on a host of factors. It is some function of the demand for the services of people trained at this level. A prime determinant of a nation's demand for agriculturists is simply the size of its agricultural industry. This factor has two dimensions— the physical size of the national unit in question and the fraction of its total economic activity constituted by the agricultural sector.

A second major determinant of the demand for agriculturists is the stage of development of the agricultural industry. In nations characterized by static, primitive agriculture, there simply is not much of directly productive value that a university trained agriculturist can do. This simple, but significant fact is reflected in the well-known syndrome of the agricultural professions in many such nations—low prestige, low salaries, a dearth of employment opportunities, and lack of interest in agricultural careers.

As nations characterized by primitive agriculture tread the path to agricultural development, the demand for trained agriculturists expands. With technical and economic modernization of agriculture, productive opportunities for the employment of agriculturists in the production, processing, and distribution functions of agriculture expand—perhaps geometrically rather than arithmetically. The private sector of the agricultural industry offers increasing opportunities for highly remunerative inputs of technically modern and professionally competent human inputs. The expanding public infrastructure always associated with a developing agriculture creates additional opportunities for effective utilization of such people. In cases where agricultural development is proceeding rapidly, the supply of trained agriculturists and the limited training capacity of indigenous agricultural colleges and universities may become the most limiting factors to the continued growth of agriculture.

Certain time lags associated with the agricultural development phenomenon present special and difficult problems. Agriculture, in the primitive state, offers few productive employment opportunities for technically trained people. In the private sector, few incentives to employ such people exist; similarly in the public sector. Incentives and the rationale for public support of agricultural colleges are not present or at least not obvious. Competent individuals find little economic or other incentives to cast their lot in agricultural careers.

At the same time, initiation of the development process necessitates substantial inputs of highly trained agriculturists in public activities and in leading, entrepreneurial elements of the private sector. Future returns to such human inputs tend to be great. The problem is that the payoffs occur in the undefined future rather than in the present. Private firm and individual discount rates of such future returns are conditioned by risk, uncertainty, and preferences for present, rather than future, income. The net result tends to be discount rates of magnitudes making such present courses of action economically irrational.

There seems to be only one solution to this time lag dilemma. This is for the society as a whole with its longer planning horizon, more aggregate set of objectives, and lower future discount rate[4] to assume the initiative, invest appropriately, offer competitive incentives, and employ the agriculturists produced in appropriately productive developmental activities. This is not an easy course of public action. Public investment decisions are made in the political arena. Other investment opportunities for scarce public resources have shorter term, more visible, and more direct payoffs; hence, they tend to be politically more acceptable and attractive. While difficult, these decisions constitute one of the acid tests of a society's commitment, desire, and will to develop.

The value which a society attaches to institutions of higher education designed to train agriculturalists depends upon the degree to which the products of this educational process develop talents, skills, and abilities useful to the society. A multitude of factors are involved in this subtle but important evaluation. Some of the more significant of these factors follow.

The key variable appears to be one of the degree to which the schools of agriculture train people capable of meeting the needs of the agricultural sector. Here, recognition should be given to the fact that the modernization of agriculture may not always be a primary or priority objective of the developing nations. If a society, for whatever reasons, desires to maintain its agricultural sector in something less than a modern state, the agriculturists required will differ both in number and in training from those required if a society desires to modernize agriculture. If modernization of agriculture is not the objective, a society likely would not be willing to invest a great deal in institutions designed to train technically competent agricultural specialists. It is more likely that such societies would attach greater value to investments in educational institutions characterized by curricula designed to train agricultural generalists capable of treating a broad array of quasi technical but largely administrative problems. If, on the other hand, a society is genuinely committed to the develop-

---

[4] Not only does the discount rate for society tend to be lower than for individuals and firms, but the society also may be able to borrow at lower rates and on more favorable terms than individuals and firms.

ment of its agricultural sector and/or if the agricultural development process has been set in motion, it probably would attach much value to investments in institutions designed to provide the more specific technical skills required of persons actively involved in this process.

In order to provide specific technical skills, attention must be given to the question of what to teach. The curriculum of a given United States university cannot necessarily be transferred to a foreign country. Indeed, the traditional notion of a four year course of study is not always appropriate. Curricula must be developed for specific country needs.

A second major factor affecting a society's willingness to invest in agricultural colleges and universities is one of the effectiveness and the efficiency with which such institutions perform. Given the kind of product required, educational institutions must constantly strive to produce that product as efficiently as possible. If they do not, the costs incurred, from the viewpoint of society, may be so great that continued investment will become quite unattractive. The developing world abounds with examples of this particular phenomenon.

A third major determinant of the value which a society attaches to such educational investment is the responsiveness of the institution to changing demands for technically trained agricultural manpower. This responsiveness must be viewed both in terms of numbers and in terms of the nature of the human agent produced. This matter is of particular significance in societies where rapid changes in agriculture are occurring. With rapid development comes rapid changes in the type of agriculturalists required for continued growth and development. Educational institutions flexible enough to respond appropriately to the changing structure of demand for trained people will continue to offer high payoff investment opportunities for public resources. Those which do not respond to such changes in the demand for trained people will not constitute attractive investment opportunities. Public support will decline; other institutions will be devised to provide the talents required for continuation of the agricultural development process.

AGRICULTURAL SCIENTISTS

The second major category of trained people of concern is that of agricultural scientists—persons with research-oriented training beyond the undergraduate level. Here, a number of matters are significant. However, attention is focused on two major areas: (1) the role of the scientist in agricultural development, and (2) the set of issues determining the investments which developing societies might most appropriately make in institutions designed to train this particular kind of human resource.

Perhaps one of the most significant, but least recognized elements in agricultural development is the role of the agricultural scientist. Despite the well-known and fundamental role that research has played in all nations which have achieved a highly productive agriculture, there has been a tendency, until recently, for developing nations and for nations assisting them in the development process to ignore one fundamental truth: the creation of a directly applicable technological, economic, sociological, and political knowledge base is a necessary condition to the development of agriculture. Agricultural development efforts endogenously or exogenously inspired in the developing nations have, for the most part, not reflected the hard fact that meaningful and positive changes in agriculture depend directly upon the magnitude and duration of investments in agricultural research, in the development of a cadre of highly competent agricultural scientists, and a set of indigenous institutions characterized by an environment in which such scientists might systematically provide the knowledge base required for the takeoff and sustained growth of agriculture. Despite the fact that there is no substitute for these types of investments, developing nations and those attempting to assist them in development have preferred to believe in the fallacy that agricultural technology is largely transferable from the developed to the developing parts of the world.[5]

This myth has, at this point in time, been exploded; the productivity impacts of indigenous science and technology have been clearly demonstrated; yet the developing nations still find themselves, for the most part, far short of the agricultural research capacity and scientific manpower requisite to development. There seems to be little question but what sustained investments of major magnitude must be made in the training of agricultural scientists and in the support of relevant agricultural research if agriculture in these nations is, in fact, to develop.

The prime contribution of the agricultural scientist to development is clear. However, he plays other important complementary roles in the development process. Knowledge created through research is useful not only in the production processes of agriculture but also as a fundamental basis for educational programs of excellence throughout the industry. Only on such a knowledge base can a nation develop effective training programs for those already engaged in agriculture, the less than university level agricultural technician, the university trained agriculturist, and the agricultural scientist.

Without a constantly expanding body of scientific knowledge, people simply cannot be educated in a manner such that they will be most productive in their particular calling.

---

[5] Basic scientific knowledge is transferable. The application of science to solution of real world problems (technology) tends not to be transferable because of differences in environment (economic, political, geographic, institutional, etc.).

Agricultural scientists have the opportunity of playing another significant role in the developing nations. In a very real sense, they constitute the elite of modern agriculture and serve as a very specific kind of intelligentsia. The agricultural scientist is the one capable of helping determine that which exists in agriculture and, that which might exist or which ought to exist.[6] In short, the agricultural scientist has the potential capability for defining in meaningful terms the development problems and issues of the agricultural sector. In so doing, he is in position to focus the attention of society on these issues. At the same time, he is in position to evaluate, although at times quite broadly, the consequences of alternative courses which the society might choose to follow.

Finally, that modern agriculture will evolve in the developing nations as a result solely of the "normal" economic, social, and political forces at play is most doubtful. At least, such will not occur rapidly enough to satisfy the expectations of the rural masses. That national objectives with respect to agricultural development will be obtained as a result of the responses to existing internal forces is most doubtful. Rather, rapid agricultural development presupposes concerted public action in many areas and at many different levels. Appropriate public action requires a specific kind of leadership which approximates quasipolitical statesmanship in the name of agricultural development. Additionally, effective management of public programs designed to stimulate the agricultural sector requires not only high level managerial skills but also a firm basis of knowledge about the agricultural industry. If agriculture in the developing world is to progress, such statesmen and managers are a necessity. A nation's corps of agricultural scientists is likely to provide a far better source for these specific kinds of talents than alternative sources. The relatively small number of a nation's trained agricultural manpower that rises to this set of challenges can make extremely important contributions to development.

INSTITUTIONAL, ORGANIZATIONAL, AND STRUCTURAL CONSIDERATIONS

If one accepts the premise that the creation of an indigenous corps of agricultural scientists and the evolution of associated programs of relevant agricultural research are essential to agricultural development, a multitude of pragmatic issues remains to be faced. One of these is the question of the time span required to implant an

---

[6] This assumes even greater importance when we consider the importance of the agricultural sector in most developing countries. In many instances, half or more of the human resource is in agriculture and a substantial part of the national products comes from that sector.

effective and adequate agricultural education and research establishment in a developing society. This particular activity is not one that lends itself to crash programs; rather it is one that must be evolved systematically through time with appropriate attention to and balance among several facets. Developing nations having no, or extremely small, cadres of agricultural scientists must concern themselves with alternative means of training such people. In the absence of effective educational machinery for producing scientists, these nations must rely on sending capable people abroad for advanced training. At some point in time, the need for trained scientists will tend to exceed the numbers that might feasibly be trained abroad. Here the issue of developing internal mechanisms for training scientists must be faced. Simultaneously with the expansion of the corps of scientists and the need to develop indigenous means of further expanding the supply, developing nations must face the issue of investing appropriately in research institutions and research programs. The question is one of priority and balance. The process requires judgment, wisdom, and above all, time.

A related public policy issue of great importance is one of determining the particular institutional organization or arrangement in which payoffs from investments in graduate agricultural education and research will be the greatest. Here, developing nations are faced with many alternative institutional forms in which they might organize these endeavors. They may elect to develop a national system of independent agricultural research institutions with responsibility only for the research function. They may tie the graduate education function to such research institutes. They may elect to associate the agricultural research function, organizationally and administratively, with the agricultural extension function. They may develop sets of institutions which have responsibility for graduate education, undergraduate education, extension, and agricultural research. Other organizational combinations of these and other functions are possible.

In the developing world, one finds examples of every conceivable type of organizational structure for agricultural research and graduate education of agricultural scientists. While there probably is no single best solution applicable to all cases, there are some guidelines useful to the process of evolving the most appropriate system.

With respect to the training of agricultural scientists, particular attention should be given to the type of system which will best serve the needs of the nation. Efficiency in training of agricultural scientists must be considered a major factor. At early stages in the development of a nation's agricultural research establishment, sending neophytes abroad to obtain advanced training is necessary and efficient. In small nations or in those with a relatively unimportant agricultural sector, this may always be the most efficient way to provide scientific manpower. In many nations, however, as the demand for and the ability of the system to absorb agricultural scientists expands, creation of indigenous machinery for expanding the supply of scientists becomes necessary, in the interest of efficiency.

As previously noted, agricultural scientists may be trained in a number of different ways. The problem is for the society in question to evolve imaginatively a system which will maximize the output of trained scientific manpower from any given quantity of resources available for this purpose.

The particular institutional environment in which graduate education takes place is a matter of utmost concern. There appears to be no acceptable substitute for the university environment if scientific training of excellence is desired. Essential inputs from the basic scientific disciplines, other applied disciplines, an environment of scholarly inquiry, library facilities, and the like are available only in the university complex. Complementarities existing among these and other factors argue strongly for implanting graduate education in the university complexes of the developing nations. There are examples abroad where graduate education is being developed apart from the university structure. While special circumstances may dictate this approach, serious questions are unavoidable about the wisdom of this approach.

Three other general principles appear significant. One of these is the necessity of assuring adequate research facilities, support and programs as a precondition to establishment of a system of graduate education in the agricultural sciences. A second is the necessity of assuring an adequate corps of senior scientific staff capable of handling with excellence graduate level courses and providing satisfactory supervision of the research endeavors of budding young scientists. Finally, the development-inspired expansion in the demand for agricultural scientists tends to create extreme pressures on indigenous graduate programs to expand both in terms of numbers and in terms of the level of advanced study offered. Here, developing graduate institutions must resist premature capitulation to these pressing demands and insist that expansion take place only as staff development, research programs, and facilities warrant.

While this chapter is limited to a discussion of undergraduate and graduate education in the agricultural sciences in the developing nations, the intimate relationship between graduate education and agricultural research leads to a few general comments relative to the organization of agricultural research institutions. There is a multiplicity of institutional forms in which agricultural research might be performed. Probably no one best structure applies to all developing nations. There are, however, a few general principles which seem to have universal application to this particular public policy matter.

To increase the probability of limited research resources, human and otherwise, being allocated to the more relevant and important problems, a nation's agricultural scientists must be subject to institutional forms characterized by built-in, continuous channels of communication with the realities of agriculture. The organizational structure of agricultural science should be such that the prime users of the products of the research investment have low-cost, easy access to research output in the most directly usable form. The agricultural sciences should be imbedded in organizations capable of providing a maximum of open communication among scientists. Finally, the developing nations should attempt to organize agricultural research in a maner such that the inherent complementarities between agricultural research and investments in agricultural education, at all levels, might be operative.

SUMMARY

Undergraduate and graduate educational institutions are key elements in the complex of public and private institutions requisite to agricultural development in the developing world. The products of these institutions constitute inputs of crucial value to agricultural development. In the most fundamental way, the human resources conditioned by these institutions form the thinking, deciding, and acting agents of development in the agricultural sector. They constitute the unique resource capable of constructing the scientific knowledge base of a modern agriculture. These institutions provide the professional human resources constituting the cutting edge of all public and private entities involved in agriculture. This cutting edge can be no sharper than that honed on human agents passing through a nation's graduate and undergraduate educational institutions.

DISCUSSION by ERLY D. BRANDAO

AFFLUENT SOCIETIES AND THEIR COMMITMENTS
TO ASSIST DEVELOPING NATIONS

THE COMMITMENT of the rich nations toward the poor nations is very relative. One certainly cannot deny that the aid channeled by the Alliance for Progress to Latin America has been sizeable. Equally clear is the fact that most of this economic assistance has been in the form of loans. Nevertheless, support in the United States Congress for this and other forms of aid showed a tendency to decrease in the late sixties. For this and other reasons the likelihood that rich countries will aid poor ones is very much reduced. These are the reasons why the gap between developed and developing countries will continue to increase daily. Perhaps developing nations expect too much from the developed ones. Conklin in discussing this point says:

> Unfortunately, the United States is almost wholly incapable of sparking the profound changes in the 'rules of the game' which are needed in most of Latin America today. We never went through the process of changing from a feudal or neofeudal system. Our forefathers ran away from this when they came to America. (1)

Herrera takes yet a stronger position on the same matter:

> Blame must also fall on a basic backwardness in some of our concepts related to basic aspects of the way in which our countries are organized, and resources are distributed within them. A typical example of this, is the backwardness of the Latin American University, taken as a whole. I ask you, "upon whom falls the responsibility to make available sufficient public funds to the universities that these can live up to their lofty mission, if it isn't upon us? . . . We cannot unbind ourselves from this responsibility, nor can we transfer it to outsiders. It is up to our communities, our governments, our intellectuals, our scientists, and our universities, and to avoid this task would be to renounce those vital elements which structure the characteristics of our communities. (2)

In connection with the third of the authors' generalizations, the real concern should be with the quality of education offered rather than with the quantity of resources that many developing countries are devoting to education.

In the case of Brazil a preliminary investigation shows that total public expenditures in the field of education by federal, state, and municipal sources, in 1968 prices, has increased from NCr5.43 million in 1960–63 to approximately NCr8.2 million in the period 1964–67. In real terms, this is an increase of 50 percent. Public expenditure in education, in 1968 prices, has been raised by 90 percent between 1960 and 1967, during which period GNP increased by only 35 percent. The percentage of GNP spent on education was increased from 2.7 percent 1960–63 to 3.1 percent in 1964–67 (3).

As the actual result of the recent university reform brought about in 1968, funds for education were increased substantially in real terms. If we compare public expenditures planned for the three year period 1968–70 with the preceding period, we may note an increase in real terms of 40 percent. If we make the same comparison with the 1962–64 period, the increase is 122 percent, which shows the substantially higher priority granted since 1960 to the formation of human capital in Brazil in terms of money invested (3).

This rapid growth of funds for education represents increases in the percentage of GNP of the following magnitude: 2.7 percent in the three year period 1960–63; 3.1 percent in 1964–67; and 3.6 percent in the year 1968. Estimates for 1969–70 show that the indicators will be raised to 4.2 percent and 4.4 percent respectively (3). If funds from the private sector are added to those of the public sector, the figure is raised to 5 percent in 1970 (4).

The new Brazilian policy through which education will receive a proportionally larger share of funds, taking the country as a whole, is being considered unfavorable to the poor northeast region. The new scheme calls for fewer federal funds in contrast with more state and municipal sources. In practical terms, this means that the northeast region apparently will lose the opportunity to establish a number of industrial plants and to finance some agricultural projects already planned by the region (4).

This example helps to illustrate, to some extent, the fundamental concept expressed by the authors when they state:

> economic development in the traditional societies tends to require rather massive injections of other forms of social overhead capital— transportation, communications, research, public services, utilities, physical resource development and the like . . . a most difficult allocative decision is posed.

The effort undertaken in terms of money invested to benefit the education sector has resulted in a spectacular increase in the total number of students enrolled within the last six years. In effect, the number receiving primary education has increased by 43 percent, those in secondary education establishments by 93 percent, and the number of university students by 100 percent. The corresponding increases among teachers and professors were 73 percent at the primary and secondary levels, and 64 percent at the university level (3).

Investments in education, science, and technology (which are essential to economic development) have so far not attained adequate levels, in spite of the fact that the budgetary allocations made by many countries for education are sizeable. At the signing of the Charter of Punta del Este, in 1962, the signatory countries agreed that funds for education should reach a level corresponding to 20 percent of the total national budgets for the next ten years, or to 4 percent of GNP. Some, but not all, countries have surpassed this goal.

Although these investments are a praiseworthy initiative, the increase of funds for education apparently has not modified the quality of teaching. In developing countries there has been too much teaching of poor quality and too little of good quality.

In expanding their conceptual framework, the authors indicate the following courses of action: (1) to invest all available public resources in human resources development, (2) to invest all available public resources in other forms of social overhead, or (3) to invest in some combination of the two. Logical reasoning suggests that neither extreme would turn out to be optimal. The developing countries would find it to their advantage to allocate scarce resources somewhere between the extremes. Nevertheless, people with power and influence might justifiably try to convince the decision makers to invest more in education, science, and technology. The expected results might be illustrated by Japan. Its determination to have universal education began almost a century ago. The fantastic development this nation presents today is related to that historical decision. In an effort to capitalize on similar opportunities in Latin America, the Inter-American Development Bank is making educational loans. Persons interested in that program are encouraged to contact the Bank for details.

SUMMARY

The conceptual framework presented is an outstanding contribution. Decision makers involved in the complex problem of allocating resources between education and a set of other public investment requirements now have an excellent guide for helping them make right decisions. Similar advantages are extended to all those persons referred to by the authors, when they state, "specific issues associated with educational investment in human resources continue to be hotly debated by those who are either academically or operationally connected with economic development in the developing nations."

Developing nations should not wait until the more developed ones make available to them continuous and large quantities of resources even if these are in the form of loans. To incur heavy loads of indebtedness is a dangerous situation which the poor countries must avoid. Agriculture can contribute in a very important way to economic development, as various countries have already demonstrated. On the other hand, economic development imposes upon agriculture the need to make adjustments and introduce changes of very great magnitude. These changes can only be made with material and human resources that are of high quality. The indispensable role of education, research, and extension in this complex problem is absolutely clear. In this field the poor countries find themselves confronted with a particularly attractive challenge—possibly the only one which will enable them to open larger doors toward development.

REFERENCES

1. Conklin, Howard E. "Pioneer settlement and agrarian reform," in *Rural development in tropical Latin America*. New York: Cornell University, 1967, pp. 123–25.

2. Herrera, Felipe. *"Prologo" la educación avanzada y el desarrollo de America Latina, Banco Interamericano de Desarrollo.* Washington D.C., 1965. (Translation by author.)
3. Reforma Universitaria, Expansão do Ensino Superior e Aumento de Recursos para Educação, *"Relatorio da subcomissão especial do grupo de trabalho da reforma universitaria,"* Ministerio do Planejamento e Coordenação Geral, Rio de Janeiro, Agosto, 1968.
4. Vaz da Costa, Rubens. *"Recursos para investimentos educacionais,"* Fortaleza—Ceará, Novembro, 1968.

DISCUSSION by GENE WUNDERLICH

GRADUATE and undergraduate institutions in the Western-oriented world are remarkably uniform in faculty structure, administration, curriculum, and student affairs. They produce students and faculty well suited to the Western mass marketing techniques. Major demanders of graduates in business, government, and education can rely, more or less, on the minimum skill level associated with the academic degree. Obviously this standardization has many advantages in a highly integrated, mass-producing economy. However, the pattern may not be most efficient for a developing country seeking innovative solutions to rather basic problems.

The present institutional structure of Western universities evolved from guilds of students (Bologna, eleventh century) and masters (Paris, twelfth century) at first emphasizing the professions of medicine, law, and theology. Medieval universities played an important part in public and ecclesiastical affairs. Many universities, as objects or instruments of national policy, were reorganized in the nineteenth century, and in Italy, Spain, and France autonomous regional universities were established. Although the first universities in the United States were sponsored by religious groups (Harvard, William and Mary, Yale), they became secularized and later, to a degree, nationalized through federal grants and subsidies. The democratization of education in the United States through the Land Grant College system in the 1860's may well be one of the world's major innovations in higher education. A question now before us is: Is the Land Grant University innovation of the mid-nineteenth century in the United States an appropriate form for developing countries in the late twentieth century?

Democratization of education in the United States has provided a broad base of minimum skill levels for industry and government.

A large pool of literate, if not brilliant, technicians, administrators, and educators was able to carry out an industrial revolution which in turn provided a capital base for further scientific achievement and technological development. Mass education provided a common value base which transcended several internal crises. Education provided one form of social mobility.

On the other hand, the democratization of education in the United States was supported by external capital and industry, vast natural resources, and a comfortably small population. The United States, in other words, could afford to be more liberal with its educational resources than may be possible for some presently developing economies. These countries may have to tailor their educational programs more carefully.

EDUCATIONAL REQUIREMENTS FOR DEVELOPMENT

Education for economic development as it is now known at least, suggests a high priority on scientific and technical skills. A substantial portion of those skills will be oriented toward primary industries, namely agriculture. The fund of knowledge about agriculture in developed countries is great enough to suggest the concentration on operation, i.e., undergraduate training, rather than on invention, i.e., graduate training. To some extent the same may hold for heavy industries and the professions. In trade, finance, and planning, on the other hand, emphasis might tend more toward the inventive and hence graduate training. In no way is it possible to generalize for all developing countries, however.

One feature required of all educational systems in virtually all countries experiencing (or seeking to experience) growth is innovation. Educational innovation must be available to meet conditions of change. Educational innovation in this context means the changes in the structure and processes of education necessary to provide needed skills quickly. Can the fickle demand, which in one year calls for 100,000 agricultural engineers and three years later calls for 100,000 systems analysts instead, be accommodated?

Flexibility comes at a cost. Specialized, technical skills can be developed but often at the expense of breadth of education. A specialized education runs the risk of obsolescence. A general purpose education runs the risk of insufficient depth to accomplish anything. Even very large educational institutions with wide diversity of skills must choose their areas of concentration.

From the viewpoint of a national education system, flexibility can be attained either by encouraging major organizational shifts in the structure of the institutions ("reforms") or encouraging internal flexibility in curricula, staff, and projects within the institution (changes in "instrument variables"). National policymakers probably will be most interested in major reforms because changes in curricula, staff appointments, and degree requirements would not individually affect national objectives such as economic development. Furthermore, the traditional nature of many universities may be resistant to change. The creation of new educational institutions may be more effective and efficient than modifying older ones. In traditional economies educational institutions may exert as conservative a force as peasant agriculture.

TAILORING HIGHER EDUCATION FOR DEVELOPMENT

National differences in economic opportunities will call for different educational curricula and organization. Although broad variations in the level, style, and content of training are possible, fundamental choices must be made by national policymakers in terms of the requirements for economic development. Some of the choices will be among education for:

1. administration, government, politics, and law to develop orderly economic, social, and political processes
2. agricultural, mechanical, and informational skills to adapt and disseminate technology
3. science, engineering, and basic research to discover and evaluate knowledge
4. humanities and arts to use economic development in the service of other objectives

Confronted with certain broad policies of desired economic attainment and the realities of low income, technological backwardness, population pressure, poorly utilized resources, and other characteristics of a developing country, national policymakers may wish to question the traditional procedures for training. Should educational processes be oriented to lifetime careers of individuals? Should teaching and research be conducted at the same location? Should education be project oriented or discipline oriented? What operational devices such as research centers, professional organizations, grants, and sabbaticals, encourage needed innovations? In partial answers to these questions, two dimensions of higher education might be examined in combination: (1) the academic degree, and (2) continuing education.

DEVELOPING SLOWLY BY DEGREES

The bachelor's, master's, or doctoral degrees represent terminals of structured units of education—basically units of education time.

These terminal degrees also are the planning units around which most universities and colleges are built. The highly institutionalized processes of curriculum modification and degree requirements permit only limited flexibility in the educational institution. The degree process requires a lock-step adherence to year-in, year-out schooling from kindergarten to doctorate with only minor variations. In this process occupation is intended to follow, not to lead or combine with the life process of education.

Imagine the elimination of the terminal degree concept. A fuller expression of inherently flexible man might be obtained by a closer association of education with occupation. With education analogous to savings or investment, and occupation (application or activity) analogous to expenditure, the educational process could be regarded as continuous. One would invest in education, and spend in vocation on a sustained basis.

The conventional Western view of continuing education is still oriented to the terminal degree accompanied by an occasional "retread." It presumes the graduate to be basically uneducable. Alternatively we might assume an educational point system for the individual. At any time in his career, his educational attainment could represent an accumulation of points rather than one, two, or more degrees.

The challenge of educating persons with life experience (those who may have been occupied with something other than school) is as real to developed countries as to developing countries. However, reasons for questioning the terminal degree institution would differ between developed and developing countries. Some of the reasons for abandoning the terminal degree concept in developing countries are that it is expensive, inflexible, and often nonfunctional. The terminal degree institution is not well adapted to educating older people. The degrees are associated with wealth and status, tending to separate, rather than level, social strata. Degrees represent large indivisibilities in education, so "small-investors" may not enter the education market. Thus, resources that might have been channeled into education are used where the payoff is not as high.

No single device or system will be adequate either to continuing education or education for innovation, but some alternatives to the long, expensive process of formal education might be considered, especially in those countries with limited resources. At best, education can be a nation's most valuable input for development. At worst, it can be a waste of time.

7

RESEARCH INSTITUTIONS:

QUESTIONS OF ORGANIZATION

VERNON W. RUTTAN

THE RESEARCH INSTITUTE and the university represent alternative methods of organizing professional resources to produce technical, social, and cultural change. In this chapter, two case studies will be used to illustrate some of the advantages and disadvantages of these two institutional patterns. The first case study focuses on the evolution of the academic sub-discipline of agricultural economics. The second focuses on the emergence, in the agricultural program of the Rockefeller Foundation, of the international institute as a primary device for organizing professional resources.

Generalizing from these two cases, it is argued that in societies characterized by a highly developed infrastructure linking the university to other public and private institutions, education and research conducted within the framework of the traditional academic disciplines and professions represent an effective link in the total system devoted to the production, application, and dissemination of new knowledge. The same academic disciplines and professions, when transplanted into societies where such an infrastructure does not exist, rarely become forceful agents of technical, social, or cultural change. Agricultural economics will be used to illustrate this point subsequently. If developing countries are to overcome the technical and institutional barriers to economic growth they must engage in a

An earlier draft was read at the Conference on "The Role of the Professional as an Agent of Economic, Social and Political Change," Berkeley, California, May 24–26, 1968. I am indebted to David Hopper, John M. Richardson, Clifton R. Wharton, Jr., Sterling Wortman, Arthur Mosher, Richard King, and Lowell Hardin for criticism of an earlier version of this chapter.

pragmatic search for patterns of institutional organization of professional resources, rather than adopting either a "classical" or a "land grant" university ideology as a model.

Examination of these two cases is conditioned by a perspective (bias) that a basic deficiency of Western academic and professional organization is its conservative (reactionary) response to the evolution and reform of its own structure. The deficiency is particularly apparent in the difficulty of the university in the modern technical-scientific economies of the West in adapting its research and teaching to a situation in which the great bulk of scientific activities takes place outside the university.[1]

Seitz has argued that in the United States the universities are evolving in a direction that is destined to turn them into what might be termed "degree factories." That is, they are being turned into extensions of secondary schools in which basic disciplines are taught and in which the student may gain rudimentary experience with the research process.[2] By and large this experience will be gained under the direction of gifted amateurs rather than professional research scientists.

EVOLUTION OF AGRICULTURAL ECONOMICS
AS AN ACADEMIC SUB-DISCIPLINE[3]

Agricultural economics is a field of applied economics. Its scope and its relationship to other social and natural science disciplines has changed over time in response to: (1) the social, economic, and technical changes impinging on the agricultural sector, and (2) progress in economic theory and in other related social and natural science disciplines.

Prior to 1900, agricultural economics did not exist in the United States as a field of specialized study, either within general economics departments or in colleges of agriculture. The rapid growth of agricultural economics as an academic field, between 1900 and the early twenties, reflected the emerging interests of a number of men who had been trained in the agricultural disciplines; in factors affecting the costs of production; and in the economics of farm management—particularly in problems such as the economics of enterprise selection, choice of production methods, and the financing and growth of the

---

[1] Robert Solo, "The University in Functional Social Systems," mimeographed (Dept. of Economics, Michigan State University, East Lansing, 1968).
[2] Frederick Seitz, "Science, the Universities, and Society," *Am. Scien.* 56 (1968): 296.
[3] This section draws very heavily on a paper by Vernon W. Ruttan, "Agricultural Economics," Dept. of Agricultural Economics, University of Minnesota, Staff Paper 69–17, June 3, 1969. The survey was organized under the joint auspices of the Social Science Research Council and the National Academy of Sciences National Research Council.

firm. It also reflected the growing interest of a number of economists in problems of agricultural policy, the behavior of agricultural commodity markets, and the economics of land use. The interests of both the production scientists and the economists were clearly oriented to the use of social, economic, and technical change to improve both agricultural productivity and the quality of rural life.

Throughout the development of agricultural economics there has been continuous debate regarding the appropriate scope and method of the field in an effort to overcome the ambiguity resulting from its multidisciplinary origins. In 1959, the joint Social Science Research Council Committee on Agricultural Economics—American Farm Economic Association Committee on New Orientations in Research commissioned a series of papers to review the progress and problems being faced by the field.[4] The initial paper in the series identified excessive fragmentation along geographic and sub-disciplinary lines as the major factor limiting the effectiveness of agricultural economics.

These criticisms remain valid. Yet this very parochialism and fragmentation of agricultural economics has also represented a source of strength. Its parochialism has contributed to the interest of agricultural economists in focusing their attention on the economic problems of states and localities and of individual farm production and marketing firms. Its fragmentation has contributed to the interest of agricultural economists in examining specific commodity demand, supply, and production relationships. Close association with the experimental and statistical methodology employed in applied biology made agricultural economists particularly receptive to methodological developments leading to greater precision in: (1) quantification of economic and technical relationships, (2) empirical testing of hypotheses and generalizations, and (3) providing quantitative guides to the effect of alternative private and public sector decisions.

The fragmentation of agricultural economics along sub-discipli-

---

[4] These papers were: George K. Brinegar, Kenneth L. Bachman, and Herman M. Southworth, "Reorientations in Research in Agricultural Economics," *J. Farm Econ.* 41 (August, 1959): 600–19.

Vernon W. Ruttan, "Research on the Economics of Technological Change in American Agriculture," *J. Farm Econ.* 42 (November, 1960): 735–54.

Marc Nerlove and Kenneth L. Bachman, "The Analysis of Changes in Agricultural Supply: Problems and Approaches," *J. Farm Econ.* 42 (August, 1960): 531–54.

Robert L. Clodius and Willard F. Mueller, "Market Structure Analysis as an Orientation for Research in Agricultural Economics," *J. Farm Econ.* 43 (August, 1961): 515–53.

Karl A. Fox, "The Study of Interactions between Agriculture and the Nonfarm Economy: Local, Regional, and National," *J. Farm Econ.* 44 (February, 1967): 1–34.

A sixth paper on the economics of agricultural development was also discussed by the committee. The scope of the problem appeared too broad for treatment in a single article and a new set of papers was commissioned. The papers have been published under the title of *Agricultural Development and Economic Growth,* Herman M. Southworth and Bruce F. Johnston, eds. (Ithaca: Cornell University Press, 1967).

nary lines also may have accounted for the ease with which it has expanded from its initial emphasis on problems of production economics and farm management to encompass: (1) marketing of agricultural commodities and factor inputs, (2) commodity, supply, demand, and trade relationships and policy, (3) land and natural resource economics, and (4) problems of agricultural development and economic growth.

In spite of these strengths, agricultural economics is facing a number of serious challenges to its future as a field of applied economics. Two trends which have serious implications for the way in which professional resources are organized in the future have emerged with particular force during the last two decades:

(1) Agricultural economics has evolved away from a multidisciplinary field to increasingly acquire the organizational and cultural characteristics of a sub-discipline of economics. One major consequence of this development is that problems that are defined as "interesting" by the sub-discipline carry an increasingly heavy weight relative to problems that are defined outside the discipline in the choice of research strategy, objectives, and methods.
(2) This trend is reinforced by a rise in private sector research in agricultural economics relative to public sector research. This is particularly true of applied problem-solving research. Appropriate objectives of public sector research have become less obvious.

One result of these developments is that academic public sector research is increasingly directed to problems that are of interest to other economists. Both of these developments are functional in a society characterized by a highly developed institutional infrastructure linking the university to other private and public institutions which are directly involved in the conduct and management of economic affairs. They would be highly disfunctional in a society which has not yet developed such an infrastructure.

THE AGRICULTURAL PROGRAM
OF THE ROCKEFELLER FOUNDATION

United States technical assistance programs in agriculture have been organized around three patterns or models. Perhaps the most familiar is the "counterpart model." This is the situation where individual scientists employed by United States technical assistance agencies work in close cooperation with individual scientists in national research, educational, or operating program agencies.

A second pattern might be characterized as the "university contract model." The "university contract model" has typically been employed where "institution building" has represented a major objective of the technical assistance activity. Frequently, the institution building objective has involved, either explicitly or implicitly, positive assumptions with respect to the relevance of the "Land-Grant philosophy" or the "Land-Grant experience" to the solution of technical and social problems of the host country.

A third research and/or training "institute model" has also been widely employed. The institute model has typically been employed when working within the framework of existing institutions would be subject to such severe limitations as to hamper the achievement of the technical assistance program objectives.[5]

In this section the emergence of the international research and training institute model within the context of the agricultural program of the Rockefeller Foundation will be traced. Both the technical accomplishments and the production impact of the Rockefeller Foundation program in Agricultural Sciences in Latin America and Asia have been adequately reported in both professional and popular literature.[6] Therefore, the focus here will be on the manner in which the organization of professional resources has evolved in order to meet the program objectives. The program objectives themselves have been stated primarily in terms of the invention, introduction, and diffusion of a new biological and chemical technology. The measure of the success of these efforts that have been adopted by Foundation scientists and administrators has been primarily in terms of increases in the national average yield and of national output of key agricultural commodities, particularly wheat, corn, and rice.

The Rockefeller Foundation Agricultural Sciences program was initiated in 1943, with the establishment of the Office of Special Studies (Oficina de Estudios Especiales), in the Mexican Ministry of Agriculture.[7] Field research programs were first initiated with wheat and

---

[5] The typical operating situation frequently involves elements of more than one of these ideal type models. A common criticism of United States AID country directors or contract officers is their failure to distinguish between the appropriate roles of direct hire and university contact personnel. See John M. Richardson, Jr., *Partners in Development: An Analysis of AID-University Relations, 1950–66* (East Lansing: Michigan State University Press, 1969).

[6] A. T. Mosher, *Technical Cooperation in Latin-American Agriculture* (Chicago: University of Chicago Press, 1957), 100–26; L. M. Roberts, "The Rockefeller Foundation Program in the Agricultural Sciences," *Econ. Botany* 15 (October–December, 1961): 296–301; Ralph W. Richardson, Jr., "A Pattern of Practical Technical Assistance: The Rockefeller Foundation's Mexican Agricultural Program," *Agri. Sci. Rev.* (USDA-CSRS) (1964); E. C. Stakman, Richard Bradfield, Paul C. Mangelsdorf, *Campaigns Against Hunger* (Cambridge: Harvard University Press, 1967); Delbert T. Myren, "The Rockefeller Foundation Program in Corn and Wheat in Mexico," ed. Clifton R. Wharton, Jr., *Subsistence Agriculture and Economic Development* (Chicago: Aldine, 1969).

[7] The decision to initiate the program was made following the report in 1941, of a survey team consisting of Richard Bradfield (Professor of Agronomy and Head of the Department of Agronomy, Cornell University), Paul C.

corn. The program later expanded to include field beans, potatoes, sorghum, vegetable crops, and animal sciences. A common pattern of staffing was followed for each commodity program.[8] A specialist from the United States was brought in as each commodity program was initiated. Each specialist assembled a staff of young Mexican college graduates who were trained in research methods and practices as part of the research program rather than through a formal program of graduate studies.

In retrospect, the staffing program adapted by the Foundation, centered around a project leader for each commodity, did have one major limitation. This can be illustrated by comparing the relative progress of the wheat and corn programs. The wheat program achieved technical success earlier and its impact on yield per hectare and on total wheat production has been greater than for the other commodity programs. New wheat varieties were being distributed to farmers by the fall of 1948. By 1956, the production impact was sufficient to make Mexico independent of imported wheat. The rapid progress of the wheat program was clearly related to (1) the special competence of the early leaders of the wheat program in the fields of plant pathology and genetics, and (2) the fact that stem rust was a dominant factor limiting wheat yields. Improvement of corn yields was much more complex. In addition to a more complex set of biological factors the institutional considerations involved in seed multiplication, distribution, and diffusion were more difficult.

In situations where the technical, production, and organizational problems were relatively complex, their solution requires contributions from a broad spectrum of biological and social scientists. In such cases the staffing pattern worked out during the early years of the Mexican program was not entirely consistent with rapid progress in the solution of research and production problems. In these more complex situations a multidisciplinary team approach emerged as a more appropriate strategy than the simple commodity program approach of the early years. The problem of successful integration of social scientists into the project teams was, however, never successfully solved in the Mexican program.

A major source of strength in the success of the Rockefeller Foundation program in Mexico was its economical use of the scarce professional manpower available in Mexico, both at the beginning and throughout the program. The shortage of professional manpower and of indigenous educational resources was conducive to the development

---

Mangelsdorf (Professor of Plant Genetics and Economic Botany, Harvard University), and E. C. Stakman (Professor of Plant Pathology and Head of the Department of Plant Pathology, University of Minnesota). The team was sent to Mexico as a result of a request to the Rockefeller Foundation from the Mexican Ministry of Agriculture following a visit to Mexico by Vice-President Henry Wallace. (See Stakman, Bradfield, and Mangelsdorf, 1967).

[8] Sterling Wortman, "Approaches to the World Food Problem" (Paper read at Southwest Agricultural Forum, Tulsa, Oklahoma, January 19, 1967).

of an internship system which intimately linked professional education with investigation.

In 1943 there was not a single Mexican in the field of agricultural sciences with a doctoral degree and only a few with a masters degree. By the end of 1945, the Office of Special Studies employed 7 Rockefeller Foundation scientists and 25 Mexican "interns." Even at its peak, in the late fifties, the Rockefeller Foundation staff in Mexico consisted of less than 20 scientists. By 1963 over 700 young Mexicans had served for one or more years as interns in the Oficina de Estudios Especiales. About 250 of the best interns had received fellowships for study in universities in the United States or elsewhere. There were 156 Mexicans with M.S. degrees and 85 with Ph.D. degrees in the agricultural sciences. Of the 27 interns who entered the program in the first two years, all but 4 were still engaged professionally in the field of agriculture *in Mexico* in 1963.

By 1963, agricultural science had been successfully institutionalized in Mexico.[9] On December 30, 1960, the Office of Special Studies was dissolved and merged into a new National Institute of Agricultural Research under Mexican direction. After an emotionally painful two-year disengagement, the Rockefeller Foundation program and staff in Mexico were reorganized into a new International Center for Corn and Wheat Improvement.

The significance of the disengagement is that it is symbolic of the fact that Mexico has succeeded in building into the fabric of professional life the acceptance of agricultural science as a career service into which men could enter with confidence that their contributions would be rewarded, both in money and in professional recognition.

On May 14, 1963, advanced degrees in the agricultural sciences were conferred for the first time in Mexico. Mexico's new capacity to produce trained manpower in the agricultural sciences is developing in response to the demand for scientific manpower generated by the success of the initial thrust of the technical revolution in Mexican agriculture. The dramatic technical revolution of the past two decades did not, however, depend on the existence of graduate training in the agricultural sciences in Mexico, nor did it draw significantly on the skills of large numbers of Mexican scientists trained in the United States and elsewhere.

The establishment of the International Rice Research Institute (IRRI), in the Philippines, in 1962, represents a second major landmark in the evolution of the agricultural science program of the Rockefeller Foundation. The IRRI was jointly financed by the Ford and Rockefeller foundations. It was established as an international

---

[9] Charles M. Hardin, "The Responsibility of American Colleges and Universities: Definition and Implementation" (Paper read in Section O of the American Association for the Advancement of Science, New York, December 28, 1967).

research and training institute rather than as a component of a national ministry of agriculture. It was staffed by an international team of scientists representing eight different nationalities.

The multidisciplinary competence that would be required to solve the biological problems of higher yield potential and to achieve rapid increases in total national and regional output was recognized and carefully structured into the staffing plan.[10] An intensive program of seminars and research program reviews was initiated to focus the efforts of the diverse multinational and multidisciplinary team on a common set of objectives and to achieve complementarity among the several disciplines. This singleness of focus was thought necessary to invent, introduce, and diffuse a new high-productivity rice technology.

The location of the IRRI in Los Banos, adjacent to the University of the Philippines College of Agriculture (UPCA), made professional resources available to the IRRI that had not been available in Mexico. The UPCA had already developed relatively strong departments in several fields of agricultural science. Joint appointments of IRRI staff to the UP graduate school strengthened this capacity. This arrangement permitted many of the IRRI trainees to work toward M.S. degrees under the direction of an IRRI member while simultaneously engaged in a highly complementary research "internship" at the Institute.

The typical research scholar or intern at the IRRI has emerged from this training with greater personal research capacity and a higher level of sophistication with respect to research strategy and relevance than most graduate students from the developing countries who complete either M.S. or Ph.D. degrees in the United States graduate schools.

Within six years after the initiation of the research program at the IRRI a series of new rice varieties with yield potentials roughly double those of the varieties that were previously available to farmers in most areas of Southeast Asia has been developed and is now being disseminated to substantial numbers of farmers. In some areas this process has proceeded far enough to have a dramatic impact on aggregate production.[11]

---

[10] "The scientific staff has been cosmopolitan from the beginning . . . as shown by the following list: agronomy, Moomaw, Hawaii; plant breeding and genetics, Beachell and Jennings, United States, and Chang, Taiwan; soils, Ponnamperuma, Ceylon; plant physiology, Tanaka, Japan, and Vergara, Philippines; plant pathology, Ou, Taiwan; entomology, Pathak, India; chemistry and biochemistry, Akazawa, Japan, and Juliano, Philippines; microbiology, MacRae, Australia; statistics, Oñate, Philippines; agricultural economics, Ruttan, United States; agricultural engineering, Johnson, United States; communications (and sociology), Byrnes, United States," Stakman, Bradfield, and Mangelsdorf, p. 298.

[11] These developments have been widely reported in the popular press typically in a highly exaggerated form. For a more careful assessment see International Rice Research Institute, *Annual Report: 1967* (Los Banos, 1968); E. A. Jackson, "Tropical Rice: The Quest for High Yield," *Agricultural Science*

The significance of the Rockefeller Foundation experience, both in Latin America and now in Asia, goes well beyond the impact of the new wheat, corn, and rice technology which has been invented. The significance of the experience is the evolution of an institutional pattern for the organization of scientific resources which can be replicated for a wide variety of crops and localities with a reasonable probability of success. It is now possible to organize a multidisciplinary team of biological, physical, and social scientists capable of inventing a new highly productive biological and chemical technology for crop production and to make this technology available to farmers in a form that they are capable of accepting within the relatively short period of five to ten years.

IMPLICATIONS FOR THE ORGANIZATION OF PROFESSIONAL RESOURCES IN DEVELOPING ECONOMIES

What are the implications of the two cases examined above for the organization of professional resources to induce change in developing countries?

Agricultural economics has evolved, over the last five or six decades, into an academic subdiscipline directed primarily to: (1) the refinement of theory and method and (2) supplying increasingly precise information about the economic consequences of private and public action. The results of both types of inquiry are regarded as inputs into decision-making systems for which the researcher assumes no responsibility for either direction or control.

In spite of its relatively short history and its initial problem solving orientation, agricultural economics in the United States has acquired most of the organizational and cultural characteristics which are typical of other fields of science or academic disciplines. Problems that are defined within the discipline or the field of science carry an increasingly heavy weight relative to problems that are defined outside of the discipline in the choice of research strategy, objectives, and methods.

The United States is characterized by a highly developed institutional infrastructure linking the university to other private and public institutions involved in technical, social, and economic change. In societies where such an infrastructure has developed, research and education within the framework of the traditional academic disciplines and professions have represented an effective link in a larger system devoted to the production, application, and dissemination of new knowledge.

Review, USDA-CSRS, Vol. 4 (1966); S. C. Hsieh and V. W. Ruttan, "Environmental, Technological, and Institutional Factors in the Growth of Rice Production: Philippines, Thailand, and Taiwan," *Food Research Institute Studies,* 7 (1967): 307–47.

The same pattern of academic and professional organization, when transplanted into societies where the institutional infrastructure which it presumes does not exist, rarely performs as an effective instrument of technical, social, or cultural change. This is one of the major factors responsible for the substantial frustration involved in attempting to utilize the "university contract model" as an instrument to induce technical, social, or cultural change in developing economies. The institution building approach to the replication of either the "land grant" or the "classical" university in developing countries has rarely been productive in terms of either technical or cultural impact. The more typical result is to burden the developing country with an overextended academic bureaucracy which is unable to make effective use of the limited professional capacity available to it.

If developing countries are to overcome the technical and institutional limitations that separate the performance of the world's low and high income economies, they must make efficient use of the professional competence which represents their single most limiting resource. This implies a pragmatic search for patterns of institutional organization which permit a nation to have access to the professional competence available to it and to focus this competence directly on the critical barriers to technical, social, and cultural change.[12]

The research institute pattern which has evolved in the Rockefeller Foundation programs in Latin America and Asia is an example of one such pattern that has been exceptionally effective in situations where the institutional infrastructure linking science to the rest of the economy is lacking. This model should not be held as a solution in other situations. Rather it is illustrative of the desirability of a pragmatic rather than an ideological approach to the organization of professional manpower for the solution of development problems.

---

[12] Theodore W. Schultz, "Efficient Allocation of Brains in Modernizing World Agriculture," *J. Farm Econ.* 49 (December, 1967): 1071–82.

RESEARCH SYSTEMS

A. H. MOSEMAN

PERHAPS the most certain feature about the building of national systems for agricultural research is that neither their significance nor their processes are well understood. Those concerned with the problem have done a very poor job of communicating the relevance of institutionalized agricultural science, its structure, its functions, and the procedures through which effective research systems can be established on a national basis.

A principal difficulty is that those participating in agricultural development operate from widely divergent bases of knowledge and experience. They come from distinct scientific or professional disciplines—economics, social sciences, or the natural sciences. The variation may be within the profession, as a research scientist, teacher, or extension agent; or it may be in the scope of operational experience, at the local, state, national, or international level. Regardless of one's specific background, it is difficult to embrace the task of developing effective agricultural research institutions into national systems because of the incomplete and fractionated concept of such systems.

It is not difficult to generalize about the agricultural research capabilities of developing nations. Some changes have occurred since the early forties, when the Inter-American Institute for Agricultural Sciences was established in Costa Rica, and when the Rockefeller Foundation initiated its cooperative program in Mexico. And some progress has been achieved since the Point IV Program was initiated in the early fifties. But, over the span of twenty-five years, since the initial research-oriented efforts to improve foreign agriculture were made, one finds disappointingly little progress in the building of indigenous capability for agricultural research. In fact, in a number of the countries that have achieved independence since World War II, the agricultural research resource has deteriorated as visiting scientists have departed.

ORGANIZATIONAL PATTERNS

In a number of the colonies formerly British, there is a rather consistent pattern of central research institutes concentrating primarily on fundamental or basic studies of concern in the production

An expanded version of this chapter has been published as: Albert H. Moseman, *Building Agricultural Research Systems in the Developing Nations,* The Agricultural Development Council (New York, 1970).

of a commodity (usually a cash or export crop). Only limited attention is given to the practical or adaptive research essential for agricultural diversification and modernization. This was the pattern in India and in Pakistan with their central research institutes for jute, cotton, and sugarcane; and in Africa, where the research institutes concerned with rubber, cocoa, and oil palm were estalished to serve the broader regional areas of West Africa. The establishment of the Rubber Research Institute of Malaya, in 1927, also reflects the special interest in technical backstopping for commercial crops, with little research attention to the balance of agriculture in the country.

In India and Pakistan agriculture is considered a state subject, although research is accepted as a joint, or concurrent subject for state and central government attention. Since tax resources at the state level are limited, adequate support for research through the state ministries of agriculture is difficult to obtain. As a result, research to resolve the problems of cultivators was largely neglected prior to the more recent efforts to strengthen the applied and adoptive research, especially in India.

Research is not a major component of the colleges of agriculture or of the schools of agriculture in most developing countries. These are primarily teaching institutions with curricula and procedures strongly guided by the university to which they are affiliated.

In India and Pakistan Councils of Agricultural Research provide financial support to selected projects. In the absence of a strong national research infrastructure, however, the relatively modest and usually short-term allocations of funds to narrowly defined projects within special disciplines furnished little practical or cumulative benefit. India has taken positive steps in the past decade to develop All-India research projects and a national organization for adaptive and applied research, with ICAR funds channeled substantially to the coordinated All-India projects.

In general, agricultural research in developing nations is more personalized than organized, and depends largely upon the initiative, vigor, and level of training of individual research workers.

RESEARCH PERSONNEL

In most developing nations only a limited number of agriculturists are trained beyond the B.S. degree level, although in the countries following the British university pattern, increasing numbers with the B.S. Honors degree (essentially equivalent to the M.S. degree) work in the scientific disciplines related to agriculture. However, a rather commonly held view still contends that substantial modernization or upgrading of traditional agriculture can be achieved by individuals trained only through the B.S. school or degree level. This unfortunately is a misconception to which too many United States agriculturists contribute by suggesting that "technical assistance tasks can be handled by a good county agent or extension specialist." These words have a familiar ring as we recall the long record of controversy with respect to "solid research" versus "expedient demonstrations" in the evolution of the state experiment stations in the United States.

Actually, the tasks of crop breeding and improvement, soil and water management, disease and pest control, etc., are as complex in tropical agricultural regions as they are anywhere in the United States and often more so. The same level of research competence is required to meet them.

One would not expect students trained through the B.S. degree in general agriculture to be effective researchers in the United States. The training and experience in conceptualizing a problem and organizing an investigation to resolve or learn about it is achieved in M.S. and Ph.D. programs. Until the importance of raising the level of the professional capability of agriculturists in the developing countries is recognized, the technological input into their agriculture will continue to be largely secondhand and second-rate.

Some developing countries have substantial numbers of individuals with advanced training at universities in the United States and the United Kingdom or other foreign nations. Their contribution to agricultural development in their own country may well be limited, however, if their academic experience was concentrated on theoretical problems; if they have no indigenous leadership to help focus on significant local problems; and if they do not have an organizational base in their home country to supply budgetary and program stability.

Another serious limitation is the tendency to place responsibility for a broad scope of research in the hands of a single individual. As an example, in some countries one economic botanist at a research institute is designated as the leader for crop breeding and improvement research for a number of major economic crops such as wheat, cotton, sorghums, millets, oil seeds, etc. Even though he may have a sizeable number of lesser trained subordinates, no one person, no matter how competent, can furnish incisive and progressive leadership to this scope of research.

The lack of a strong organizational structure usually results in the frequent and rather continuous transfer of the subordinate level research workers from one project to another. Frequently a plant scientist will have worked on three to five different crops over a ten-year period with the moves motivated by modest salary advances in the new field. Such personnel contribute little in advancing technology during their careers.

The limited numbers of qualified indigenous research personnel is the most critical handicap in our cooperative technical assistance efforts.

The Minnesota Agricultural Experiment Station has as many

Ph.D. trained personnel at its Northwest Branch Experiment Station at Crookston, and at its Southern Branch Experiment Station at Waseca, as does the entire Research Branch of the Ministry of Agriculture and Cooperatives of the Government of Malaysia. And the latter organization is responsible for the nationwide program of research on all crops, soils, water management, disease and pest control, and related problems for all aspects of agriculture except rubber.

As one recognizes the importance of a solid agricultural research base—and the level of training required to make it productive—it becomes apparent that the agricultural education structure in most developing nations requires substantial upgrading. In most cases the targets for advanced training to the M.S. or Ph.D. degree levels are still much too low and inadequate. Questionable also is whether the strong emphasis on vocational training, through the level equivalent to the United States high school, will produce effective agricultural advisers or extension workers. This is especially so if they lack the capability to understand the significance of properly combining the packages of practices or inputs which have been developed and proved through today's orderly interdisciplinary research.

Substantial progress has been made in a number of countries where the scholarships and fellowships of private foundations and other organizations have produced a strong corps of well-trained scientists. Also, under the USAID contracts with the United States land grant universities the participant or training component has been utilized by the universities to train students from the cooperating countries to the M.S. and Ph.D. levels. As a result, a sizeable nucleus of such well-trained agriculturists can be found at many locations in the developing countries where the United States universities have been collaborating for a decade or more. In many countries this represents the best agricultural specialist resource available.

PROGRAM DEFICIENCIES

While the lack of well-structured research organizations and the limited numbers of trained research specialists have been the more critical handicaps in generating agricultural technology in developing countries, additional program or operational defects exist.

The concentration of attention on export crops has resulted in inadequate concern for improved production of the food grains and feed crops, or for design of diversified cropping systems for maximum productivity of land and water resources.

The emphasis of research institutes on fundamental studies has limited the attention to practical production problems. The research institutes are usually organized on a discipline basis, i.e., divisions of botany, chemistry, soils, mycology, entomology, etc., with a tight compartmentalization which limits concurrent or interdisciplinary research efforts.

The domination by nontechnical administrative personnel in development of budgets, release of funds, approval of travel, recruitment and selection of professional staff, purchase of equipment and supplies, and similar functions, is one of the more serious handicaps. This varies in different countries, but in few instances is there acceptance of the United States pattern where the director of a research institute or station is a trained scientist and the administrative functions are regarded as services to facilitate and expedite research.

The inadequacy of research laboratories and field stations or facilities is a rather general handicap, and frequently one of the most difficult to assess. A common problem for agronomic research is the lack of precision in field experimentation which results from the absence of uniform plot lands with adequate control of irrigation or moisture management; and ineffective weed, disease, or pest control.

The lack of indigenous research capability limits opportunities for cooperation by outside organizations since there must be a minimum of indigenous competence and research facility resources for cooperative adaptive research projects.

The agricultural research capability in the developing nation was generally overlooked in the initiation of United States foreign aid activities. It has received only indifferent attention during the years of cooperative technical and economic assistance and it is likewise overlooked as steps are being taken to withdraw United States cooperative assistance from certain countries, including those which are still largely agricultural. Decisions on withdrawal or diminution of support are determined largely on the evaluation of such economic indices as the rate of increase in gross national product, the per capita income, or the rate of increase in overall production over recent years.

STRENGTHENING NATIONAL AGRICULTURAL RESEARCH SYSTEMS

The question is frequently asked: Can developing nations afford the investment in national institutions for agricultural science and technology? In this regard it is well to remember that the basic structure for the United States national system of land grant colleges and for the U.S. Department of Agriculture was established in 1862, when the national treasury was strained by Civil War costs. And the strengthened state experiment station component dates to 1887 when the United States economy was significantly below recent levels.

There is a special urgency in the strengthening of national agricultural research capability in the developing countries stemming from their enthusiastic acceptance and widespread use of the new wheat and rice production technology. The Mexican wheats moved into India and Pakistan at an unprecedented rate with millions of acres in each of these countries now planted to a few varieties with a similar genetic base. Experience in the United States has demonstrated that the rapid introduction and widespread use of single varieties accelerates the biological dynamics of crop-disease–host-plant relationships. This was also well demonstrated in Mexico where the initial rust resistant varieties selected by the Rockefeller Foundation personnel were knocked out after three years of commercial growing, and successor selections with the Kenya resistance soon experienced the same fate as a result of another race of stem rust. The emergence of Races 15-B, 49-B, 139, 29, and 48 posed serious continuous threats to the new wheats developed in Mexico. The successful combating of these and other races was accomplished only through the indigenous research program in Mexico.

The protective research necessary to forestall serious epidemic losses from the recurring series of diseases which can be expected to appear as exotic germ plasm is introduced into the developing countries must be conducted largely by these nations themselves. A single center for cereal rust research at the University of Minnesota, or the Dominion Rust Laboratory at Winnipeg, Canada, was not depended upon to provide the solution for the outbreak of stem rust Race 15-B or for other races which have occurred in the wheat crop from Mexico through the United States and into Canada. These problems were met by strengthening the breeding and pathology research throughout the region. Similarly, the protective research for the new, highly productive wheat and rice crops of Asia and the Far East cannot be furnished by the limited plant breeding and plant pathology capability in Mexico or at the IRRI in the Philippines. There is no sound alternative to the development of the essential competence in the countries which are now benefiting from the borrowed technology and there is a high order of urgency in this effort.

ASSESSING THE PRESENT STATUS

The building of national institutionalized agricultural science capabilities in the developing countries has been handicapped by the lack of a clear concept of the essential elements of such a system. Not only has there been inadequate attention to the development of research institutional capability, but much of the effort that has been made has been on a fragmentary or piecemeal basis.

The vigorous endorsement of the United States land grant college form of combined education, research, and extension has generally failed to recognize that the research component, while effective on a statewide or relatively limited basis within that organizational structure, achieved national impact primarily through its contributions in the nationwide system of such state agricultural experiment stations. A single land grant type of institution should not be expected to furnish the science and technology input in a developing nation necessary to cover all functions handled by the state experiment stations, the United States Department of Agriculture, and private enterprise in the United States. Also, the extension function for the transmission of new technology in developing countries might well be handled in part by the private industries supplying fertilizers, pesticides, and machines and channeled through farmers' associations or other existing organizations.

Before proceeding with the strengthening of institutional patterns or the transfer of counterparts of United States research organizations into cooperating developing countries, a careful assessment must be made of the existing indigenous capabilities. The objective of establishing a national system of research, serving effectively all the important cropping regions of the country and associated to the maximum extent possible with educational institutions, would furnish an effective working base for the review. The pattern for extension organization might well remain flexible and undetermined until the national research organization is designed.

PLANNING ON A NATIONAL BASIS

One would not expect to plan for a developing nation the total complex and integrated system which exists in the United States, but the basic components or elements might include the following:

(1) A strong national center for background research and for conceptual and coordinating leadership for national and regional projects. The Beltsville research center provides this resource in the United States, and the similar national headquarters at Chapingo, Mexico; Tibaitata, Colombia; La Molina, Peru; La Platina (Santiago), Chile; and the Indian Agricultural Research Institute near New Delhi furnish similar "national headquarters" services in those developing countries.

(2) Regional centers for adaptive research and specialized attention to the agricultural requirements of the major cropping regions. In the United States the federal field stations, together with selected state agricultural experiment stations have served as regional headquarters for specific research projects.

(3) Localized research and/or verification and testing stations designed to fit innovations to specific soil and climatic conditions. In the United States this component is represented primarily by the branch stations of the state agricultural experiment stations.

The concentration of competent scientists from various disciplines at the national headquarters will ensure the most effective use of scarce talent in the same way that the specialized research institutes make most efficient use of manpower and laboratory-field station resources. The level of competence at the regional stations should be similar or about equal to that of the central headquarters, but with the mix of scientific disciplines determined by the nature and complexity of the problems of the region. The competence at the localized field stations should be of the B.S. degree level of training at the initial stages, with upgrading to the M.S. and Ph.D. level in time, as has occurred in the branch experiment stations in many states in the United States.

For the dissemination of improved technology, extension specialists should be located at the national and regional research centers. These individuals should be trained at least to the B.S. degree level and preferably should have graduate training and research experience since they will be expected to understand fully the significance of the individual technological advances as well as the proper assemblage of "packages of practices" which are increasingly the pattern in modern agricultural technology. These extension specialists would be responsible for planning adaptation and verification trials, in collaboration with the state or local extension workers or others responsible for transmission of new technology and other production inputs to the farm level.

In the establishment of this relatively simple pattern of research institutions one should recognize that effective results will be achieved only from research workers with the high levels of skills and training in the respective basic sciences concerned with agriculture. This cannot be substituted for by larger numbers of generalists or agriculturists with a mediocre level of training and competence.

THE RESOURCES FOR RESEARCH INSTITUTION BUILDING

A wide variety of patterns of institutionalized agricultural science has emerged in the United States and in other advanced nations. The cooperative adaptive research programs and specialized institutes, together with the United States university efforts in developing nations, have furnished experience in numerous individual efforts to increase productivity and to build selected research-education institutions in many countries of Asia, Latin America, and Africa.

A major deficiency in the past cooperative efforts has been the omission of the ultimate objective of building the indigenous institutionalized science capability into a national, self-sustaining system. A special challenge—and one of increasing urgency—is to channel or coordinate technical assistance resources now available to a developing nation as separate specialized projects so as to strengthen or build such national systems.

The prime factor in such an effort will be the recognition by the developing nation—as well as the donor cooperators—of the significance of this objective. The collaboration among donors should not be difficult but would require constant awareness of the need for modification in support or emphasis to ensure effective meshing of resources for the adaptive research goals and experience, for scientific staff development, and for the building of laboratory and field station facilities. Donor organizations will, of course, have to retain a maximum degree of flexibility in use of their resources to facilitate this coordinated effort.

REFERENCES

1. Cummings, Ralph W. Concepts of agricultural technology and strategy implications for behavioral change. (Paper read at the meetings of the American Association for the Advancement of Science, Section O, New York, December, 1967.)
2. Gregory, Wade F. *Agricultural development in Greece, Mexico, and Taiwan.* (Paper read at the CENTO Conference on Agricultural Development Policy, Istanbul, Turkey, September 11, 1967.) Washington, D.C.: ERS, USDA, 1967.
3. International Rice Research Institute. *Annual Report, 1966.* Los Banos, Laguna, Philippines: IRRI, Manila Hotel, Manila, 1966.
4. Kellogg, Charles E. Interactions in agricultural development. (Paper read at the United Nations Conference on the Application of Science and Technology for the Benefit of the Less-Developed Areas, Geneva, Switzerland, February, 1963.)
5. Krull, Charles F., et al. *Results of the second international spring wheat yield nursery, 1965–66.* Research Bulletin no. 11. Mexico, D. F.: International Maize and Wheat Improvement Center, August, 1968.
6. Moseman, A. H. The development of agricultural research and educational institutions and programs. (Paper read at the CENTO Conference on National and Regional Agricultural Development Policy, Istanbul, Turkey, September 11, 1967.)
7. ———. "New patterns of agricultural research and education in India." *Agricultural Sciences for the Developing Nations,* Albert H. Moseman, ed., Publication 76. Washington, D.C.: American Association for the Advancement of Science, 1964.
8. Mosher, Arthur T. *Getting agriculture moving.* New York: Frederick A. Praeger, 1966.
9. *A national program of research for agriculture.* Report of a study sponsored jointly by the Association of State Universities and Land Grant Colleges and the U.S. Department of Agriculture. Washington, D.C.: USDA, October, 1966.
10. Rockefeller Foundation. *Progress report: Toward the conquest of hunger, 1965–66.* New York: Rockefeller Foundation.

11. Schultz, T. W. *Economic growth and agriculture.* New York: McGraw-Hill, 1968.
12. Sprague, G. F. Agricultural production in the developing countries. *Science,* 157 (August 18, 1967): 774–78.
13. U.S. Department of Agriculture. *State agricultural experiment stations: A history of research policy and procedure.* Miscellaneous Publication no. 904. Washington, D.C.: USDA, May, 1962.
14. Vaidyanathan, P. P. I., and K. C. Naik. *Agricultural institutions in the United States of America.* Madras, India: Government Press, 1958.

DISCUSSION by MELVIN G. BLASE

RUTTAN AND MOSEMAN present an interesting contrast in their presentations. Although both make a contribution, they do so in different ways. Hence, a comparison is warranted after reviewing each individually.

RUTTAN ON QUESTIONS OF ORGANIZATIONS

Several favorable comments are in order with respect to the Ruttan paper. The implications of the evolution of agricultural economics as a sub-discipline, with its focus on self-defined "interesting" problems (a working hypothesis), should be clear. Likewise, Ruttan's plea for relevant research, which runs through the paper, should be audible to the academic community in general and the one—albeit frequently embryonic—in the less developed world. Suffice it to say, there are several worthwhile contentions put forth in the paper.

However, attention is now turned to some matters on which our views differ. In order that the issue may be joined quickly, the cases selected for study by Ruttan will be reversed and, to a degree, the conclusions reached. If one compares the Rockefeller experiences in countries not mentioned, which are conspicuous by their absence in the paper, with selected university contract programs—focusing on institution building among other things, e.g., Purdue/Brazil and North Carolina State/Peru—one may come to the opposite conclusion reached by Ruttan. Further, the question can be raised whether the former has been focused on the "right" problems. This question is especially important if one considers the creation of a viable, auto-catalytic research institution as the top priority objective of the technical assistance process. This, then, gets close to the heart of the problem: what criteria are appropriate for evaluating project performance? Clearly, these should be different for political presence projects as compared to substitute resource projects, as compared to institution building projects. Given a long enough time span, the same criteria are appropriate to the latter two, according to some observers. Even if this is granted, can one compare the output of the Rockefeller-Mexican experience at the end of twenty-five years with those of the institution building approach of United States universities of a maximum of half as long a life? Objectivity suggests not.

To be more specific, the following questions seem to be appropriate:

1. Is there a myth that United States university contract programs are by their very nature extremely unproductive—to the point of being generalized as failures?[1]
2. Is institution building a valid objective in technical assistance? If so, will it always occur as an accidental by-product of the "institute model"? If not, what are the implications for the images of donor agencies as intellectual colonialists?
3. Is the presence of highly visible results a clear indication of the relevance of the host institution or is it indicative of "fortunate right choices" made by administrators, in the case of Mexico, from the United States in 1941? Likewise, what are the implications for the importance of an economy's ability to absorb and utilize new technology?
4. What does "relevant" mean? Is it limited to increases in real output to the exclusion of effects on the distribution of income?
5. Why did the Mexican technical revolution occur if training of Mexican scientists was not of crucial importance? Were the investments in their education wise? What would have been the probabilities of success of any assistance effort, institute or contract, if assured of adequate length of life in the early forties in Mexico?
6. To what extent can the IRRI success be attributed to variety selection rather than hybridization? What role was played by the interdisciplinary team in the process?
7. Why have university contract efforts been focused so closely on internal problems of host institutions while overlooking the linkage function to be performed, as well as the crucial importance of research?
8. Why have university contracts been devoid of the singleness of purpose characteristic of the concisely stated objectives of Rockefeller programs?

Let me conclude this section by clarifying the perhaps mistaken impression that I am only critical of the institute approach. Far from it. It has been highly successful with respect to specific objectives. However, further insight is needed concerning: (1) the forces responsible for the success that has been enjoyed, and (2) the im-

---

[1] For a perspective to the contrary see I. L. Baldwin et al., *Building Institutions to Serve Agriculture*, CIC, Purdue University, 1968.

portance of alternative objectives. Finally, I quite agree with the need for a pragmatic approach, which is the basic contention of the Ruttan paper.

MOSEMAN ON RESEARCH SYSTEMS

Two points are especially noteworthy in this paper. The first is the heterogeneous nature of agricultural research institutions in the developing world. The second is the integrated nature of a national agricultural system such as found in the United States. Both can hardly be overemphasized. However, within these strengths of the paper also lie its weaknesses. Although heterogeneity is emphasized, most of the examples reflect the British tradition. Are there unique research institutions in the rest of the world worthy of mention?

In making the second point, Moseman qualifies himself as follows: "We would not expect to plan for a developing nation the total complex and integrated system which exists in the United States, but . . ." Herein lies the problem. What type of complex is appropriate for small nations? What are the international organizational implications? Can these problems ever be overcome at the same pace required by all participating nations in an international research institution? How can such a local, national, international system be synchronized? Finally, are the resources available for building such a system? If not for all of it, what criteria should be applied in determining intertemporal priorities.

While some questions remain unanswered, e.g., the role of economic analysis, Moseman has made a significant contribution. When one reviews this segment of development in the literature concerning developing countries, the totality of the view presented by Moseman is conspicuous by its absence. Needless to say, many would profit by becoming acquainted with it.

A COMPARISON OF THE TWO APPROACHES

Review of both contributions gives one an impression of greater breadth of insight on Moseman's part. While his emphasis on a research system is welcome indeed, the question of priorities is left largely unanswered. Ruttan, on the other hand, clearly commits himself with respect to where to initiate the action but in so doing confers the image of a panacea to the institute approach, his plea for pragmatism notwithstanding. Clearly, the presentations are complementary. Both should be read to obtain a balanced view.

8

EXTENSION INSTITUTIONS

J. K. McDERMOTT

WHEN DISCUSSING institutions of any kind in economic development, the fact must be recognized that the role of institutions in the performance of an economy has never been well understood in the homeland of the United States. Thus United States scientists engaged in institution building abroad have gone into the institutional building battle virtually unarmed. Good reason exists for this lack of understanding. An institution, by its nature, is so much a part of the environment that it seems almost a work of nature. Further, in the United States, institutions relevant to development emerged autonomously, i.e., not from any central design. Finally, they were remarkably effective in bringing about development.

Whether or not he is armed, the United States agricultural scientist is in a battle highly relevant to the task of development. This is not the first time that he has been relevant long before he was right. In fact, relevance is perhaps the most important hallmark of the Land-Grant College system. Problems that have taken most time are those important to some sector of the economy, but for which the right answers were not available. This system has played the dominant role in shaping the personality of the United States agricultural scientist and is playing the dominant role in institution building abroad.

UNDERLYING ASSUMPTIONS

One of these is that the stock of natural resources, or the natural environment, is not nearly as important in economic development as is the man-made environment, or the social, political, and economic

151

organization man has devised. Institutions are the components of this organization.

A second is that the performance of an economy is a function of the performances of individuals in the economy. These individuals are everyone, from the man with the hoe (whose major contribution is energy), to the highest authority on economic policy. It includes the *major domo,* landowners absent or resident, truckers, buyers of products, manufacturers and sellers of inputs, college professors and other public servants, and others. Two major determinants at any given time control the performance of the individual: (1) his own inherent characteristics (health, intellectual capacity, and attitude), and (2) his environment, or the situation in which he can perform. Thus, a brilliant person will never learn to read if his environment does not provide access to an alphabet. Nor will this same person ever be the president of a large corporation if the environment does not provide for the organization of large corporations. Institutions are the important components of that environment.

These two presumptions lead to an oversimplified definition of "institution." An institution is regarded as one of the components in the organization of a society that has important influence on the performance of the individual; or, as Commons says, collective action in control, liberation, and expansion of individual action. To define by contrast, an institution is *not* simply a specific organization or program. It has to be much more pervasive in impact, although clearly, specific organizations are necessary as a vehicle for the institution, and the performance of the organization is one determinant of the effect of the institution.

Still other presumptions underlie this discussion. United States personnel cannot escape their tradition, or the impacts their own institutions have had on them, since the institutions are pervasive. Nor should they seek to. The United States has come to terms with the demands of the Master known as Economic Development, and to a significant degree, other nations could well achieve economic development to the extent that they do become like the United States. But how like the United States, and in what? The admonition that "one can not go overseas and make the host country like the United States," has little content.

Another presumption is that the United States developed autonomously. This nation still does not understand central planning. Many of its most effective institutions had such difficulties aborning that in retrospect it is difficult to understand how they survived. The first Land-Grant College Act, for example, was vetoed by a president whose main worry was that it was undue interference with States' Rights. Even after the act was signed, varied interests struggled violently against it, wanting either to abandon the entire concept or to shape it into other directions. Curiously, those who came out of this tradition of autonomous development are now involved in a rather substantial program of trying to induce development.

This leads to the proposition that perhaps the greatest deficiency in United States personnel working in economic development abroad is the lack of understanding of the development of the United States. If one is to have much success in inducing development via institution building, an understanding of the history of the relevant United States institutions would be most useful. This does not mean that the institutions overseas must be carbon copies of those in the United States. Indeed, innovation is one of the important components of development, and the capacity to innovate together with mechanisms that encourage innovation are perhaps essential. But that, too, is one of the lessons of United States experience.

Turning to the extension institution, and following the preconceptions stated, one should recognize that extension is peculiarly a United States institution that has resisted strongly transplantation to other climes. Further, extension is a part of the Land-Grant College phenomenon. In fact, one can argue strongly the point that the extension function was the significant difference between the Land-Grant College idea and other forms of higher education. The very name "extension" means literally an extension of the campus functions to the needs and problems of a society, and in the beginning these functions were extended by the same persons who were doing the teaching and the research. This fact alone perhaps had as much influence over the eventual nature and function of extension as anything else. This may be a condition very difficult to duplicate in the process of inducing development. Regardless, the functions performed by extension are worthy of consideration.

FUNCTIONS OF EXTENSION

The most obvious and the only one commonly agreed upon is that of diffusing information developed from research. Many view this as the only function of extension. It leads to assertions that there is no reason to have an extension service until the experiment stations have generated substantial amounts of technological innovation.

Much less obvious is the role that extension played in maintaining relevance in the research and the teaching functions of the agricultural colleges, and only slight contacts with agricultural colleges in many parts of the world indicate the importance of this function. Through this relevance for dealing with practical problems, plus some political competency, extension helped to maintain good public support for the research, teaching, and extension complex. A good case can be built that extension in the United States was as important to research as research was to extension.

These were functions initiated by extension of the Center. In order to execute these functions more effectively, there was organized extension of the field, the vast and highly effective county agent organization. This organization has confused many observers, both from the United States and abroad, as to just what extension is, and what it does. In a significant sense, form has been more apparent than function, but not completely. For example, many extension services overseas, and this was especially apparent in some of the binational services so popular in Latin America up until the early sixties, were simply field services, with no stable tie to a research or teaching entity. Thus, though called "extension," they lacked the vital element of the United States system after which they were patterned. Extension was considered as the extending of information rather than the extending of the agricultural college itself into a complex interaction with the economy. However, in the United States, this form created an entire new set of functions and strengthened some incipient functions of the extension of the Center. Extension of the field, in other words, took on functions and a personality of its own and actually changed the Center in addition to facilitating execution of extension of the Center.

One of these functions was leadership development. This happened through such organizations as 4-H clubs, home demonstration clubs, local sponsoring agencies, numerous commodity producer associations, and the myriad of activities which might be called community development for want of a better name. The reaction to local problems by the field extension has involved much more than experiment station technology, and this has been true throughout the history of extension. Some groups, organized as teaching devices, such as Corn Producer Associations, Purebred Breeder Associations, and the like, served effectively as teaching devices, but they too took on personalities of their own and thus performed new functions. Extension itself has been an institution building device.

Related to leadership is the effect the extension service had on attitudes, and in particular, the high value that rural people have come to place on science and rationality in farming. In accomplishing this attitude change, extension served an evangelistic function. Farmers the world over are relatively low in status. In the United States their sons, once draped with the prestigious mantle of science, did not forget their younger brothers and while eloquently extolling the virtues of rural life they helped many others escape. They were good scientists, but they were not cold and objective. They had a mission. Some will say that the most important function extension served was to get farm boys to college. Farm families did not escape the influence of the evangelism for science. Through Farm and Home Weeks on campus and its other activities, faith in science in farming was propagated. A pride was established in the profession and norms and standards of performance were set. The very effectiveness of this evangelism led many to the belief in the one-function extension and the profound faith in science and experimentation in agricultural development.

There are still other functions of extension. Purists would rather forget it, but extension has discharged an important function in the organization of local committees that administered many other governmental programs. Extension organized the Soil Conservation Districts and the elections for price support and acreage control committees, along with many other campaigns and programs—including State Health Department campaigns for vaccinating dogs for rabies. In these activities its role was to stimulate and coordinate activities of many public agencies and even of private enterprise.

Finally, extension performed the function of compensating for almost any kind of inadequacy that existed in the organization serving rural life. Just one example out of many will suffice. A state and local government extension project was born in Indiana during the depression when a farmer attending a farm management meeting told the farm management specialist that the problem of keeping the county solvent worried farmers much more than farm management. There was no experimental evidence to bring to bear on this problem and although Indiana has won a considerable reputation for its extension program in this field, this is still not an important area of experiment station research.

The very method of organizing extension in the United States— the form—has had a great impact on function. The three-way financing has enabled the federal government to stimulate action and local people to control it. The scheme has built into it its own adjustment mechanism that has enabled one organizational scheme to span geography from Appalachia to California, and at the same time to span history from the early automobile until the space age.

One function extension has not performed in the United States— it has done little for the individual in the area of direct service. It has taught skills, taught understanding, changed attitudes, helped with organization, and in general expanded the individual's capacity to serve himself. This has resulted in great efficiencies in public programs to stimulate agricultural development, efficiencies that other governments relying on direct specific action programs have not achieved.

This discussion of the functions performed in the United States inevitably has to have substantial inaccuracies. Yet just as surely it has to have substantial relevance. If nothing more, it serves to call attention to the complexity of the task of understanding the workings of a society, even before one starts tampering with these workings. This complexity is further complicated when the society is not one's own.

This discussion should lead one to an attitude of humility[1] as he faces the task, and it should also lead to a reappraisal of the task of institution building, which has been seriously underestimated. At the same time it should not lead one to despair. Clearly intercultural innovation has been taking place throughout history. Further, the very complexity of the problem indicates that many things can happen in the field of human organization and accomplishment and do happen whether or not humans understand it. Finally, extension contributed to great changes in the United States, and in the beginning knew less about the processes of change than is known today.

APPLICATION TO DEVELOPING COUNTRIES

How does one translate all this to the task facing the world?

First, transformation from traditional to rational agriculture requires that efforts be made to get agriculture moving,[2] i.e., make it dynamic. Simply raising it to a higher level of stagnation is not development. Once agriculture becomes dynamic, it is no longer adequate for fathers to teach sons, or oldsters to teach youngsters. Society has to devise other mechanisms to replace the family as the teacher.

Just how a society can discharge this teaching function depends on many factors. Extension in the United States built on a century's experience in personal improvement—manifest in horticultural societies, farm magazines, fairs, and chautauquas. It geared into a public school system that taught literacy, at least, and later even taught agriculture. It also was accompanied by the growth of the input industry which played a significant role in teaching, as did other agricultural agencies. It also engaged persons who came out of the very area into which the teaching returned.

In this environment, United States extension exhibited some other characteristics worthy of note. It had almost an exclusive rural orientation, worked with a fairly commercial clientele, focussed largely on the technology of production, and operated in an economic environment marked by a relatively good price structure and by relatively small labor shortages.[3]

---

[1] Humility in itself, not to be confused with meekness, is a considerable asset for one with the temerity to involve himself in foreign economic development. Humility consists of a recognition of the limited understanding we have of the process of development, a great respect for the power of the tradition in which one operates, and an honest esteem for colleagues of various nationalities imprisoned by their traditions. This probably adds up to a personality trait which could be called either courageous humility or humble courage.

[2] The use of the wording of the title of Arthur T. Mosher's book, *Getting Agriculture Moving* (New York: Frederick A. Praeger, 1966), was intentional.

[3] This clarification was suggested by A. J. Coutu in a critique of an earlier draft. In discussing the technological focus he calls attention to the steady stream of innovations flowing from experiment stations and other research entities as well as the interaction between agriculture and the research sources facilitated by extension. While extension is engaged in general activities, one must not lose sight of its great role in technological development.

The role of extension in developing countries cannot be stated by recipe. It has to be fitted into the situation in a pragmatic way, adapted to the needs of the country as analyzed by those in power to articulate needs, and modified to the resources that can be mobilized for it. Human resources, both technical and administrative, are just as important as financial, or perhaps more so, since competent administrators can often solve the financing problem. Another important element is the experience the country has had with extension or extension type programs and the complex of agencies that exist.

Such a call for pragmatism[4] puts perhaps an unreasonable burden on the foreign aid technician and his counterpart. The temptation to follow United States form is great, and it may be just as great for the host country person.

Some examples of different situations may be suggestive of the innovations needed. They are not guidelines.

One can buy various amounts of extension. A country faced with an urgent need for increased production of a single important commodity may want to buy only the diffusion of a standardized technique. Such diffusion can be facilitated if the technique is accompanied by other elements, such as credits to buy needed inputs and price supports. This type of direct operation resembles that of a firm, and extensioners involved in it are, in a sense, package salesmen. Success of this type of operation will depend as much upon capital, management, and other criteria of the firm as on institution building criteria and must be evaluated on these criteria.

Not all countries, however, can reduce their agricultural development problems to the need for increased production of one or a few commodities. More countries fall into this category than conventional wisdom would have it. In these situations the welfare of rural people may be the first end, with production increase as one means to that end. This was the original objective of the Brazilian extension service and influenced greatly its evolution. The Brazilian general purpose type of extension closely resembles the United States prototype. Its success in Brazil would indicate that many countries can afford such a service.

The distinction between center extension and field extension is especially useful in adapting extension to the landscape. It not only provides a flexibility in strategy by opening new alternatives, it is an important step in partially freeing the technicians from the rigidities of the form of the latter day United States model, although it comes

⁴ Vernon Ruttan calls attention to the need for pragmatism in a defense of the international research institute in Chapter 7. He closes with these sentences: "This model should not be held [international research institute] as a solution in other situations. Rather it is illustrative of the desirability of a pragmatic rather than an ideological approach to the organization of professional manpower for the solution of development problems." If sight is lost of the pragmatism and the desire to be useful so characteristic of the land grant concept in the United States, then indeed it is irrelevant.

directly from the United States experience. Center extension is much less expensive than field extension. It could serve either a specialized teaching or research institution, and if no other alternative exists, it could be created by diverting resources from the other functions. It not only initiates a diffusion process, but also puts the institution in contact with agriculture. Legion are the comments of the isolated research and teaching institutions around the world, and the great lack of relevance that flows from the isolation. In most countries there do exist field agencies ostensibly serving farmers. They are highly variable in their effectiveness, but many are potentially useful organizations, and few are living up to their potential. A well-designed and administered center extension could have an impact. At least the alternative needs to be explored.

This strategy was employed by the Rural University of Minas Gerais-Purdue University project in the state of Minas Gerais, Brazil. There existed a relatively good field organization, ACAR,[5] and a history of almost a decade of fruitless attempts to integrate the field extension with the Rural University so that it would look like Purdue. In fact the attempts were worse than fruitless, because they created between these two organizations tensions and suspicions that otherwise had no reason to exist. Working through the field organization the university's center extension was able to have contact with agriculture, diffuse information, and have some impact on the field extension.

Still another purpose was served in Minas Gerais. In the state the veterinary faculty belonged to another university, and there existed still another faculty of agriculture. By leaving the field extension autonomous, either of those faculties had a completely viable alternative to create its center type of extension. In fact, the Veterinary School of the University of Minas Gerais initiated extension work very soon after Rural University. Conceivably this innovation could be introduced into Indiana if the other three state supported universities should demand access to the state's field extension which is now the property of Purdue University.

When creation of a field extension is necessary, the Brazil experience strongly suggests two important elements: (1) start it modestly so the inevitable errors will be small, and (2) build in corrective devices. One seldom knows enough to innovate correctly. Strategy must make of error a teacher, not a threat.

The rather successful field extension in Minas Gerais was started in four counties, in 1949, under the technical guidance of a former Farm Security Administration person, at the time working for the American International Association, as a supervised credit program. Within fifteen years the organization had been expanded throughout the state, similar organizations had been started in about fifteen

---

[5] Assoçiaca de Credito e Assistencia Rural.

other states, a national federation had been formed, and the organization had evolved itself into an organization much more like United States extension than United States Farm Security.

In this experience, the field extension looks very much like the United States County Agent system, but it grew at a pace determined by the Brazilian administration. For example, the county extension committees were added fairly late, but apparently fairly effectively. Also, this is not a pure service, and some of its achievements have been in the area of building roads and schools, and improving health and nutrition. Yet it has been attentive to the problems of technology. Its weaknesses with regard to technology were a result of low production of schools and experiment stations more than inherent weaknesses in the service. This organization has many of the other attributes of a real institution, pervasive in its impact. It has greatly influenced teaching in the schools of agronomy. Most dramatic has been the addition of home economics and extension methods to curricula. It has improved the market for agricultural graduates, it has instituted new employment methods and standards imitated by other agencies, and it has developed a mystique of service.

LESSONS LEARNED

If one can risk generalizations from this caselet, these lessons emerge. Put little faith in shortcuts to economic development. Enough is not known to cause abrupt turn arounds in economies in which tradition has built an inertia over several centuries. The success of direct action, firm-like operations is not incompatible with this assertion.

A second lesson is that if an institution is to have any chance for survival and effectiveness, it must have built into it the capacity to analyze its environment and determine its role in it, and to adjust its program when necessary. Further, it must develop the habit and the confidence to exercise this ability. Policy and program designed by technicians outside the system run the risk of allowing a weakness to exist or even develop that can prove fatal.

AGRICULTURAL LOGISTICS PROBLEMS

Extension in most of the developing countries will encounter the situation in which the supply of inputs is not adequate. This was alluded to in describing the very simple type of extension as "package" sales organization. It has also called attention to the compensating function extension performed in the United States. This point needs further clarification. When the problem of lack of inputs exists, agricultural extension cannot ignore it. The strategy selected to attack it, however, is highly important.

Package programs have one very great peril. If extension is the purveyor of packages, dramatic results can be obtained on a limited basis in the short run, but the question must be asked: Where can this program go? It will immediately encounter a lack of capital and will be stopped by this lack. One thing extension cannot do is provide all of the services needed by a commercial agriculture. Nor can any other public agency of which extension may be only a part. There is a way out. Extension can be a mechanism by which other individuals, firms, or agencies, can be stimulated to perform some of these functions.

Perhaps what distinguishes extension as an institution from extension as simply an organization, is whether or not it can influence other entities in the economy, or whether it is limited to the programs it can execute directly. Such an argument incurs the risk of being criticized as being too ideological, and may indeed cause technicians to be ideological. The fact is that institutions are not built in a vacuum. They are built only through an active, even aggressive participation in an economy. It probably matters little how a program starts when faced with inadequacies elsewhere in the system. It does matter that something is started and it does matter what direction it takes once it is started.

Coutu[6] has also called for the establishment of operating experiments on alternative means of initiating effective extension institutions. He suggests not only careful and objective study of the efforts already underway, but also "that other approaches be structured over four and five year periods in the form of pilot experiments."[7]

The extent to which extension needs to, and can, work in the field of organization, attitude change, and such nontechnical problems as building roads and schools and health, are decisions that need to be made case by case. Certainly they should not be excluded from extension's role by definition.

Finally, in listing considerations important to determining a role for extension, one must recall that if the concept of extension has any real meaning it must be considered a part of a larger complex which includes a research component. Arthur Mosher once asserted that the agricultural college needed to develop a role as "powerhouse for development."[8] This can be interpreted that the agricultural

---

[6] This suggestion was made in the same critique of an earlier draft of this paper which has already been cited.
[7] The time period is important. Carlos Buritica hypothesizes that one reason for extension's limited success in Colombia has been a lack of persistence. Carlos Buritica, "Extension in Colombia," *Agricultura Tropical*, publication of the Colombian Association of Engineer Agronomists, 24 (August, 1968) 26–32.
[8] He made this point orally in a conference of the CIC-AID Rural Development Research Project in Chicago, late 1965. Whether the concept has been expanded in publication is not known.

college cannot really be looked to for certain definite and specifiable functions, but rather as a sort of generalized source of innovation and other forces for development. If one follows this analogy, extension must be regarded as the transmission line necessary to distribute power to the right places in the economy. Thus, extension must be something more than a large organization serving farmers, if it is to have any sort of definable meaning.

The transmission line analogy is not adequate to understand extension, because extension must also serve the research center. The research center, apart from all considerations of agricultural development, needs this sort of contact with the economy. Autonomy of the field extension does not *per se* preclude its providing these functions to and for the research center. Whether the powerhouse for development is an international research institute, or a so-called Land-Grant College perhaps has little difference in the short run. In the long run whether a country has its own powerhouse or must depend upon the good will of foreign authority to provide this function will make a difference.

SUMMARY

In summary, this chapter has tried to make the point that the institution of extension is something considerably more than an organization. It must have pervasive impact on individual behavior, not simply render good results to those whom it is able to reach directly. It also asserts that extension is typically a United States institution, and a thorough understanding of that institution and its institutional setting will lead to a more useful determination of the role of extension in a foreign setting. The various functions of extension in the United States have been identified, calling attention especially to impacts on attitudes and on the relevance of research and teaching as well as its diffusing function. Finally, extension must, to a large extent, somehow seek its own role in a foreign setting. Its organizational mechanism must provide for rather prompt and even profound adjustments as it does. While some considerations are suggested for the use of extension institutional mechanics, the clear fact remains that with the present state of knowledge, the greatest burden falls upon the technician, foreign and national, on the spot to adapt the concept of extension to its new habitat. In that chore he will likely find himself better served by pragmatism than ideology.

DISCUSSION by A. J. COUTU

THE UNIQUE United States institution of agricultural extension has been well characterized by McDermott. He also correctly related some essential attributes of United States extension personnel if the functions he outlines are to be made operative in developing countries. His reference to the need for United States personnel to have a greater knowledge of United States development, necessity for reference points other than the current situation in the United States, and the capacity to innovate are most essential.

Some additional characteristics of the United States extension experience, their implications abroad and some probable avenues for more viable extension activities outside the United States are discussed here.

UNIQUE U.S. CHARACTERISTICS OF AGRICULTURAL EXTENSION

Throughout the many United States technical assistance efforts abroad, there is little evidence that the United States agricultural extension institutions have been adaptable. Some insight into this limited success can be gained by study of the unique characteristics under which the extension functions have been and are being performed in the United States.

A brief listing of these unique characteristics might include its truly rural orientation, commercial farm clientele, primary focus on technical questions of how and how much, as well as operating in an environment of labor shortages and throughout a period where relatively favorable economic incentives have prevailed. The first point is quite obvious in that United States extension activities have been directed and performed by people who left farms in order to work on behalf of the rural component of United States society.

The clientele issue is most significant—United States extension personnel work with the commercial farmer or those low income (scarce capital assets) situations highly motivated toward change. Most definitely, until the last few years, few if any extension functions were carried out with subsistence type farmers or with people now classified as rural nonfarm residents.

Starting in the late thirties when rates of growth in the agricultural sector reached 5 to 6 percent per year in productivity per man, the extension service concentrated upon technological changes relating to questions of "how" and "how much." Very little effort was devoted to questions of public policy, farm enterprise organization, regional specialization and trade or the impact of change in commercial agriculture on the rural nonfarm population. This was a mutual characteristic in that a steady stream of innovations was emerging from private and public research activities which overshadowed many policy issues. Also, the nonfarm sector was able to absorb many of the rural to urban migrants.

From the period of the late thirties through the present time, substantial rural to urban migration has been a reality. This element accounts for the tremendous interest in mechanical types of change—an incentive due to rising farm wage rates.

A most important characteristic was the presence of other incentives for the commercial farmer to innovate. Foremost among these have been relatively favorable factor-product price rates; realization of the gains in a highly competitive system of early adoption of innovations; large transfer payments to the commercial farmer in the form of public markets, conservation payments, long term-low interest credit, and among others, improved rural transportation.

DEVELOPING COUNTRIES AND THE EXTENSION FUNCTIONS

Most of the characteristics described above are not to be found in the developing countries. Efforts to adopt the United States extension system are not conducted in large part by those recently migrated from agriculture. The emphasis is not on commercial farmers but rather those with very high discount rates and scarce assets. Similarly there has not been a steady stream of proven innovations emerging from research institutions in indigenous countries. When proven biological changes have been present the rate of adoption and desire for knowledge have been great.

In still another area—mechanical innovation—the situation of surplus rural labor is very different.

Perhaps the most limiting factor relating to success in transferring the United States agricultural extension institution is the lack of economic incentives. In many emerging countries factor-product price ratios favor the urban consumer, not the agricultural producer. Certainly the scarcity of public capital along with substantial disbelief in the significance of the agricultural sector has minimized transfer payments to the agricultural sector.

Because of these differences in the characteristics or the setting in which extension functions are performed a vast amount of innovativeness, on the part of United States extension personnel working abroad, will be required to increase its rate of adaptation. A critical need if extension functions are to become effective in emerging countries is to establish operating experiments on alternative means for their performance. An objective study is urgently needed of various United States university extension efforts underway in emerging countries. Also, other approaches to this difficult issue must be structured over four and five year periods in the form of pilot experiments. Under either approach suggested above there must be a purposeful experimental design and objective criteria established for measuring the postulated relationships.

SOME UNSTRUCTURED PERUVIAN EXPERIMENTS

For many reasons, most of which are apparent to readers of this volume, no well-structured experiments on the performance of extension functions are underway in Peru at this time. Rather, joint efforts of some Peruvians and members of our staff in this area are quite informal.

The efforts that are underway include:

1. An attempt to create viable national commodity programs with a close knit research and extension staff. Also being tried is a concentration of effort in growth centers or areas with a comparative advantage for selected commodities. In addition, an orientation to commercial producers, a close linkage with credit agencies, selection of outstanding extension personnel for these programs, and increased monetary rewards to extension personnel chosen to work in the National Commodity Programs are being attempted.
2. An attempt to distinguish the type of personnel and programs that are oriented to the subsistence farmer. Hopefully, such efforts will focus more on increased output possibilities from changing the use of non-purchased inputs and emphasis on biological type innovations.
3. Another attempt not yet implemented includes efforts to service the private extension services operating within the country.

SUMMARY

United States personnel abroad should not lose sight of the extension functions reviewed by McDermott. That they must innovate, if viable extension institutions are to develop in emerging countries, cannot be denied. However, at the same time a more realistic approach would further clarify characteristics or settings essential to progress. If a reasonably favorable set of characteristics does not exist, then structured innovation or experimentation should be high on the list of alternatives.

DISCUSSION by WILLIAM A. WAYT

McDermott has done an excellent job of placing some important issues in perspective. His expression that a viable institution is more than an organization, that relevance is crucial, and his emphasis on the functions the institution performs rather than the particular form it assumes, deserves more attention by practitioners working in a foreign environment.

McDermott observes that United States personnel abroad often lack understanding of the development of the land grant college, especially the extension function, in the United States. If the practitioner abroad had this historical perspective he would likely not be so dogmatic in his insistence on trying to reproduce the particular form exhibited by the institution in contemporary America. He would be aware that the form evolved with changes in specific functions to be performed, and that at present the organizational charts are not identical in all fifty states. McDermott could have elaborated further on this when he speaks of the ability of the extension service to span time and geographic space in the United States.

The essence of extension is that it began its work with rural people and their problems, transmitting information, expressing the way people think about their problems to the research scientist and to community leaders. The motto of "Strive to Know Why—This Teaches How and When" has been as applicable to problems of marketing, transportation, farm supply, and local government as to agricultural production techniques. This is the basic idea expressed by a United States extension adviser in an African country when he pointed out that the "field service" of the ministry of agriculture worked with "chickens, pigs, maize, and ground nuts—not people." The role of extension in fostering and encouraging other organizations (marketing cooperatives, livestock improvement associations, Rural Electric Cooperatives, etc.) has in large part grown out of the "people with problems" focus.

McDermott stated that extension in the United States "has done little for the individual in the area of direct service." A different perspective might yield a different interpretation. Although the agent has been interested in using the activity as a teaching or demonstration vehicle, he has, among other things, culled chickens, castrated livestock, performed soil tests, identified crop pests and disease, and analyzed farm records for individual farmers. The individual client may have been initially motivated by the desire to learn—or to have the extension agent help him do the job! One reason so little attention of agricultural extension agents has been devoted to veterinary problems or farm law may be that even in the land grant uni-

versity these subjects are taught in professional schools where the
"extension function" (service) is expected to be performed for a fee
by professional practitioners.

Extending information about agricultural technology and improved practices in the United States has not been the exclusive domain of agricultural extension agents representing the land grant
college. Practitioners abroad should be less dogmatic in conveying
this image. The work of the Soil Conservation Service and vocational
agricultural instruction through the public schools have complemented (and at times competed with) the efforts of the extension
service. Commercial firms in both agricultural supply (machinery,
fertilizer, pesticides, feeds, etc.) and farm product procurement also
have been channels of technological information. The present work
emphasis and operational activities of extension personnel in the
United States represent accommodation and modification by the existence of these and other institutions serving agriculture. The form
of agricultural extension abroad also must be in harmony with the
other institutions with which it interacts in that culture.

McDermott points out the necessity to make agriculture dynamic
and with such agriculture it is no longer adequate for fathers to
teach sons agricultural practices. This deserves considerable emphasis. Changes in attitudes and practices probably take place most
dramatically between generations rather than within generations. We
are aware of the "generation gap" in the contemporary United States.
This problem has long been recognized and institutions built to assist
in solving it. Youth clubs and young farmers' organizations are
vehicles for transmission of ideas to younger people and through them
to mature farmers.

"Strive to Know Why—This Teaches How and When" is an
idea that is transferable from one culture to another even though the
specific practices and techniques may not be directly transferable.
Soils, climates, and other natural features as well as economic forces
vary widely within countries so that locally tested research results are
likely to be needed for years to come. Further, these must be interpreted. If extension is conceived as being only a vehicle for transmission of research results to the farm clientele (as it it in some
countries that believe they have an extension service like the United
States) their agents approach farmers emptyhanded.

The role of extension in helping publicize and recognize the
practices of superior farmers with locally tested research results
should not be minimized. This serves as a method of keeping the
extension agents' recommendations "practical," with emphasis on
those new techniques and innovations that are feasible. One can
assume "in whatever culture, the local cultivator may be illiterate—
but he is not stupid." If local cultivators do not readily adopt new
technology or proposed practices there may be hidden reasons. It

may be as profitable to examine the proposal critically as it is to critically examine the cultivator who refuses to change. Such examinations may reveal barriers in factor-product-price relationships, marketing structures, and/or a series of other ingredients not understood by the extension agent or ministry proposing the new system. However, all the ingredients to change are not expressed in factor-product-price relationships. In one African country an impediment to using a new technology that promised significantly higher yields was described as follows:

> Good crops or poor crops are regarded as being more dependent on season, natural happenings, etc., than the result of the activities of the cultivator. Such things are largely in the hands of the appropriate gods or spirits. If one individual obtains yields that are significantly better than those of his neighbor's, they are led to suspect that he has used some occult or supernatural power to steal or transfer a part of his neighbor's yields to his plots. The farmer and his family who experienced better crops are likely also to experience misfortune, such as having his house burned or face the local punishment for witchcraft.

These penalties are very real and *are not* administered by the supernatural powers. Such a social structure provides strong incentives for the individual not to obtain superior performance alone. The scientific idea of cause and effect relationships of practices to higher yields will be much more acceptable to the community (and to the individual) if ten cultivators can be persuaded to try the new technology at the same time. Perhaps this is an illustration of the need for pragmatic examination of the situation called for by McDermott. It also underscores the need for extension or change agents to be evangelists for science in agriculture.

9

AGRICULTURAL CREDIT
INSTITUTIONS

TED L. JONES

An understanding of the economic development process requires an approach similar to that followed by system analysts in solving problems. The importance of one factor cannot be understood except in terms of other closely related factors. Belshaw defined economic development as ". . . a continuing social process leading to a progressive increase in average output per head, among the people in a society."[1] This definition refers to a process because economic development involves closely related variables and is continuous over time. Economic development is also concerned with the social sector because as the process continues, changes occur in the technical and institutional environments of society as well as in physical output.

Economists are compelled to focus their economic knowledge and training on current problem situations. Since World War II, the focus has been upon increasing the rate of economic development in the emerging nations, and at least maintaining the rate of economic development in more mature nations. But the profession's record as problem solvers, or even as explainers of the economic and social relationships involved in the economic development process (particularly in developing countries), is far from perfect.

In one sense, economists have felt restrained to offer their explanation of the development process by emphasizing the historical determinants of production—land, labor, capital, and management. Recently, technology has earned the right to be added to this august list. These determinants do place limitations on production, per se. With

---

[1] Horace Belshaw, *Agricultural Credit in Economically Under-developed Countries* (Rome: FAO Publication, 1959), p. 5.

a given amount of land, labor, capital, and technology, the manner in which people organize will determine the level of production.[2]

Too often, in the past, economists have attempted to simplify the development process by calling attention to one limiting factor and then trying to remove this restraint as if it were not related to other variables. As a result, programs have been designed and conducted to solve the problems of education, production, marketing, capital, credit, cooperatives, etc. This approach has not been very fruitful.

Probably the capital problem has received the greatest amount of attention. "In the view of many economists, capital occupies the central position in the theory of economic development."[3] Kindleberger quotes many economists who state that capital occupies the key role in the development process, but he also quotes just as many who question the importance of capital as the key factor in development.[4] Capital should not be considered the primary determinant of economic development, but the importance of capital in increasing production and per capita income cannot be disregarded. Gadsby points out that differences in capital resources, more than any other factor, distinguish the agriculture of developing countries from that of economically advanced countries.[5]

THE CAPITAL FORMATION APPROACH

Nurkse presented one of the first applications of the capital formation explanation of growth in developing countries. In explaining the vicious circle of poverty he said:

> There is small capacity to save resulting from a low level of real income. The low real income is a reflection of low productivity, which in its turn is due largely to the lack of capital. The lack of capital is the result of the small capacity to save.[6]

Spitze stated that a good understanding of the determinants of capital formation is necessary to understand the capital and credit problems

---

[2] Lyle W. Shannon, "Cultural and Related Restraints and Means of Overcoming Them" (Paper read at the Conference on the Economic Development of Agriculture, Ames, Iowa, November 9–12, 1964), p. 1.

[3] Charles P. Kindleberger, *Economic Development* (New York: McGraw-Hill, 1958), p. 83.

[4] Ibid.

[5] Dwight Gadsby, "Capital and Credit," chap. 7, in *Changes in Agriculture in Twenty-six Developing Nations—1948 to 1963*, U.S. Department of Agriculture, Foreign Agricultural Economics Report No. 27 (November, 1965): 77; also see Peter T. Bauer and Basil S. Yamey, *The Economics of Under-developed Countries* (Chicago: University of Chicago Press, 1957), p. 113.

[6] Ragnar Nurkse, *Problems of Capital Formation in Under-developed Countries* (New York: Oxford University Press, 1963), p. 5.

in a changing agriculture.[7] The capital formation approach to economic development is widely held by many economists, but certainly is not universal.[8] Most economists agree, however, that normally the productivity of labor will be increased when used with capital inputs and total production normally increases—other things being equal.

The conclusion reached here is that capital formation problems are only one group of problems which needs to be analyzed and solved in order to increase the rate of economic development. Assuming that capital problems are present, some of the questions that must be answered are: (1) What kinds of capital to add? (2) When to add the additional capital? (3) How much capital to add? (4) Into what sectors and enterprises should capital be injected? (5) How obtain the needed capital? (6) How should capital be injected?

The last point leads to the discussion of agricultural credit institutions, as one means of injecting capital into agriculture, thereby possibly increasing the rate of agricultural development.

OBJECTIVES OF
AGRICULTURAL CREDIT INSTITUTIONS

Each country has its own unique combination of human agents, land, capital resources, and technical possibilities—as well as its own economic, social, legal, and political institutions. Agricultural credit institutions have their own unique objectives. Nonetheless, the general objectives of agricultural credit institutions should include the following points:

1. To increase the rate of economic development by facilitating the injection of capital into agriculture by making, supervising, and collecting agricultural loans supplied to farm producers and agricultural marketing and supply firms.
2. To upgrade the capabilities of the agricultural credit staff as well as provide for the expansion of the number of trained agricultural credit personnel.
3. To provide the lender services needed so that, over time, the agricultural credit institution will be viable and efficient.

---

[7] R. G. F. Spitze, "Determinants of Capital Formation—Conceptual and Factual Considerations," Chap. 2 in *Capital and Credit Needs in a Changing Agriculture*, ed. E. L. Baum, H. G. Diesslin, and E. O. Heady (Ames: Iowa State University Press), p. 19.

[8] Many writers believe that the role of capital has been overemphasized in explaining the economic development process. These include: Lauchlin Currie, *Accelerating Development* (New York: McGraw-Hill, 1966); Gottfried Haberler, *Stability and Progress in the World Economy* (New York: Macmillan, 1958); Charles Kindleberger, *Economic Development* (New York: McGraw-Hill, 1958); Everett Hagen, *On the Theory of Social Change*, (Homewood: Dorsey Press, 1962); J. K. Galbraith, *The Liberal Hour* (Boston, Houghton Mifflin, 1960); Albert Hirschman, *The Strategy of Economic Development* (New Haven: Yale University Press, 1958); and others.

One of the assignments concerning this chapter was to support or refute the hypothesis that agricultural credit institutions are critical in determining the rate of agricultural development. The parameters of the expected role of agricultural credit institutions to agricultural development must be estimated before this hypothesis can be supported or refuted.

Galbraith stated that in every agricultural community, developed or developing, farmers seek credit in order to acquire two broad types of capital assets. First, farmers seek credit to become owners of land or smaller nonrenewable assets. These assets are now in the possession of others. Here credit is required to facilitate the transfer of existing capital, or existing productive equipment, from one person to another. Second, farmers seek credit to bring capital into existence that does not now exist—such as better seeds, livestock, machinery, etc.[9]

The position is taken here that many agricultural credit institutions in developing countries have been given the assignment of increasing the rate of agricultural development; however, their terms of reference were too narrow for most to succeed. In other words, due to the apparent need for capital, and in an attempt to meet the demands of a local populus, agricultural credit institutions were established and were expected to increase, within a very limited time, the rate of agricultural development. Credit institutions were often established with a minimum amount of information available concerning other limiting factors, which could have prevented the best organized and operated agricultural credit institutions from meeting their objectives.

THE ROLE OF CREDIT IN AGRICULTURAL DEVELOPMENT

The initial injection or expansion of agricultural credit as a source of capital does not always bring about an increase in agricultural production. Agricultural credit can be a powerful economic force for development if used to inject appropriate capital inputs into agriculture that are not otherwise available to farmers from their own financial, physical, and labor resources.[10] Mosher classified production credit to farmers as an important accelerator of agricultural development. He emphasized that farmers must spend additional sums of money on improved seeds, fertilizers, and implements to increase production. Such expenditures must be financed either out of the savings

[9] John K. Galbraith, "The Supply of Capital for Under-developed Areas," Proceedings of the International Conference on Agricultural and Cooperative Credit, vol. 1, ed. Elizabeth K. Bauer, Berkeley, Calif., August 4 to October 2, 1952.

[10] Ralph U. Battles, "Agricultural Credit—A Powerful Force in Agricultural Development but Not a Panacea," Mimeographed (USDA, Washington, D.C., December, 1966), p. 1.

of the farmers or by borrowing for the period between the date when supplies and equipment are purchased and the time when the agricultural products can be sold.[11]

A recent FAO publication pointed out that the incentives and the possibilities of using capital for increasing agricultural production are more limited in the early stages of rural development than is often realized. The productive element in agricultural credit generally increases in the later stages of agricultural development. Although a rapid increase of long and medium term credit is essential for continued development of agriculture, this evolution depends to a great extent on the conversion of the millions of small subsistence farm units into more advanced types of enterprises. The transformation from traditional agriculture to commercial agriculture depends on the existence of an adequate market for agricultural products. In other words, a need for agricultural credit and increased agricultural production must also be accompanied by an effective demand for the product at prices that are profitable for the farmer.[12] To summarize, agricultural credit is only one of the many factors in the complicated process of increasing agricultural production.

Far from being a panacea, agricultural credit is not the harmless patent medicine that it is often thought to be.[13] Agricultural credit ceases to be an economic force facilitating agricultural development if it attempts to finance farmers, either individually or collectively, who *do not* have a potentially adequate economic base. If the individual farmer lacks sufficient financial, physical, or labor resources within his family, together with those supplied through the proceeds of a loan to increase his production and income so the loan can be repaid with interest and at the same time improve his level of living, no economic purpose will be served by the granting of agricultural credit. A loan on an uneconomic basis becomes a grant, and may destroy repayment discipline thereby contributing to the deterioration of the financial strength of the credit institutions.[14]

Many agricultural credit institutions and projects for increasing agricultural development have produced inadequate results or failed completely primarily because important economic, social, political, and cultural institutions were not sufficiently analyzed before the agricultural credit institution was created or reorganized. The tendency to view agricultural credit as an isolated subject has resulted in inadequate lender services which have produced inadequate returns to the

---

[11] A. T. Mosher, *Getting Agriculture Moving* (New York: Frederick A. Praeger, October, 1965), p. 141.
[12] *Agricultural Credit through Cooperatives and Other Institutions* (Rome: FAO Agricultural Studies, no. 68, 1965), pp. 1–2.
[13] Ibid., p. 3.
[14] Battles "Agricultural Credit," p. 1.

resources employed.[15] Some governments of developing countries, advanced countries, and international agencies providing technical assistance have started credit programs without having first studied the other important institutional restraints and satisfied themselves that these projects had a reasonable chance of success.

INSTITUTIONS INFLUENCING AGRICULTURAL CREDIT INSTITUTIONS

Agricultural credit institutions must be fitted to the economic, social, political, legal, and cultural institutions that prevail in the country if they are to facilitate agricultural development.

The supply of, and demand for, agricultural credit is, to a considerable degree, the result of the environmental setting within which the credit institution and the agricultural firms operate. When the environmental considerations are developed to the extent of favoring or inducing capital investment, effective programs of agricultural credit may be achieved. Conversely, deficiencies and maladjustments of the environmental considerations inhibit economic development and restrict effective investment in agriculture, thereby making effective and continuing programs of agricultural credit difficult to achieve. Different types of agricultural credit systems have been operative with varied degrees of effectiveness under both favorable and less favorable environmental conditions. This poses such questions as: (1) What are the basic principles governing effective programs of agricultural credit in different environment settings? (2) What guidelines can be formulated for establishing and operating viable and effective agricultural credit institutions? (3) Under what conditions, or environmental constraints, must these guidelines be modified? Knowledge of the relationships of the environmental components are necessary if agricultural credit and planning personnel can reasonably expect to organize and operate agricultural credit institutions so that agricultural producers can employ agricultural credit productively, benefit from its use, and increase the rate of agricultural development.[16] Economists need assistance from other disciplines to evaluate the nonagricultural institutions. If possible, an interdisciplinary effort of economists, anthropologists, political scientists, and sociologists could be very fruitful.

To be effective, agricultural credit institutions initially must fit

[15] *Agricultural Credit through Cooperatives and Other Institutions,* pp. 9–10.
[16] C. D. Curry, D. M. Sorenson, J. O. Early, and D. L. Stansbury, "Some Environmental Considerations Influencing Agricultural Credit in Developing Countries," mimeographed (Agricultural Finance Center, Department of Agricultural Economics and Rural Sociology, Ohio State University, May, 1967), p. 1.

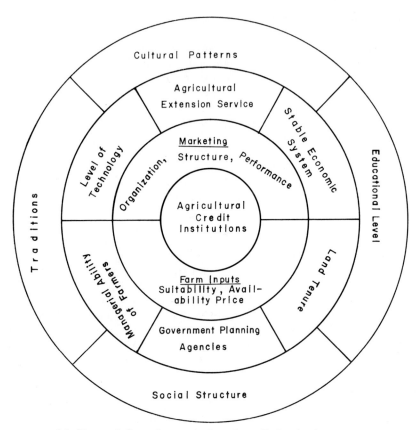

FIG. 9.1—Forces influencing agricultural credit institutions.

into the present environment in the country when the agricultural credit institution is established. This is not to imply the other environmental institutions are fixed in the long run, but simply to recognize that in the short run the environmental situation must be accepted as given. Some of the environmental forces that influence agricultural credit are shown in Figure 9.1. Agricultural credit institutions must operate initially in a given marketing organization, structure, and performance environment, and this environment can be determined from research efforts. Also, the suitability, availability, and price of off-farm inputs (capital) must be known in order to establish operating procedures of the agricultural credit institution that will work. The marketing and nonfarm input institutions are influenced by the social structure, educational level, cultural patterns, and traditions.

The objective of this chapter is not to delve into detail on the influences of different political, economic, social, legal, and cultural institutions on the organization or operating procedures of agricultural credit institutions. However, selected examples will be cited before a suggested research methodology is presented for fitting the credit institution into the existing environment. One example concerning the influence of the land tenure system upon the type of agricultural credit institution is as follows:

> If the primary agricultural producer is a part of an extended family and is farming tribally-owned land, or if the farm producer is a small farmer who is either renting farmland from large farmers or working as hired labor on larger farms, then the credit institution that requires farmland as security for loans will be unable to operate.
>
> If, on the other hand, the agricultural producers are freeholders and hold title to the land, even though the acreage or size of unit may be small, real estate may be taken as security for a loan.

This is not to imply that agricultural credit cannot be injected into environmental settings where the individual producers do not own their land. It does imply that the major type of loan that can be made will be for seeds, fertilizers, and other annual operating expenses that can be repaid from the sale of the crop at harvest time.

The types of loans must reflect the basic kinds of agricultural production in the area. In many countries, the basic types of agricultural production will vary from region to region thus requiring different types of loans and operating procedures for different areas within the same country. If the major types of crops in a region are annual grain crops, the major type of loan used for annual operating expenses may be self-liquidating. In this situation, if the market is adequate, the farmer is expected to be able to repay the loan from the proceeds of the sale of the farm products. If, on the other hand, the annual crops are primarily domestic food crops, with a very limited market, and the major income producing crops are tree crops, such as cocoa and rubber, then the agricultural credit institution will need to make loans for four to five years before income can be earned and the loan repaid. The eligibility requirements could also limit prospective borrowers to those farmers with "X" number of acres of tree crops in production in order to obtain a long term loan. Of course, there may be combination loans to producers that have both annual and tree crops that earn money income for loan repayment within the first year.

SUGGESTED RESEARCH METHODOLOGY

The first objective of analyzing the agricultural environmental setting is to determine the supply of agricultural credit. Farm producers may then be classified on the basis of present repayment ability to estimate the effective demand for agricultural credit. After the farm producers have been classified and the other environmental factors analyzed, lender services needed to increase the rate of agricultural development can be developed.

Figure 9.2 shows one method of conceptualizing some of the environmental restraints with which an agricultural credit institution must deal if it is to be effective. In general, farm producers can be classified on the basis of the level of technology employed, using a power base as an indicator. The "low" designation would represent the power employed in agricultural production by the human agent using such simple tools as the hoe and shovel. A limited amount of animal power could be in this subgroup but the vast majority of the power would be the human agent—the man with the hoe. The "medium" level of technology would include the groups of farmers who use animals as the major source of power in agricultural production, but complemented by human power. The farm machinery is improved over that used by the "low" level group, but it is still simple animal drawn equipment.

The "high" level of technology is when mechanical power, either gasoline, oil, or electric, is employed in conjunction with animal and human power. The size in terms of horsepower of the mechanical tools may range from very small to large horsepower ratings.

The marketing organization, structure, and performance and the off farm input supply environment are more difficult to conceptualize. The "poor" classification applies when marketing services do not exist or are very inadequate. For example, roads suitable for trucks or railroads do not exist (products are transported out of the production areas and inputs are brought into the areas by head loads or beasts of burden). Nonfarm inputs such as labor, machinery, fertilizer, seeds, insecticides, herbicides, improved livestock, building materials, etc., are either not available, or of poor quality, or are so expensive that farm producers do not employ them in production. In terms of marketing and off farm input supply environment, this group represents traditional agricultural producers.

Marketing Organization, Structure, and Performance and Off-Farm Input Environments		LOW (Hoe-Agriculture)	MEDIUM (Animal Power)	HIGH (Mechanical Power)
Poor	Food Crops			
	Export	A	B	C
Fair	Food Crops			
	Export	D	E	F
Good	Food Crops			
	Export	G	H	I

FIG. 9.2—Level of technology used by farm producers.

The "fair" classification could be typified as when a limited number of institutional marketing firms exist, but they are ineffective (limited number of buyers maintain control by keeping the producers perpetually in their debt, etc.). Although limited highways and railroads do exist, orderly movement to market on a regular basis is not possible. The supply of off-farm inputs is incomplete, of poor quality, or very high priced in terms of productivity.

The "good" marketing organization and input supply environment is when institutional marketing services are well developed and effective. Roads, railroads, or other transportation systems are well developed and commodities can move to market on a regular basis. The supply of off-farm inputs is adequate, of good quality, and reasonably priced in terms of productivity.

The conceptualization of areas A, B, C, etc., as shown in Figure 9.2, implies effective and efficient lender services will not be the same in all areas. Before the determination of the types of lender services required to increase agricultural development in any of the areas, additional information is required.

Assume that subsection E, or any of the other subsections could be delineated. Additional research efforts in the form of surveys of farm operations would be required to obtain the types of information shown in Figure 9.3. Farm producers may be classified in several different ways. One method of classification would be to determine the characteristics of the farmers that are in the agricultural credit feasibility area at the present time. Subsistence farmers by definition are not in the money economy. Therefore, these farmers do not have repayment ability and are outside of the credit feasibility area.

Partially subsistence farmers are defined as those farm producers still predominantly subsistence, but who earn some money income from the sale of agricultural products. With the present farm or-

---

Classification of farmers to determine credit feasibility group

    1. Subsistence
    2. Partially subsistence
    3. Commercial

Effective demand for agricultural credit

    1. Farm size, type, estimate of managerial ability
    2. Productivity of capital

Present supply of capital (credit) in agriculture

    1. Sources, terms, interest rates, etc.
    2. Quantity and kind

Lender services required to increase rate of agricultural development

---

FIG. 9.3—Additional information required for establishing and operating an agricultural credit institution.

ganization and level of income, this group of farmers could repay small annual operating loans.

Commercial agriculture is defined as farm producers who generate farm income from the sale of agricultural products from their presently organized farms and have repayment capacity for both short and long term loans.

ESTIMATE OF EFFECTIVE DEMAND
FOR AGRICULTURAL CREDIT

The classification of farmers into whether or not they are in the credit feasibility area is based on ability to pay from farm income. However, the ability to pay and willingness to pay agricultural debts are two entirely different concepts. An estimate of the willingness of agricultural producers to repay agricultural loans must be derived from the analysis of the social and cultural traditions of the society.

Connolly[17] has developed a conceptual macroagricultural economic model for the purpose of identifying the feasibility area within which agricultural credit can best be used to accelerate capital formation and agricultural development. The simplified model of the agricultural sector within a country is represented graphically with the following assumptions for the static model: (1) constant price level, (2) consumption as a linear function, (3) net foreign and government investments are consolidated into consumption and investment, and (4) savings equal investment. All forces are in equilibrium.

Basically, Connolly has added the food consumption function to the basic Keynesian model shown in Figure 9.4. The agricultural credit feasibility group conceptually is one with income levels greater than Y_3.[18] The triangle area F, E_3, G, graphically represents repayment ability, which is a function of the income level. Income equal to Y_1 is sufficient to meet food expenditures labeled E_1 (Figure 9.4). An income level less than Y_1 does not provide sufficient income for food expenditures. The income level between Y_1 and Y_3 would provide sufficient income for food expenditures, but insufficient income for desired consumption expenditures for other goods and services. An income level of less than Y_3 represents no payback ability from the present organization and income of the farms.

If supervised agricultural credit is used in the developing country, then the lower limit parameter E_3 Y_3, may be moved to the left as represented by line E_2 Y_2 in Figure 9.5. Parameters E_3 Y_3 and E_2 Y_2 now delineate the upper and lower limits of the feasible super-

[17] Chancy C. Connolly, "Identifying and Measuring the Agricultural Credit Feasibility Area for Capital Injection in a Country with a Probability Measure for Credit Repayment" (Agricultural Finance Center, Department of Agricultural Economics and Rural Sociology, Ohio State University, March, 1966).
[18] Food expenditures $= a_1 + b_1 y$, with $F =$ food consumption; $a_1 =$ level of food consumption; $b_1 =$ propensity to consume food; and $y =$ farm income.

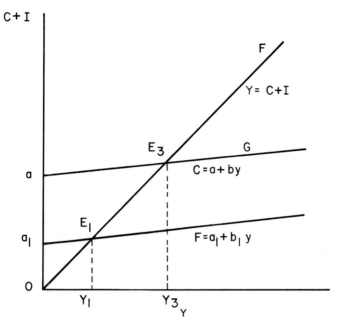

FIG. 9.4—Conceptualization of food and other consumption expenditures and agricultural credit feasibility groups.

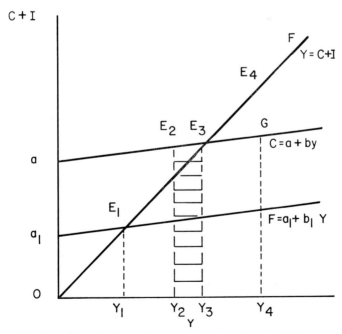

FIG. 9.5—Conceptualization of agricultural credit feasibility groups, by level of income.

vised agricultural credit group. Supervised agricultural credit could be used for an income level greater than Y_3, but the need for supervised credit in this area is not as great.[19]

After the agricultural credit feasibility group is conceptualized the magnitude or size of the group must be determined by obtaining a measurement of the size of the agricultural credit feasibility area. The number of farm units with payback ability from present farm organization and income can be estimated.[20]

Another method of estimating the effective demand for agricultural credit is by estimating the marginal productivity of capital. Chen used a Cobb-Douglas production function to estimate the marginal productivity for both fixed capital assets and working capital assets in several different areas in Taiwan.[21] The results of these estimates were then compared with the existing lending policies of the credit institution. For example, if the lending institution is making loans for particular assets that have lower marginal productivities estimates than other lending alternatives, it would serve as a signal to delve deeper into the returns earned by the assets.

SUPPLY OF AGRICULTURAL CREDIT

The farm survey of individual operators would also reveal the quantity of agricultural credit used in production as well as the source, terms, interest rate, and security required by existing lenders. In many developing countries, the only institutional agricultural credit is from governmental owned or sponsored credit institutions. But in most developing countries, money lenders provide the largest quantity of agricultural credit. If the effective demand for agricultural credit and the supply of agricultural credit being used can be estimated for the farmers with repayment ability, the magnitude of the financing requirement in terms of loan funds can be determined.

TYPE OF AGRICULTURAL LENDER SERVICES NEEDED

The ultimate objective of analyzing the environmental situation in depth is to determine the kind of agricultural lender services needed

---

[19] Connolly, "Identifying and Measuring the Agricultural Credit Feasibility Area," pp. 7–9.

[20] Ibid., pp. 9–13. A sample of farm balance sheets and income statements could provide the data to classify the farm firms according to volume of farm income. A frequency distribution of farm income can be derived. Next the probability of farm income being greater than, or equal to consumption can be computed for the different levels of income. From these data, estimates of the probability of loan repayments for specific borrowers could be made.

[21] For additional information concerning the use of the Cobb-Douglas production function, see G. Tintner and O. H. Brownlee, "Production Functions Derived from Farm Records," *Journal of Farm Economics* 16 (1944): 295–304;

to increase the rate of agricultural development. The analysis could also indicate that at the present stage of economic growth a greater return would be expected from developing institutions other than credit; for example, improving the marketing system, improving the input supply system, etc.

The types of agricultural credit services needed in developing countries are conceptualized as follows: (1) supervised credit, (2) balanced credit, and (3) commercial agricultural credit.

Supervised credit is defined as the making of agricultural loans (often credit in kind for operating expenses), with financial and farm management or technical assistance provided at the farm level. Annual farm plans in conjunction with a long range farm plan are usually prepared. Financial management assistance is provided by the agricultural credit specialist analyzing balance sheets and income statements. The credit specialist assists the borrower in keeping sufficient farm records to prepare the financial statements for use in farm planning and in agricultural credit usage.

The financial management and technical assistance features increase the cost of operating the agricultural credit institution, and also increase the probability of loan repayment and greater production. Due to the limited number of individual farmers that can be served by an agricultural credit specialist, the supervised credit institution should not be expected to cover all of the total costs from interest income. However, the agricultural credit institution must keep supervision and technical assistance cost at a low level without sacrificing the services required to increase the rate of agricultural development.

Balanced credit is where loans or credit in kind are made to individual farmers along with financial management assistance, but without technical assistance or intensive supervision at the farm level. The agricultural credit specialist considers both repayment ability and security of the farm borrower in the credit analysis. Normally, a complete farm plan will not be prepared, but the agricultural credit specialist will assist the borrower with the analysis of balance sheets and income statements to estimate the influence of the credit used by the borrower. Agricultural credit specialists will be able to serve more farm operators with this type of lender service than could be served under supervised credit. The cost of lender services will also be reduced.

Commercial agricultural credit is defined as making loan funds to individual operators without technical assistance at the farm level and with limited financial management assistance. Loans will be based primarily upon the security offered by the borrowers. Only

Earl O. Heady, "Production Functions from a Random Sample of Farms," *Journal of Farm Economics* 28 (1946): 991; and Hsing-Yiu Chen, "Structure and Productivity of Capital in the Agriculture of Taiwan and Their Policy Implications to Agricultural Finance" (Ph.D. diss., Ohio State University, 1957).

large plantations or estates will be eligible for this type of lender service in most developing countries. The total cost of agricultural credit services per dollar loaned would be less for this type of lender service than for either supervised or balanced credit.

NEED FOR AGRICULTURAL CREDIT TRAINING PROGRAMS

Any discussion concerning the influence of agricultural credit institutions upon agricultural development would be incomplete if the need for well-trained agricultural credit personnel was omitted. The shortage of well-trained agricultural credit personnel is one of the greatest restraints that precludes the establishment of efficient and effective agricultural credit institutions. The form of business organization of the agricultural credit institution may be private corporations, cooperatives, governmental corporations, or any other form; the environment may be analyzed perfectly; and the operating procedures for providing the lender services needed may be more than adequate, but unless the agricultural credit personnel are sufficiently trained in making, supervising, and collecting loans the agricultural credit institutions will not succeed or survive. The development of an adequately trained credit staff is essential if a faster rate of economic development is expected.

The level and status of training of agricultural credit personnel varies widely among developing countries. Most developing countries have some type of inservice training programs in various stages of development. Many of these inservice training programs are being developed by assigned host country training personnel who do not have the necessary background or training to conduct a well-organized, integrated program on a continuous basis. Some countries send a limited number of agricultural credit specialists to other countries for credit training.[22] If the major emphasis on training of agricultural credit specialists is dependent upon training in other countries, then many credit workers will not receive adequate training due to budgetary, time, and language limitations.

One method of filling the training gap would be to organize a highly trained cadre of experienced personnel to go into developing countries to train the "trainers" of the host country. A cadre of three or four individuals could assist in organizing the training program, in training the trainers, and in conducting a pilot training program within a three to four month period. The major advantage of

---

[22] Agricultural credit specialists from developing countries have received training in agricultural credit in the United States for many years. A new training program to broaden the subject matter training received by foreign participants was initiated in the fall of 1966 at the Agricultural Finance Center, the Ohio State University. This International Credit Training Program was financed by the Agency for International Development.

this program would be that thirty to sixty specialists, within one institution, would receive training at one time. The agriculural leader services required for agricultural development would be emphasized and tested within the environment in which capital would be injected.

CONCLUSION

The functions of agricultural credit institutions are limited to: (1) mobilizing loan funds from the economy (not always possible in developing nations in the early stages of development), (2) supplying loan funds needed to purchase productive assets (capital) for agriculture that otherwise could not be obtained by farmers, and (3) furnishing or coordinating technical assistance, if needed, at the farm level in the form of financial and managerial assistance.

Agricultural credit institutions can accelerate agricultural development if the economic, social, political, and legal institutions in the economy have been correctly analyzed and the agricultural lender services needed in the environment are provided. After the environment has been analyzed and lender services determined, the major tasks facing the individuals responsible for the credit institution are to organize or reorganize the credit institution, to develop operating procedures, and to staff the institution with the best available personnel.

The above generalizations are the results of appraising typical credit institutions in developing countries. Too often the agricultural credit institutions that were established in developing countries were only transplanted from more advanced countries. Too often the basic organization and operating procedures that had evolved over many years in more productive environments were expected to work, as is, in the developing countries. The actual result was an injection of credit (and capital) into the agricultural sector, with only limited amounts, if any, of increased agricultural production moving into commercial marketing channels. Frequently, the income level of the farm borrowers was not increased. The repayment record was often very poor. In some cases capital and loan funds were dissipated without accelerating development. In those cases the agricultural credit institution was either dissolved or reorganized with another injection of capital from government, a new set of operating procedures, and with many, if not all, of the same credit personnel remaining in the organization at the same level of training.[23]

---

[23] This conclusion assumes the loan funds for agriculture will come primarily from government in the early stages of development. If loan funds are inadequate, the best organized and operated agricultural credit institution will have a limited impact upon development.

Agricultural credit technicians and consultants have spent too much of their limited time drafting credit legislation, preparing detailed operating procedures, and emphasizing low interest loans. The real limitations that prevented agricultural credit institutions from being an effective instrument of development have not been recognized as: (1) failure of the credit institutions to fit into the environmental structure, and (2) the insufficient level of training of the credit staff to make, supervise, and collect agricultural loans.

The methodology suggested here is one approach to fitting agricultural credit institutions into a given environment. After the environment is analyzed, the time required to determine the optimum lender services will be reduced. Then the limited supply of loan funds and trained human agents can be expected to make a significant contribution in the developmental process.

DISCUSSION by WILFRED H. PINE

ADMINISTRATIVE PROBLEMS, lack of understanding credit principles, customs, and other conditions often prevent successful commercial credit operations in developing countries. Particular attention needs to be given to the borrower's understanding of his obligation to use credit productively and to repay loans. Rather than credit in all circumstances, grants may result in more gain to the economy.

Credit extended where production would be increased the most could mean using funds for the larger farms where (1) better management may be available, (2) costs to make loans are less, (3) less supervision is needed, and (4) repayment is more likely. On the other hand, assistance to the masses of small farmers may be a more important objective. But then a realistic view recognizes that politics and favoritism often determine where funds go.

Jones refers to the relatively successful farmer owned and operated credit cooperatives in Taiwan. Like credit, cooperatives often are proposed to solve problems of small farmers in developing countries. Attitudes as well as management frequently interfere with the successful operation of credit cooperatives. Farmers often feel less obligated to repay loans obtained from their cooperative than from other private sources. However, money costs of management may be less (low wages of management) and knowledge of needs and uses of funds greater with the use of local credit institutions.

Trained personnel and supervision of credit institutions to prevent large sums of money from disappearing cannot be overemphasized. Simple balance sheet or resource statements are needed, not so much to identify collateral as to indicate the resource situation and opportunity to use credit productively. In many situations the value of assets is difficult to determine and many borrowers have insufficient rights in suitable resources to pledge as collateral. Credit agencies usually find taking collateral impracticable; it can be a hazardous job.

Although equity considerations may call for a wide distribution of capital, incentive and motivation in using credit productively are important. Distinguishing between credit and grants is more difficult for public than private sources of credit. Failure to separate farm and family expenditures frequently is a serious problem. Productive use of credit ultimately will permit greater consumption. However, the future usually is highly discounted. Credit, it is hoped, will be used productively with the increase in production shared by consumption and saving, with the latter becoming a source of capital.

Appropriate credit helps to combat practices of loan sharks. Shark practices keep many farmers at low levels of living and prevent savings from being used for farm capital.

As noted by Jones, roads, storage facilities, marketing systems, suitable tenure arrangements, and extension education are essential for effective operation of credit institutions.

More information is needed concerning kinds of capital and places to use capital in developing countries. What are the gains in providing credit in small amounts to large numbers of farmers with high costs and poor repayment records? How much subsidy is needed and will the public gain exceed the subsidy? Are there alternatives such as credit in kind rather than money, that may be more productive?

DISCUSSION by PHILIP M. RAUP

ONE OF THE key points made in this chapter is that credit policy is not universally applicable to agricultural development problems. Ability to make effective use of credit is an indicator of a level of development yet to be reached in some countries, and in some sectors in almost all countries.

In this sense, some discussions of credit policy are parallel to the consideration of incentives that can be given through income tax policy, the benefits that can flow from the bargaining power of labor unions, or agricultural policy that is concentrated on price supports. The hard core poverty problem is largely bypassed at home and abroad.

Even where the level of technology and degree of monetization of the economy make a discussion of credit relevant, the problem of inflation can make it farcical. An inventory of developing countries in terms of those in which the degree of inflation on average in the past decade has equaled or exceeded the average rate of interest on development loans would be revealing.

Needed institutional changes should especially be considered before meaningfully considering the use of credit to promote development. And the barriers to institutional change are typically rooted in deep seated attitudes and beliefs. Traditional society ceases to be traditional as soon as it becomes aware of the alternatives that are precluded by its conventional beliefs. In this transition, attitudes toward time play a crucial role.

A concept of time as a part of the production process, and of the possibility of forecasting when making economic choices, is essential to the creation of an economic climate in which exploring the use of credit to promote economic development becomes relevant. Talk of credit policies in agricultural development planning in a society that does not yet have a concept of time as a cost of production is fruitless.

There are societies or cultural groups of this kind. For them, any proposals to use credit to promote development probably are premature. This may be the case with some of the inland peasant and migratory tribal groups in the Maghreb states, or in Libya. It may also be the case with some of the Indian communities in the mountain states of Latin America.

Some tentative hypotheses regarding the nature of this transition in attitudes toward time can be drawn from a current comparative study of barriers to agricultural development in Greece and Tunisia, sponsored by the University of Minnesota and the Agricultural Development Council.

In this study, communities have been found in which families appear to have little concept of elasticity in the production function but do exhibit a concept of elasticity in the consumption function, i.e., families do not believe they can prosper by working harder or more effectively. Their presumption seems to be that they are working as hard and as effectively at present as is humanly possible.

They do believe they can prosper if given more capital, or more land, or both. But their behavior suggests they regard the marginal productivity of any added input of their labor as near zero, given their existing input mix. Since more capital in the past has been difficult or impossible to obtain, and land typically unavailable, the only remaining avenue for advancement has been to reduce consumption. The role of credit in this situation is to nurture the idea that increased command over capital will lift the marginal productivity of added labor inputs above zero, and justify an increased work effort. But if consumption had been depressed in the past, the first results of more credit normally will be an increase in on-farm consumption. To have a beneficial impact on marketed output, the initial injection of credit may need to be large enough to overcome this "consumption effect."

One of the more bizarre aspects of increased personal incomes during certain phases of development has been the rising demand for gold to hoard, or to use for dowries and gifts. The net decline in visible world gold stocks after 1965 is widely believed to have been in good part a consequence of improved incomes in countries in which gold is still a traditional symbol, and gold jewelry the expectation of every bride.

In this situation, to condemn the dowry system or the social compulsion for conspicuous consumption is too simple. What is needed is a careful maturing of the idea that productivity is not exclusively determined by nature or the gods. Without a concept of elasticity in the production function, to extend agricultural credit will do no good. It may in fact do harm, for the credit is virtually certain to be exhausted in superior levels of consumption with possible negative effects on agricultural output.

Where credit policy is relevant to agricultural development planning, as it typically is, it is frequently surprising to find no reference to supporting legal and commercial codes of conduct (the subject of a subsequent chapter in this book). The function limitations on the size of the business firm are often determinant. An inadequate commercial code, or lack of a court system to enforce contracts, may be associated with a defective land tenure system in which landlords dominate local justice. The only people who can be trusted are members of your own family, and not all of them!

In this setting the effective size of firm is limited to the business that can be managed by one family. This is still the limit to firm size in many countries. This limit guarantees small scale agricultural marketing agencies, consequent high risk, and hence high cost credit. A revolution in business ethics is needed if an expansion in the availability of credit is to be effective in promoting development.

This emphasizes the need for reform and development of the legal structure under which credit institutions are organized. The institutional structure that is most defective in many developing countries is the structure of law and commercial practice that regulates the conduct of business.

Economic history provides examples of the effectiveness of codes of commercial behavior that have promoted economic growth, or facilitated the penetration of ethnic or trade oriented groups into developing areas. The following examples are noteworthy:

1. Germanic penetration into Central and Eastern Europe was promoted by a superior municipal law, which was designed to facilitate trade and commerce.
2. Jewish commercial success has often been promoted by an ethic that made possible the expansion of size of firm beyond that of the immediate family, and that increased business efficiency by making a man's word his bond.
3. Chinese penetration into the commercial life of South and East Asia is explained in part by a similar group ethic that substituted an unwritten code of conduct for more formal commercial law.
4. Although routinely damned by their neighbors, the success of the Lebanese in the Middle East is in good part due to their more efficient codes of commercial law and business practice.

Economic historians thus have much to tell us about the role of credit, and the institutions supporting credit, in processes of economic development.[1]

More use of the work of the anthropologists is also relevant to a study of the role of credit in economic development. Among recently published works some of the most pertinent are those by Julian Pitt-Rivers,[2] Sidney Mintz,[3] Alice G. Dewey,[4] and F. G. Bailey.[5] And, one is surprised to find so little reference to the work of Raymond Firth and B. S. Yamey.[6]

---

[1] Awareness of the significant role of credit and commercial institutions in promoting development is one of the unifying themes in the collection of essays by Alexander Gerechenkron *Economic Backwardness in Historical Perspective* (Cambridge: Harvard University Press, 1962), Chapters 1–3.

[2] Julian Pitt-Rivers, *Mediterranean Countrymen* (Paris: Mouton and Company, 1963), and especially the chapters by Pierre Bourdieu, "The Attitude of the Algerian Peasant toward Time," pp. 55–72; and Ernestine Friedl, "Some Aspects of Dowry and Inheritance in Boeotia," pp. 113–35.

[3] Sidney W. Mintz, "Peasant Market Places and Economic Development in Latin America.," Occasional Paper No. 4, The Graduate Center for Latin American Studies, Vanderbilt University, Nashville, Tennessee, (July, 1964).

[4] Alice G. Dewey, *Peasant Marketing in Java* (Glencoe, Ill.: The Free Press, 1962).

[5] F. G. Bailey, "The Peasant View of the Bad Life." *The Advancement of Science* (London), 23 (1966–67): 1–11.

[6] Raymond Firth and B. A. Yamey, *Capital, Saving, and Credit in Peasant Societies* (London: George Allen and Unwin, Ltd., 1964).

10

RURAL GOVERNING INSTITUTIONS

NICOLAAS LUYKX

One of the tasks of nation building and of development is to bring members of the national community into a network of relationships and institutions which enable them to participate actively in decisions affecting their individual and group welfare.[1]

DISCUSSIONS of rural government are usually restricted to the formal village level councils, headmen, and other structures officially recognized as the lowest tier of administrative authority. These are the institutions focused upon when grants of "local government autonomy" are made. Community development programs frequently go further to recognize the importance of "natural leaders" and informal social structure within the localities. Beyond this point there are few attempts to build workable linkages with a wider arena of public affairs. However, the concept of "rural governing institutions" includes the complex of all formal and informal institutionalized organizations, roles and activities which affect the course of public affairs in rural areas.[2] As seen in the categorization on pages 191 and 192, many of these have normal linkages well beyond the physical boundaries of the rural communities in which they have at least part of their impact.

Valuable comments on earlier drafts of this article by Kusum Nair, John W. Mellor, William J. Siffin, and Robert D. Stevens have led to a number of improvements in its substance and organization. The writer nonetheless accepts full responsibility for any remaining defects.

[1] Milton J. Esman, "The Politics of Development Administration," in *Approaches to Development: Politics, Administration and Change,* ed. John D. Montgomery and William J. Siffin (New York: McGraw-Hill, 1966), p. 63.
[2] Nicolaas Luykx, "Rural Government in the Strategy of Agricultural Development." In *Approaches to Development,* pp. 114–18.

In developing structures appropriate to the processes of modernization, there should be more concern for the integration of rural governing institutions into a system of planning and implementation which joins the community to its external relationships, than with the establishment of narrowly focused local government structures which, through concern over autonomy, direct the attention of the locality inward upon itself.

Most development stimuli come from sources external to the community. The more efficient the distribution system for ideas and materiel, the more intensive and relevant the nature of interaction, the greater the number of people involved (in one way or another) in decision making and execution, the more likely it is that change will be viable and dynamic.

DYSFUNCTIONAL PRESSURES TOWARD RURAL SEPARATISM

The situation at present in the rural areas of most developing countries is that there are barriers between national and local levels of government and activity that are reinforced by attitudes which encourage separatism rather than interrelationship. These barriers prevent mutual understanding and interfere with the successful formulation and implementation of integrated development programs.

Among the factors which contribute to the existence of these barriers are: (1) generally low levels of literacy and background knowledge among rural people, (2) generally low levels of competency among government officials in technical matters and in the means of effectively transmitting information to rural people, (3) prevalence of low-income conditions, (4) relative inaccessibility of many rural areas, (5) general lack of identification of government officials with their rural compatriots, (6) absence of attitudes among government officials favoring the objective evaluation of program results, (7) concentration on forms and formalities rather than on pragmatic approaches in the meeting of goals or the performance of functions, and (8) frequently unrecognized aspects of social relations and personal security in government employment which affect motivations and outlook.

The reaction of many sovereign national governments to difficulties in articulating with rural areas has included formal grants of "local government autonomy" accompanied by lists of mandatory and optional functional responsibilities well beyond the technical and financial means of the established local structures. Implicit, and occasionally explicit, in such policies are a separatism and rural fundamentalism which place greater emphasis on the differences in the concerns of the nation and locality than they do on their present or future commonality.

Antibureaucratic, anticommercial, and antipolitical sentiments lead to the implicit espousal of a form of isolationism. In this situation rural people are seen as dependent largely on themselves in order to provide for their own welfare and defend against the traditional administrative, economic, and political exploitation to which they as a group have been subjected by other elements in society.

Symbolic of the potential power of formal local governments, in the usual set of arguments, is the power to tax—to mobilize and to allocate their own resources as they see fit. After generations of real or imagined tax robbery by higher administrative authorities, such sentiments are understandable. This right is highly treasured and imbued with symbolic value well beyond the functional value such capacities have for the achievement of development.

The reason for emphasizing this point is not to attack it but to argue that it stops short—far short—of achieving potential strengths. The obstacle it presents is the drive for insulation from the world of ancient "enemies" (bureaucrats; landlords, traders, and moneylenders; and demagogues).

THE INSTITUTIONS OF "RURAL GOVERNMENT"

Modernization is built on expanding functional interrelationships. As transformations take place in administration, in the economy and in politics, the potential for exploitation is likely to be diminished. Greater command over the requisites of power will expand local capacities for effective competition in external arenas. Hence, the justification of isolation will diminish with time.

The marketplace will provide powerful stimuli for development via the price mechanism. Technological stimuli also may come via the market, but the strongest consistent source of information will be through technical specialists in the nation-building departments serving health, education, agriculture, and so forth.

In order to institutionalize the necessary communication and supply processes, a number of structures may have to be adapted in order to channel and focus activities. These will become part of, and interact within, the complete set of rural governing institutions that is made up of the following:

A. *Formal, or explicit, governing institutions:*
   1. *Those lower-echelon administrative units recognized or established by the central government as the formal "local governments,"* such as village councils, village headmen, village assemblies, and local administrative committees. These may exist in two or more tiers depending on the background of the personnel involved and their manner of selection and action.

2. *Those field representatives of the central government who operate within rural areas,* such as teachers, extension agents, health workers, police patrolmen, community development workers, and district chief administrators or higher-echelon administrative coordinators.

B. *Informal, or implicit, rural governing institutions:*
1. *Those local organizations or activities promoted by the central government on an "unofficial" or "semi-official" basis,* such as cooperatives, farmers associations, community development projects, parent-teacher associations, volunteer guards, and patriotic political activities.
2. *Those forms of public organization and action which are customary and traditional among rural people,* such as religious organizations and their ceremonies, commercial agents and trading patterns, partisan political activity, land tenure and credit arrangements, public discussion meetings, ad hoc contributions to autonomous public works, and even patterns of interpersonal deference and respect.[3]

Such a broad definition of "rural government" paints a useful picture of diverse interaction in rural public affairs. It lays out one terminal of an administrative continuum that reaches to the national capital. It shows rural government partly as an arm of the national government, and the national government partly as an upward reach of rural government. In such terms, the stability of the nation and the stability of rural localities are more clearly seen as interrelated.

The capacities for mobilizing the effective participation of rural human and material resources are also seen as greater than those falling only within the jurisdiction of formal local governments (even when supported by the "natural" or informal leadership of the community).

The development of these capacities will be taken up in the following sections which deal with considerations regarding the nature of the processes, and of the structures of rural government.

CONSIDERATIONS OF PROCESS

Decision-making and execution—the direction, management, and control of rural public affairs—are the key processes of rural government.[4] However, since government is identified not only by its processes of action but also by the organizational structures through which these processes flow, both aspects need to be considered.

---

[3] Ibid.
[4] With certain adaptations, this follows the concept of "government" expressed in M. G. Smith, *Government in Zazzau 1800–1950* (London: Oxford University Press, 1960), pp. 15–33.

Some specialists would argue that structures of government are considerably less significant than the processes which flow through them.[5] This is largely because the structures of government are situation-specific while the processes are more nearly universal. To use an analogy, by the same token that green plants, fish, and humans have different structures for the common process of respiration; so also New England townships, Indian villages, and Soviet collective farms have different structures that direct, manage, and control the public affairs over which they have jurisdiction.

Therefore, short of an encyclopedic discussion, few useful statements can be made about structure at this point. More will be said after a consideration of the processes which flow through them. Consequently, the discussion of "structure" will be taken up in a later section. At this later point guidelines are offered for the structuring of rural governing institutions with capabilities to serve development needs.

The processes of government are both political and administrative. Government at any level involves the crucial processes of public decision-making and execution which involve a variety of formal and informal organizations and structures. At the heart of the matter is the "political" question of who it is that has the legitimate right, the skill, the experience, and the power, not only to make public decisions and to implement them but to defend such processes from encroachment and competition.

PARTICIPATION UNDER CONDITIONS OF INEQUALITY

Participation in public decision-making—oftentimes discussed in terms of the norms of egalitarian democracy—actually takes place in a real world of almost total inequality. No two individuals are exactly alike; some have more skill, some have more knowledge, some have better health, some have more status, some have more power, and so forth.

The striking feature of low-income countries is the breadth of inequality between a relatively small urbanized elite and the majority of the population—especially in terms of wealth, power, and education. The nascent middle class in developing countries is made up largely of government employees who are upwardly mobile and whose formal administrative relationships are geared to the hierarchical flow of authority. Their professional attitudes are colored by status and income differences among themselves, and between themselves and rural people (and others who are menial workers). Even village society is, to a greater or lesser degree, built upon status differences among its members. Wealth, caste, religion, politics, race, family, or other fac-

---

[5] *Local-level Politics,* chap. 1, ed. Marc J. Swartz (Chicago: Aldine, 1968).

tional dividing lines separate individuals and groups and order their relationships.

Among all these disparate groups there are one or more subsets of shared goals. Where these goals include consistent aspects of the welfare of individuals, groups, and sovereign state, then there is a common purpose along the axis of achievement of this particular set of goals through development activities.

Among those with the power to make decisions, sensitivity to development needs and the ability to form consensus will be major traits. Efficacy rather than ideology will be the test of developmentally relevant rural governing institutions. One writer identifies the essence of democracy as respect and consideration for the individual but raises the question of "how much?"[6] It may be no more than he can command or defend, or than will be commanded or defended on his behalf by others in sympathy with him or with fundamental principles.

FUNCTIONAL OBJECTIVES AND PROGRAMS—AN INITIAL REQUIREMENT

The determination of what is to be done is a primary concern. Operational programs have to be developed around consistent and realistic objectives. Objectives are more often implied than specific, as may be seen in the fulfilment of a role expectation, or in the direct melioration of a perceived problem or need. In any event, without an agreed-upon set of goals, involving large and leading segments of the population, program objectives would be untenable and local institutions and individuals would have no more than nominal involvement in purposeful change. Even though most critical decisions may be made at relatively high levels external to the community, intermediate objectives are within every program, and lower-order decisions are to be made at each level of jurisdiction.

BUILDING DEVELOPMENT CAPACITIES

The needs of a traditional society differ from those of a modernizing one. Developing societies go through transitions which present unfamiliar tasks and problems. Individuals and institutions need the capacities to perceive the sequential nature of development, and to do things that have, to a greater or lesser degree, not been done before.

In traditional situations the passage of the seasons is paralleled by agricultural, ceremonial, and other activities that are cyclical and conservative of the status quo. Life stages from birth through death

---

[6] Charles Hyneman, as cited in David Braybrooke and Charles E. Lindblom, *A Strategy of Decision: Policy Evaluation as a Social Process* (New York: Free Press of Glencoe, 1963), p. 85.

in successive generations are paralleled by the inception, completion, deterioration, and destruction of crops and physical facilities.

In the same way that farmers in traditional agriculture may be looked upon as relatively efficient in allocating their resources within a traditional context,[7] so also the formal and informal institutions of rural government may evolve to a relatively effective level in meeting needs that are familiar in village custom.

This is reflected, for instance, in the management of autonomous public works, such as the construction of buildings in the Buddhist temple compounds in rural villages in Thailand.[8] Here, traditional institutions interact to meet needs with which they have become familiar over the course of generations. The principal initiative in decision-making and planning is taken by key elements in the village leadership, the head priest of the temple, the laymen associated with the temple's temporal affairs, and the formally recognized village headman. If the cooperation and material support of the villagers is crucial to the success of the project, they are called to a meeting and asked to ratify the decision and pledge support. The design of a temple and the manner of organizing its construction is known from preexisting structures, from religious teaching, and from participation in prior activities.

Considerable amounts of physical and human resources may be involved as needs are identified; plans are formulated; consensus is formed; materials, manpower, and money are assembled; tasks are assigned; performance is supervised; and public accounts are rendered.

In such settings, roles are learned from example and apprenticeship. In a well-integrated traditional society virtually no scope or need exists for autonomous structural change in local institutions. But the acquisition of a development potential—to direct, manage, and control new activities unfamiliar to local traditions—requires such structural changes. Before any restructuring of rural institutions can be accomplished, however, the powers and skills of organization and training would have to achieve an effective level of relevance, competence, and potency.

ORGANIZATION AND TRAINING

Farmers in developing countries, although socially integrated through kinship and other systems, are weakly *organized* in an economic sense. They are dispersed atomistically as smallholders, share croppers, or laborers. They are vulnerable in their dealings with commercial traders, money lenders, landlords, or employers. Separate-

[7] Theodore W. Schultz, *Transforming Traditional Agriculture* (New Haven, Conn.: Yale University Press, 1964), pp. 36–52.
[8] Nicolaas Luykx, "Some Comparative Aspects of Rural Public Institutions in Thailand, the Philippines and Viet-Nam" (Ph.D. diss., Cornell University, 1962), pp. 327–29.

ly, they lack the resources and scale of operation to take advantage of opportunities to employ many kinds of technological advances.

The *training* needs of rural people derive from their minimal educations beyond socialization into community traditions and apprenticeship to traditional roles and occupations. In the areas of literacy, hygiene, vocational skills, problem solving, and so forth, they have had little formal preparation.

Established local governments suffer from similar deficiencies. Although accredited to undertake many functions, they are generally not fitted into hierarchical governing systems that would provide leadership, coordination, and guidance to these local bodies, and supplement their meager resources.

Over the past decade or so in rural Thailand steps have been taken to build local competencies to make development decisions. The Thai government has organized a simple, vertically linked "planning" procedure, and is training village level committees.[9]

"Village Development Committees" have been formalized in rural districts where the Community Development (CD) Department has established field offices. The members of the committee are, in a formal sense, elected. The village headman is usually the chairman, occasionally with only honorary status. The head teacher of the local school is usually the committee's secretary. Five to nine other members are elected from the village. The CD worker acts as coach and guide to the committee.

Within each of the 71 provinces, local land revenues and other minor incomes are retained for reallocation within the province—largely to the localities in support of their formal requests for minor public works such as wells, canals, school buildings, and bridges. The planning and allocation process moves back and forth between the province level and the village level via the intervening echelons.

The Ministry of Interior has given broad decision-making authority to the provincial governors with regard to the accomplishment of rural development over and above the work of the line agencies serving agriculture, education, public health, and the like. Through frequent touring, and formal and informal meetings with administrators, the governors publish their views on desirable local rural development projects, consistent with their training, the policies of the Ministry of Interior, and their interpretations of needs in the province. The chief administrative officers of the subordinate "districts" perform a similar activity in relaying the policies expressed by their provincial governors. There is, in this process, a clear downward-flowing stimulus that reaches the CD workers, the village headmen, and the local school teachers.

At the outset of the project submission season, the local village development committee, with the assistance of the CD worker and the

---

[9] Ibid., pp. 93–98.

teacher, prepares a request for the funding of a specified project that is of its own choosing. However, the statements emanating from the governor and the chief administrator of the district are not lost on the committee. The prepared requests go through two stages of collating, editing, and priority setting by higher level committees as they pass upward through administrative echelons. The aggregated requests arrive at the province-level office of the "Accelerated Rural Development" (ARD) program where they are integrated into the draft budget which the governor presents to a province-level legislative body known as the "Provincial Assembly." The assembly makes only minor changes in allocating the land revenues to the designated projects.

In the long run the hope is that this procedure will result in a genuine expression of popular desires in feasible form. At present, however, the outcome of the procedure is a local response to central initiative, helped along at each stage by central government field officers taking the role (however expertly or inexpertly) of organizers, tutors, and guides. The procedure takes traditional institutions and procedures as its point of departure (i.e., informal consultations among leading individuals and groups in the planning and execution of autonomous public works, such as in the construction of the temple buildings noted above). The procedure also accommodates the traditionally unequal status positions of government personnel and rural people. Despite these differences, means are devised for opening up the channels of communication in both directions. Traditional procedures of leadership initiative and consultative response are used to shape locally agreed-upon plans. These are then processed upward in response to an initial downward stimulus. Coordination and integration of the diverse requests are the principal activity at each ascending echelon.

Other somewhat more elaborate endeavors to build integrated development oriented governing systems were undertaken under the Rural Works Program in East Pakistan.[10] Here again, both *organization* and *training* are applied to a specific *program* or set of objectives.

The echelons of government in East Pakistan start at the *union* level and include the *thana,* the *sub-division,* the *district,* and the *division* in ascending order, finally terminating at the *province* level (East Pakistan). The most important local government units are the councils at the union, thana, and district levels, which were established in 1959 under "The Basic Democracies Order" of the military government of Ayub Khan.

The members of each union council are chosen from electoral "wards" which today contain about 1,250 people. About ten such wards are in each union. Union councils have broad optional authority for administrative activities involving community welfare.

[10] A. K. M. Mohsen, *The Comilla Rural Administration Experiment: History and Annual Report 1962–63* (Comilla, East Pakistan: Pakistan Academy for Rural Development, October, 1963).

The union councils receive 35 percent of the land tax as well as other revenues.[11]

Although there is considerable variation among thanas, this level of jurisdiction encompasses an area of approximately 100 square miles and an average population of between 150 and 200 thousand. The membership of the thana councils is made up of the elected chairmen of the union councils, on the one hand, and the appointed thana-level government officers serving agriculture, education, and several other nation-building departments on the other hand. The day-to-day co-ordination of thana council affairs is assigned to an appointed government official known as the "circle officer." He serves officially as the vice-chairman and secretary of the council. The chairman is the sub-divisional officer (SDO) who is an appointed government officer with jurisdiction over all of the half-dozen or so thanas that make up each sub-division.

The thana council is a significant coordinative body which does not have a base of local revenues to finance its activities. Coordination takes place horizontally as members of the bureaucratized nation-building departments have opportunities to interact with their comparable numbers in related fields. Integration takes place as four levels of the governmental hierarchy meet and interact at one table. The union council chairmen are village-level leaders, representing rural-based interests and values. The officials representing the nation-building departments at the thana level are individuals who have made the transition from rural origins to the lower rungs of the bureaucratic hierarchy and town society. The circle officer is a member of the "East Pakistan Civil Service" (EPCS), ranking somewhat higher in status but still lower than that of the SDO who is a young man near the beginning of his career in the elite "Civil Service of Pakistan" (CSP).

The developmental and administrative interests of the central government, the provincial government, and the rural people were seen as giving a clear opportunity for realistic and coordinated in-teraction within the structure of the thana council. However, custom-ary patterns of social and administrative behavior were a major im-pediment. Status differences were explicitly or implicitly invoked by those holding advantageous positions. Field officers of the nation-building departments resisted coordination across bureaucratic lines.[12]

The initial optimism following the issuance of the Basic Democracies Order in 1959 was followed by disappointment as it became clear that union and thana council members were not accomplished

---

[11] Elliot Tepper, *Changing Patterns of Administration in Rural East Pakistan* (East Lansing, Mich.: Asian Studies Center, Michigan State University, August, 1966), p. 107.

[12] Mohsen, *The Comilla Rural Administration Experiment*, pp. 18–19.

planners and that their immediate capacity to cope with development needs was low.[13] However, union councils did appear to be
able to develop and execute public works projects such as flood control embankments and drainage canals. These initial successes led
to a pilot project which developed procedures for a Rural Works
Program for the entire province of East Pakistan, utilizing large
amounts of PL480 wheat for part of its financing.[14]

The pilot project's methods for identifying projects, assigning
them priorities, collating union council and thana council projects,
securing technical opinions from agencies such as the Water and
Power Development Authority (WAPDA), training local "project
committees" (chaired by union council members) supervising locally
hired labor, using PL480 wheat in partial payment of wages, measuring physical accomplishments, maintaining records and accounts, and
establishing effective working relationships between government
officers and council members, were all incorporated into the manual
of procedures and/or the training programs that were held for officers
involved in the provincial Rural Works Program.

> There are two partners, the Government officials on the one hand
> and the local leaders on the other. The officials have the responsibility
> for helping the local leaders in planning and execution and in admin-
> istering funds. The local leaders have the responsibility for selecting
> projects, setting priorities, mobilizing local labour, making payments
> according to the rules, and getting the work done.
> Among the officials the greatest responsibility falls on the SDO and
> the circle officer, as they are chairman and vice-chairman of the thana
> council and so the supervising officers for the union councils. The circle
> officer as vice-chairman and secretary of the thana council is the execu-
> tive chief in the programme; the SDO is its chief supervisor and guide.
> An essential service rendered by the SDO is obtaining the necessary ad-
> vice from WAPDA and other authorities.
> The tasks of training the local leaders falls directly on the circle
> officer, and the success of the programme depends on this training.[15]

SUPPORTIVE SERVICES

Public and private services are scarce in the rural areas of developing countries, and those that are performed are usually at mini-

---

[13] Ibid., pp. 23–24.
[14] Initially the wages of laborers on the Works Program were paid partly in
cash and partly in wheat. Subsequently, payments to laborers were made entirely in cash, although imports of PL480 wheat continued as a mainstay of
Works Program financing. Wheat consumption by the rice eating East Pakis-
tanis was never a problem under the pricing policies adopted by the government of Pakistan. See John W. Thomas, "Rural Public Works and East
Pakistan's Development" (paper read at Harvard University Development
Advisory Service Conference, Sorrento, Italy, September 5–12, 1968), p. 24.
[15] Mohsen, The Comilla Rural Administration Experiment, p. 36.

mal levels. In addition to service needs in education, health, transportation and communication, physical protection and security, and justice, rural people have a variety of needs in the promotion of productivity and income. Organizational and production planning assistance; and access to credit, to other production inputs, to technical information, and to stable markets are among the prerequisites of a developing economy which people are unable to provide or ensure from their own resources.

The pilot project in rural cooperatives initiated in Comilla, East Pakistan,[16] is a system of village level primary societies integrated under a "Central Cooperative Association" which acts as a servicing headquarters for all the cooperatives within the 100 square mile area of the thana. The system operates a large-scale savings program and a loan program making it, in effect, a rural bank. An extension education program is conducted using elected persons from within each primary cooperative as intermediaries. These persons attend regular training sessions and return to their home areas obligated to implement their training on their own fields and to pass their training on to other cooperative members. A machine station operated by the central cooperative association runs a motor pool and a maintenance shop for irrigation pumps, tractors, and other equipment available for rental by primary cooperatives. A grain mill, a cold storage plant, and a dairy processing unit are also operated by the central cooperative association as business ventures to enhance the market strength of the entire membership. Additional endeavors are directed at widening the role of women in rural society, at adult literacy, the mobilization of rural youth, and family planning.

In those fields where the pilot projects have achieved persuasive results, the Pakistan government has attempted to incorporate the methods of operation into the activities of its service agencies.

DISCIPLINE

By "discipline" is meant the blocking off of clearly undesirable behavior patterns from the available range of feasible choices. Whereas the foregoing factors of *organization, training,* and *supportive services* enhance the capacity of individuals and groups to make and carry out developmentally relevant decisions—once decisions are made their

---

[16] A. Aziz Khan, *A New Rural Co-operative System for Comilla Thana: Sixth Annual Report, Rural Co-operative Pilot Experiment* (Comilla, East Pakistan: Pakistan Academy for Rural Development, May, 1967); and Nicolaas Luykx, "The Comilla Project, East Pakistan" (Paper read at International Seminar on Change in Agriculture, University of Reading (England), September 3–14, 1968), reprinted in *Change in Agriculture,* ed. A. H. Bunting (London: Gerald Duckworth, 1970).

implementation needs to be ensured through *discipline* if goals are to be achieved and scarce development resources are to be conserved.

In the course of technological change new measures for the increased productivity of economic resources and for other improvements in welfare are developed and adapted to specific situations. They present a net addition to the range of alternative opportunities, or feasible choices. However, the wider the range of opportunity becomes, the slower will be the rate of acceptance of the most efficient alternatives and the slower will be the overall pace of development.[17] The objective, then, in striving to accelerate the process of change, is to narrow the scope of action to the minimum number of relatively efficient proven options.

As new possibilities open up, older and less effective opportunities need to be withdrawn through some mechanism.

The cost-price squeeze, new or rising taxes, the threat of poverty or loss of status, or declining satisfaction in the face of new wants and ambitions are among those forces which bedevil farmers into changing their behavior patterns in favor of greater productivity. However, these pressures are not exerted evenly or automatically, and, more likely than not, a large proportion of farmers may unwittingly drift in contentment toward obsolescence.[18]

What is needed are new and more dependable mechanisms for prodding farmers into accepting innovations.

Further improvement of extension education is, of course, a potential bulwark in pursuing such an objective.[19] More concern in

[17] ". . . *the rate of adoption and diffusion of new techniques, and the requisite changes in farmers' values, attitudes, and practices will be in inverse ratio to the range of available alternatives.*" Kusum Nair, *The Lonely Furrow: Farming in the United States, Japan, and India* (Ann Arbor, Mich.: University of Michigan Press, 1969), p. 231. Kusum Nair goes on, in the same passage, to point out that the level of operative efficiency in agriculture is determined not by the highest limit of potential "but by the *floor* of economic and technical feasibility and social expectation below which it is impossible to farm." Thus farmers are, it seems, more responsive to "push" factors (such as "discipline") than they are to "pull" factors (such as new, more effective opportunities).

[18] This is a theme which runs throughout *The Lonely Furrow* (cited above). In the first eleven chapters this issue is explored through word portraits of a selection of United States farmers. In subsequent chapters comparisons are made with Japanese and Indian farmers and a number of challenging principles are elicited which offer explanations to the question of why farmers change.

[19] John W. Mellor, "Toward a Theory of Agricultural Development," in *Agricultural Development and Economic Growth,* ed. Herman M. Southworth and Bruce F. Johnston (Ithaca, N.Y.: Cornell University Press, 1967), pp. 49–50; Max F. Millikan and David Hapgood, *No Easy Harvest: The Dilemma of Agriculture in Underdeveloped Countries* (Boston: Little, Brown and Co., 1967), p. 77; and Arthur T. Mosher, *Getting Agriculture Moving: Essentials for Development and Modernization* (New York: Frederick A. Praeger, 1966), pp. 131–33. These references note the problems faced by farmers in coping with expanding alternatives. While the need to move farmers toward more productive opportunities is perceived, the procedures recommended place the burden

extension may have to be given to providing farmers with the operational skills in applying increasingly complex innovations than to improving their analytic and decision-making powers per se. The refinement of a farmer's decision-making capacity may be necessary to some extent but only to enable him to operate rationally within a narrowed range of relatively more sophisticated choices. In practice, few farmers perform analyses themselves but evaluate the analyses of others on the basis of results and respect. Basic and applied research (including local demonstration-test plot trials) could take care of most of the decision-making problems if effectively integrated with market and institutional considerations.

The price mechanism is another means but its application may be slowed by indifference, attitudes towards risk, localized distortions, nature of market structure, weak involvement in market activities of those who are predominantly subsistence farmers, or numerous other factors. Like extension, prices have considerable potential for influence[20] and would have to be included in any attack on the problem of blocking off inferior choices. However, like extension, their application is insufficiently certain and still relies on individual action.

As development proceeds, functional interdependence becomes more characteristic of individuals and institutions previously more nearly self-sufficient. Economies of scale and strength through solidarity provide previously unobtainable welfare advantages for the members of various subgroups and groups which join to comprise more or less integrated development systems. The factors of organization, training, and supportive services, discussed in previous sections, enhance the absorptive capacity of the system and its components for technology and innovation. Here discipline becomes important as a concept representing dependable institutionalized means for culling inferior alternative behavior patterns from the widening range of choice. On the one hand discipline blocks off the alternative of inaction, and on the other hand discipline blocks off the alternative of independent action which is detrimental to the common interest.

Although recognizing the values placed on individual self-determination, expression may be destructive of the common good.

> The real and very serious dilemma covered up by this verbal fuzziness about the ideal of voluntariness is that *there is little hope in South*

---

of decision on the farmer, leaving the extension worker with the role of informant and explicator. This may be a presumption based on United States extension experience and values. More needs to be learned about decision-making as a shared process and the extent to which the burden of analysis and drawing conclusions may be shifted away from farmers.

[20] In elaboration of the significance of prices, John W. Mellor makes the point that price changes in and of themselves give new alternatives. The endeavor is to get farmers to respond to changes in relative profitability which come about through relative price changes with or without technological change. Extension uses communication methods to intensify the effect, and further price manipulations may give additional amplification. Private communication, August 26, 1969.

Asia for rapid development without greater social discipline. To begin with, in the absence of more discipline—which will not appear without regulations backed by compulsion—all measures for rural uplift will be largely ineffective. In principle, discipline can be effected within the framework of whatever degree of political democracy a country can achieve; in the end nothing is more dangerous for democracy than lack of discipline.[21]

Yet this cannot be undertaken to any useful outcome unless the social decision-making process can hit upon a *program*—that is, a preferred pattern of behavior.

The point about discipline may be reinforced with a final illustration, also taken from the pilot project in rural cooperatives at Comilla, East Pakistan. Membership in the cooperative system is voluntary, but its members obligate themselves to follow a program that takes full advantage of the development services provided by the central cooperative association through the local primary cooperative societies. Failure to do so, either on the part of an individual or an entire primary society, leads to remedial steps. Initially, special consultation, assistance, guidance, and instruction are provided. If necessary, pressures for compliance can be, and are, exerted by withholding essential services, such as credit and irrigation facilities, that are not available in any comparable form from alternative sources. As a last resort, mortgaged assets may be sold to recover defaulted loans, although this is rarely necessary. The existence of these sanctions, coupled with the will to apply them, is essential for the protection of the integrity and security of the cooperative system and its members, taken as a whole. It protects each primary society from the vagaries of an individual member, and it protects the entire system from the vagaries of a single cooperative.

CONSIDERATIONS OF STRUCTURE

As noted earlier, governmental and social structures are situation specific. Their particular traits depend on the norms of the society in which they are introduced.[22] In this section, the discussion will draw on illustrative material already presented from Thailand and East Pakistan in order to examine general guidelines with regard to: (1) whether structures should be general or specific in their purposes, (2) whether structures should be formally representative or non-rep-

---

[21] Gunnar Myrdal, *Asian Drama: An Inquiry into the Poverty of Nations* (New York: Pantheon Books, 1968), p. 895.
[22] Samuel Humes and Eileen M. Martin, *The Structure of Local Governments throughout the World* (The Hague: Martinus Nijhoff, 1961), in which the summary descriptions of the local governments are presented separately for a long list of countries. The treatment is encyclopedic. The introductory section, in which some generalizations are offered, is brief.

resentative,[23] and (3) the level of jurisdiction at which these structures should be established.

An *administrative* consideration is the breadth and diversity of functions assigned to, or assumed by, a governing institution. In many instances such structures, especially those formally constituted as "local government," have a fairly broad spectrum of mandatory and optional functions. They may range from the maintenance of records on births, deaths, marriages, and land holdings to the levying of "taxes" and their allocation to local welfare needs.

Other institutions may have relatively narrow functional jurisdictions. This is especially true of the implicit or informal institutions within communities. The ad hoc, special-purpose nature of most informal structures is in keeping with the ad hoc approach to problem solving traditionally taken by villagers.

The evidence suggests that in the early stages of development interests can be aggregated more easily around a need or a function than around an institution. The inference is that special-purpose institutions are more likely to operate effectively than general-purpose institutions—especially where organization for development is in its early phases.

Most needs appear one at a time according to a priority ranking and development skills can be taught one at a time more feasibly than several at once. For instance, in an area beset by alternating flood and drought, the needs for supplemental plant nutrients and for plant protection measures are only perceived once water has been brought under control. As another example, concerns over the management of local revenues and local school curricula may only arise after skill and confidence in the management of public affairs is acquired through the handling of rural public works. The Rural Works Program in East Pakistan has as one of its main benefits the training of local government councilors in the planning and execution of substantial activities.[24]

Of the institutions which were associated with the construction of Thai temple buildings, the priests and the temple lay committee were associated only with temple affairs. Similar special-purpose institutions exist to meet other ad hoc needs in the same villages.[25]

The committees which formulated requests for small rural development projects in Thailand were constituted for just this purpose at the village level. The Rural Works Program in East Pakistan was

---

[23] The categories "general-purpose" and "special-purpose," and "representative" and "nonrepresentative" are taken from the previously cited work, pp. 3–6.
[24] Tepper, *Changing Patterns of Administration in Rural East Pakistan*, p. 119.
[25] Luykx, "Some Comparative Aspects of Rural Public Institutions in Thailand, the Philippines and Viet-Nam," pp. 303–42.

planned and carried out by the newly organized union and thana councils which, although constituted as general-purpose institutions, engaged themselves almost exclusively in Works Program activities.

The final case of the cooperative pilot project in East Pakistan clearly involves rural institutions designed to serve multiple purposes. These are relatively sophisticated structures which place heavy demands on organizational skills, training, and other supportive services, as well as on disciplinary control, for their efficient functioning.

REPRESENTATIVE OR NONREPRESENTATIVE

A *political* consideration is whether governing structures are representative of local interests and, if so, to what degree.

Elected bodies may be representative if they are selected openly by some electoral process and have the power to act on behalf of the interests they represent. Bodies that have no effective say or influence in public affairs are not representative, even if they are popularly elected. Very often such bodies act as instruments to legitimize actions taken by others. The "Provincial Assemblies" in Thailand, even in the period following martial law, are dominated by the appointed provincial governors, regardless of the manner in which the members are selected.

Nonelected bodies, skillful in consensus formation and sensitive to local needs, may also be fairly representative of local interests even though they are selected by appointment, inheritance, or other nonrepresentative means. For instance, the Thai central government, traditionally autocratic in its relationships with rural people, has modified its autocracy and adopted greater representativeness of local interests. This has come about not so much by democratization (despite the democratic forms adopted) as by sensitizing its officers to the realities of rural conditions. These officers, nonetheless, retain final authority and control in their own hands. Thai government officers in rural areas have adopted more of a downward focus of attention in their work, and the criteria for their professional evaluation are expanding into the realm of operational effectiveness in the field. Key administrative officials in the provinces spend much of their time touring rural areas and making contact with rural people. In so doing they usually involve their subordinates and colleagues as well.

Bodies such as cliques, factions, secret societies, and the like may be regarded as nonrepresentative because they are concerned only with the narrow range of special interests of their restricted membership.

The best guidelines for the degree of representativeness that is expected or tolerable in newly organized institutions likely will be found in the degree of representativeness to which individuals and groups are accustomed in other institutions. A conditioning element will be the strength of positive and negative inducements to accept variations from accustomed norms.

In the illustrations discussed earlier the pattern of action placed major responsibility on leadership.

In the case of construction of temple buildings in rural Thailand, the Buddhist priests are representative in that they set the pattern of idealized morality. The laymen involved in the management of temple affairs are drawn from the pool of respected persons in the village. The headmen are locally elected and have freedom of action in their villages.

In the case of the submission of requests for small-scale rural development facilities by "Village Development Committees" in Thailand, these committees, in effect, have a mixed membership of ex-officio and elected committeemen. The same is true for the membership of the Pakistani thana councils. In the cooperative pilot project in Pakistan there is a similar mixture of elected officers of the primary cooperative societies in interaction with regular employees elsewhere in the system. Member control over the Central Cooperative Association—the headquarters of the system—is exercised through the elected membership of the central association.

Integrated training and action situations such as these are conducted through interrelationships analogous to those between teachers and students. The preferred pattern of behavior is established and communicated by the formally nonrepresentative elements (who are the "teachers" in the analogy). They organize the participants for training and, in many cases, for the action which is to follow, as well. They maintain control over the situation. Government officers or other specialized trainers, tutors, coordinators and guides are accepted, although not selected, by the participant population. The degree of their sensitivity and responsiveness to the local situation tempers the degree of their formal nonrepresentativeness.

On the other hand, the formally representative element, which is locally selected, acts on behalf of the population it represents. Its members (who are the "students" in the analogy) act to adopt a feasibly modified behavior pattern as a result of their participant experience. In time, these modifications are expected to diffuse into the population by structured and unstructured processes involving the elected representatives as models or, in turn, as teachers and trainers.

THE LEVEL OF JURISDICTION

Between the level of the smallest residence area or hamlet and the national capital there are intervening layers of hierarchically ordered administrative echelons. The location of any particular institutional structure within this vertical array is relevant. Also relevant is the relative location of different institutions in relation to each other.

Where the scale of development activities is organized at the village level, the scale of establishment for the institution primarily concerned is the same. Small village-centered public works projects evidently can be planned and carried out through village-level institutions.

As the scale of public works and other concerns is elevated to effect certain coordinative efficiencies, village-level institutions alone no longer suffice. Rural drainage, road and other public works facilities servicing areas as large as a union, thana, or even a district (in the East Pakistan case) were planned and managed at those levels of jurisdiction.

The cooperative pilot project in East Pakistan was founded on a basis of village-level primary cooperative societies in order to coordinate village level interests in water utilization, loan distribution, shared tractor services, and the like. However, the central servicing headquarters which supports the entire system is operated at the thana level of jurisdiction so that economies of scale can be achieved in the operation of machine stations, rural banking facilities, a training and supervising establishment, and processing and marketing facilities.

An additional consideration is that rural development activities which are structured at the village level operate within the same jurisdiction as a host of traditional structures which may entrench themselves against the external threat to their values posed by the rural development activity. For these, and for other reasons, the geographical and social village may be too small a unit for the effective planning and implementation of change. A next higher level, such as a commune, district, or block may be a more functional size of jurisdiction. At such a level it may be easier to discover, assemble, and develop local competencies to make public decisions, to coordinate with government technicians, and to aggregate interests in modernization that do not fly in the face of the many local institutions with tradition-oriented values.

SUMMARY

The rational approach to the achievement of development objectives is exemplified in the technology of "planning." Information gathering, analysis, the delineation of alternatives, and deliberation are components that lead to rational choice. Opportunities for broad participation take place in the planning stage as individuals and groups pour information such as facts, interpretations of facts (including the rationalization of special interests), desires and needs (together with priority rankings) into the planning mill along with other material (including an evaluation of the constraints posed by prior commitments and an assessment of the administrative resources for implementation). Some of the planning inputs may be highly processed at lower echelons and may arrive at the highest planning level in forms that may be fitted into the final plan with relatively little adaptation. Additional opportunities for participation appear at the implementation stage where the pattern of activities authorized in the effective "plan" are programmed for action.

In order to enlist rural governing institutions in the broad task of nationally integrated development, and in order to broaden the base of participation in decisions and action affecting welfare, the conventional roles of rural governing institutions need reevaluation. Viability in a modernizing world is increasingly dependent on inter-relationships and on the preservation of the common interest. An aspect of the fundamental political nature of central-local relations that is often overlooked is the common stake both sectors have in overall national development. Developmental goals are achieved at the price of interdependence and the acceptance of coordination.

Before rural governing institutions can be adapted or created to fit effectively into such a pattern, their capacities need to be developed from the levels which served to maintain a satisfactory static state in traditional surroundings. Four main elements contribute to the development of new capacities appropriate to the progressive nature of modernization: (1) *organization* as a means of structuring the division of labor, and as a means of providing political and economic strength in approaching specific development objectives, (2) *training* in technical and problem-solving skills which permits dealing with emergent situations, (3) *supporting services,* appropriate to the objectives, which compensate for needs which participants cannot provide for themselves, and (4) *discipline* which channels and conserves the variety of scarce resources applied to the development process.

The structural characteristics of rural governing institutions are not open to prescription because of their close relationship to the norms of the societies in which they are established. Special-purpose structures seem better adapted than general purpose ones to the earlier stages of rural modernization because of the direct relation to specific functional objectives and the relative ease in focusing the four elements noted above. Representativeness in these structures is related more to the sensitivity of leadership than it is to the manner in which it is chosen. The level of jurisdiction of a structure is a function of the level of operation of the development activities for which it is responsible.

REFERENCES

1. Braybrooke, David and Charles E. Lindblom. *A strategy of decision: Policy evaluation as a social process.* New York: Free Press of Glencoe, 1963.

2. Esman, Milton J. The politics of development administration. In *Approaches to development: Politics, administration and change.* Ed. John D. Montgomery and William J. Siffin. New York: McGraw-Hill, 1966.

3. Humes, Samuel and Eileen M. Martin. *The structure of local governments throughout the world.* The Hague: Martinus Nijhoff, 1961.

4. Hyneman, Charles. *Bureaucracy in a democracy.* New York: Harper and Bros., 1950.

5. Khan, A. Aziz. *A new rural co-operative system for Comilla thana: Sixth annual report, rural co-operative pilot experiment.* Comilla, East Pakistan: Pakistan Academy for Rural Development, May, 1967.

6. Luykx, Nicolaas. Some comparative aspects of rural public institutions in Thailand, the Philippines and Viet-Nam (Ph.D. diss., Cornell University, 1962).

7. ———. Rural government in the strategy of agricultural development. In *Approaches to development: Politics, administration and change.* Ed. John D. Montgomery and William J. Siffin. New York: McGraw-Hill, 1966.

8. ———. The Comilla project, East Pakistan. Paper presented at the International Seminar on Change in Agriculture, University of Reading, September 3–14, 1968. Reprinted in *Change in agriculture.* Ed. A. H. Bunting. London: Gerald Duckworth, 1970.

9. Mellor, John W. *The economics of agricultural development.* Ithaca, N.Y.: Cornell University Press, 1966.

10. ———. Toward a theory of agricultural development. In *Agricultural development and economic growth.* Ed. Herman M. Southworth and Bruce F. Johnston. Ithaca, N.Y.: Cornell University Press, 1967.

11. Millikan, Max F., and David Hapgood. *No easy harvest: The dilemma of agriculture in underdeveloped countries.* Boston: Little, Brown, and Co., 1967.

12. Mohsen, A. K. M. *The Comilla rural administration experiment: History and annual report 1962–63.* Comilla, East Pakistan: Pakistan Academy for Rural Development, October, 1963.

13. Mosher, Arthur T. *Getting agriculture moving: Essentials for development and modernization.* New York: Frederick A. Praeger, 1966.

14. Myrdal, Gunnar. *Asian drama: An inquiry into the poverty of nations.* New York: Pantheon Books, 1968.

15. Nair, Kusum. *The lonely furrow: Farming in the United States, Japan and India.* Ann Arbor, Mich.: University of Michigan Press, 1969.

16. Schultz, Theodore W. *Transforming traditional agriculture.* New Haven, Conn.: Yale University Press, 1964.

17. Smith, M. G. *Government in Zazzau, 1800–1950.* London: Oxford University Press, 1960.

18. Swartz, Marc J., ed. *Local-level politics.* Chicago: Aldine, 1968.

19. Tepper, Elliot. *Changing patterns of administration in rural East Pakistan.* East Lansing, Mich.: Asian Studies Center, Michigan State University, August, 1966.

20. Thomas, John W. Rural public works and East Pakistan's development. Paper presented at the Harvard University Development Advisory Service Conference, Sorrento, Italy, September 5–12, 1968. Cambridge, Mass.: Development Advisory Service, Center for International Affairs, Harvard University, Economic Development Report No. 112 (Mimeographed).

DISCUSSION by W. J. SIFFIN

"How CAN rural governmental institutions be shaped as effective tools of national development?" Luykx makes two important contributions to this question. He offers a perspective and a set of "strategic premises," or guidelines for action. At the same time, his statement is loose and incomplete. This is a limitation, not a flaw. Luykx opens up an important field of inquiry. Neither he nor anyone else might be expected to also close it in one brief statement. However, other things can and should be taken into account beyond those treated in Luykx's paper, in examining the relation of rural local government to national development.

Luykx themes out some of the elements of an analytical perspective. His cases illustrate one way to sort and assess the facts and look for the lessons. And he does not limit his terrain to formally labelled rural governing institutions. Appropriately, Luykx notes that there are other governing institutions too, the "informal, or implicit, rural governing institutions" not officially designated as elements of local government.

The conceptual apparatus used by Luykx in studying these institutions can be strengthened by pinning down the term "governmental," and elaborating and refining the term into a concept.

In speaking of "the institutions of 'rural government' " he lists quite a number of kinds of organizations and forms of action. Luykx defines by reference or illustration. Implicit in this analytical action is the assumption that some sort of *delineating quality* distinguishes "governing" from "nongoverning." Otherwise we have no logical basis for talking about rural governing institutions as distinguished from rural institutions generally. The next step in conceptual development is to specify that quality.

Granting that concepts are never truths, it seems useful to conceptualize the idea of government in terms of the exercise of a certain kind of power—the power to establish and enforce collective goals. In this sense, of course, "government" is a feature of all organizations, so long as questions must be answered about aims and ways in which they shall be pursued.

The important thing about goal setting—often thought of as "politics"—is its ultimately nonrational character. The potency of government lies in its capacity to specify and carry out aims that do not have to be fully determined or justified on the grounds of "reason," i.e., as irrefutable and unambiguous deductions from consensually held higher principles. The essential sustaining premise for such decisions is neither accuracy nor the soundness of the logic that lies behind them; it is *legitimacy*.

In all but the most primitive societies government is an institution—a "problem solving" mechanism for determining goals that are binding upon those within its jurisdiction, and for seeing that those goals are pursued.

"Goal-setting" involves setting new goals; resolving conflicts over established goals (which also tends to affirm or modify them); and "keeping the system going" by doing things necessary to carry out goals.

Decisions about goals are often decisions that the existing pattern of value allocation shall be maintained. This not surprising. The legitimacy of the governmental process lies in rather widespread agreement on what is acceptable, if not always on what is just and desirable.

Thus, there is a Janus-like quality in the idea of legitimacy. It implies and acknowledges that goal setting occurs as a matter of right. But it also implies that what is right will depend upon what the relevant actors will buy. For, at the heart of it all, the potency of government stems not merely from organizational resources and technical proficiency, but from more elusive wellsprings of collective human willingness to accept the goals set by those who can never fully justify their acts by reference to objective criteria.

A grasp of this idea of "government" sensitizes us to a crucial problem—the problem of enhancing the developmental relevance and capability of actual governmental institutions, which is also, commonly, a problem of adjusting—sometimes even challenging—the legitimacy of an existing arrangement.

When political goals are truly developmental—when the object is to change or supplant an existing pattern of value allocation—then the problem of contriving and nurturing effective government can indeed be parlous and perplexing. The called-for potency will not come forth automatically. It is not preexistent. And one would not be wise to accept unquestionably the premise that rational organization, effective training, and adequate supporting resources will be sufficient to produce large changes in the real substance of that complex but vital process, government.

Developing the conceptual aspect of Luykx's perspective also makes it easier to deal with the important problem of integrating rural governing institutions with their larger setting.

The modernization of local governing institutions is bound up with higher level intervention in those institutions. Strategies of local governmental development must take account of national political system characteristics.

Luykx offers illustrations from Pakistan and Thailand. From his discussion and the above conceptualization one may infer a general thesis—that the local might be integrated with the larger by organizationally differentiating goal-setting and goal-execution.

In the case of Comilla, for example, changes in rural local behavior, in statuses, and in the effective rules of the game, were achieved. At least four factors combined to produce these changes: (1) exogenous (to the locality) authority of a complex kind, persistently applied, supported by (2) substantial infusions of resources, (3) appeals to the perceived self-interest of sizeable numbers of local actors, and (4) a scaled set of disciplining sanctions, tied rather directly to individual variance from desired behavior. In plain language, changes in local behavior occurred—among individuals and in rural local governmental organization. These changes had been chosen as goals, and a strategy of trying to achieve them was devised *outside* the initial domain of rural local government. Key factors in the relative success of the venture appear to have been *resources*, including technical and managerial skills preexistent or produced in the course of the venture, *goals* that focused rather clearly and demonstrably upon the self-interest of local people; and the *absence* of any truly effective resistance.

The primary locus of governmental goal setting in the Comilla case lay outside the local level. The relation of supralocal government to the locals was tutelary. And local action at Comilla grew out of a combination of outside impetus and local acceptance. Integration occurred through a restructuring of initial-state relations between rural local governing institutions and the higher levels of Pakistani government. An essential feature of that change was a substantial separation of the goal-setting and goal-executing aspects of government. The former were centralized; the latter remained substantially decentralized during the course of the experience described by Luykx.

The second order effects of the Comilla venture may have been further governmental developments at the local level. Local structures established to carry out developmental goals may evolve into goal-setting mechanisms—acquiring an inherent legitimacy, resolving conflicts over who gets what, and performing these operations in accordance with norms or principles compatible with national or provincial goals. Such an intent might, in fact, be built into a strategy of rural local governmental development. But will such local governmental institutions, achieving goal-setting capability, remain integrated with ever-evolving provincial and national aims and needs? Will a division between local execution and higher level goal-setting cause local goals to be set that fail to take account of local realities? (It all too often happens.)

Such speculations are remote to tangible concerns with training managers and technicians and farmers, promoting new enterprise systems, building cooperative associations, and fighting the battles of the day and week and season to improve the immediate terms of human existence in rural areas. Yet we must give thought to these abstract questions, if only to avoid succumbing to a seductive simplism—the assumption that technically efficacious and relatively rational organizations will more or less automatically take care of the political aspects of society and community. It *can* work that way, with luck; but it is not necessarily so.

To some extent we can reduce the high social opportunity costs of undue innocence by undertaking a reasonably broad and systematic analysis of situations, problems, and strategies. So we may ask—and begin to answer: Under what conditions—initial-state conditions, and conditions of intervention—are new and suitable institutions of local governance likely to emerge? Under what conditions, and in what ways, may functional aspects of governance best be assigned to different locations within the vertical spectrum of government? More light on such questions would be helpful for dealing with the problem Luykx has posed.

Luykx is not predisposed to favor smashing, radical, discontinuous changes in behalf of development. He says it may be possible to find "one or more sub-sets of shared goals" among the various elements of society in a low income country that can serve as the source of a consensus on developmental efforts. In such cases, "efficacy rather than ideology will be the test of developmentally relevant rural governing institutions."

I share this ideal as an ideal; it is a hopeful perspective from which to begin the quest for a developmental strategy. But I am not very sanguine. If, to pursue development, one must really find within the broad reaches of society "a common purpose along the axis of achievement of this particular set of goals"—"the welfare of individuals, groups, and the sovereign state"—then he is probably in trouble. To posit such a state is to posit the absence of any really large issues of developmental politics. As Luykx observes, in such circumstances development will be a matter of applying technology to expand productive resources, with no real disagreement over goals or values within society.

In reality, development creates new values; it attacks old ones; it changes the way values are distributed in society. Development is by definition a positive-sum game at the overall level, over some span of time. But to the Kulaks, the late nineteenth century Japanese peasants, present day East Pakistani consumers, and a lot of groups in a lot of societies, the subgame is not, in the short run in which we live, so positive.

Luykx sees education and technology as prime measures for combatting the deleterious effects of developmental change. Yet these very measures have effects that can be quite deleterious. The problem is so confoundingly complex. For instance, experience with feed grains suggests that large-scale technological infusions have profound redistributive effects within the rural sectors of societies. Not even Comilla-like strategies, marked by competence, continuity, and tutelary humanism, offer complete answers or assurances to questions about the orderliness of change under such conditions.

That vast problems can emerge out of our efforts at rural development, including rural political development, does not mean we should flee into fatalism. It does mean that we must beware of parochial pragmatism, however enthusiastic and dedicated. Once seized, the tigertail of managing change can never be let go. Significant redistributions of value within society may involve the redesign of authoritative goal-setting mechanisms, and the whole process will be paramountly political. Prodding and bedeviling those farmers is political. Redistributing resources within agriculture, and between agriculture and other sectors, is political. Undermining a class of landlords or merchants or money lenders is political. Not only are the actions political, requiring political power; so also are the consequences political. The secularization and rationalization of society and culture is political too. An increasing awareness of and involvement in a larger world—one concomitant of the integration of local structures with provincial and national settings—is fraught with political implications. It may, for example, involve an enlarged sense of dependence upon that larger world, with—or without—a sense of efficacy within it, while older ways and sources of identity, status, and meaning erode.

Thus our concern with the role of rural local governing institutions in national development extends beyond achieving "a responsive, integrated development system [with] . . . enhanced absorptive capacity for technology and innovation . . ." *unless* that absorptive capacity is explicitly perceived as including the capacity to manage the problems of value allocation, and to avoid too many negative sum subgames.

Our thinking and strategizing about rural local government must be integrated into a view that is larger than local, and also larger than technological—one that takes account of the political dimensions of development. This is a big order. Politics is tricky and political development is elusive. But we can build on the framework that Luykx has given up—if we strive for a powerful, systematic, conceptual basis for analyzing situations, defining problems, designing strategies, and assessing results. Only in this way can we avoid devastating discontinuities in societies—particularly in their rural sectors—as we strive after development with all the technology at our command.

DISCUSSION by J. PRICE GITTINGER

LUYKX has correctly stressed that modernization in agriculture is "built on expanding functional inter-relationships." Strikingly, he finds no need to mention any necessity for formal integration between agriculture and other sectors as an essential—or even important—part of planning for economic development. He prefers, apparently, to leave integration between sectors to other mechanisms, economic and political. In this, he is in step with the other leaders of the development profession

In this context, it is interesting that Luykx implicitly calls upon us to treat local government as having, among its other roles, a function of achieving the integration upon which modernization is built, since "developmental goals are achieved at the price of interdependence and acceptance of coordination." This is a useful standpoint from which to look at development investment in agriculture and to consider some of the forms which it might take.

A fascinating insight in Luykx's presentation—given to us almost as a sidelight—is his comment that much of what we normally consider first among the tasks of local government—schools, management of local revenues, and the like—"may arise only after skill and confidence in the management of public affairs is acquired through the handling of rural public works." Here, perhaps, those concerned with investment in agricultural development may be guilty of putting the cart before the horse. We have an inclination to feel that project implementation is too tricky to be left to local government, that only experienced local bodies could undertake such a task. Perhaps our vision has been too narrowly focused on the economic objective, and we may be missing out on what might be a useful by-product of development expenditure. Careful project design can serve not only the objective of increasing the wealth creating capacity of a rural community, but also the critical capacity of the community to bear much more of the innovative governing function so necessary for continuing economic and social development.

Here, too, is a tie in with another recent call to reexamine some of our institutional arrangements in agricultural project investment. Chambers suggests we think of checking consistency between demands on administration in rural investment proposals, restraining demands for information, weighing indirect administrative costs, and preferring "administration-sparing" policies (1). Perhaps we should be paying more overt attention to project design which can encourage buildup of local government capacity to bear part of the administrative burden while at the same time furthering the growth of local government competence which can lead to increasingly development oriented local public administration.

Both Luykx and Chambers tend, however, to underemphasize the place of one administrative mechanism which economists commonly have considered of extreme importance: the market. I have been accused elsewhere of "market mongering" (there was some excellent company, it might be added), and there is some truth in the comment (3). Even so, investment design which can make use of the market can reduce the administrative burden and at the same time simplify administration in a manner which will permit more effective responsibility being assumed by local governments. Luykx notes the market can be a source of technical information, but suggests technical specialists in the nation building departments will be the "strongest consistent source" of technological stimuli. Here is one area where his emphasis may be misplaced; it seems likely that in most open economies the market will be the more important source and could be made to be even more so if investment design were to take account of it. One thinks, for example, of seed multiplication projects where extension education aimed at commercial handlers could greatly—and efficiently—increase the information transmitted through already established channels which have a strong self-interest both in seeing that the information is adapted for the locality and that it is properly utilized.

The market may well have to perform another administrative function which will face many developing nations. Luykx refers to the compelling presentation of this by Nair (2). The discipline which seems inescapable in the development process can hardly be enforced in most developing nations through any other channel but market forces, suitably manipulated and reinforced through tax and other policies. Luykx notes how investment design in the case of the Comilla cooperatives permitted the rather indirect discipline of the market to be reinforced through a local governing institution.

If our concern is with improving the quality of rural life and making it possible for communities to grow both continuously and largely through their own efforts, then Luykx has led us in a fruitful direction of inquiry. Those more immediately associated with the economic development aspect of this concern than with the social can now reflect on some of our suggestions to development administrators. Do the forms which investment takes pay adequate attention to the necessity to build the "commonality" of the concerns of the nation and the locality which Luykx identifies as one weakness in much present rural administration. Luykx provides some useful reminders. Investment for development provides one of the easiest to use common goals which can involve "large and leading segments of the population . . . in purposeful change." Perhaps investment can be more purposefully utilized for this objective if it is explicitly recognized. The possibility of accelerating local government competence through aggregating interests around an investment activity shows in a somewhat different light an aspect of investment organization which practical administrators tend to prefer on the grounds of administrative efficiency. Perhaps both efficiency and social goals could be better served if the parallel between them were more carefully considered in organizing special-purpose implementation agencies. Some additional functions in implementing projects might be devolved in the expectation they will influence patterns of local government competence.

Can local government bodies shoulder more of the training function in project implementation, for example? Almost everyone has noted at one time or another how much faster he had to learn when he was teaching than when he was a student. Finally, careful design of investment forms and institutions can help overcome that weakness in development programs which nags in the back of the minds of those of a basically liberal persuasion—the "representativeness" of local institutions. Luykx has shown how investment forms have been one means to promote a sensitiveness on the part of local leaders, permitting them to be "skillful in consensus formation and . . . fairly representative of local interests even though they are selected by . . . nonrepresentative means."

REFERENCES

1. Chambers, Robert. Executive capacity as a scarce resource, *Intern. Dev. Rev.*, 11 (June, 1969), 5–8.
2. Nair, Kusim. *The lonely furrow: Farming in the United States, Japan and India.* Ann Arbor, Mich.: University of Michigan Press, 1969.
3. Lipton, Michael. Traditional agricultures: A question of perspectives, *Asian Rev.*, 2 (October, 1968), 28–35.

11

LEGAL SYSTEMS

W. LAWRENCE CHURCH

For many, the title, "Legal Systems" might evoke a picture of a comparative study of some of the countless substantive statutes which have been drafted to help foster economic development, e.g., various land reform statutes designed to speed rural development in many parts of the world or a comparative review of the commercial law of civil and common law countries. There is obvious merit to such efforts; but such a study is not the goal of this chapter.

Substantive laws are nothing more than the embodiment of political, social, and economic policies. Thus, each law, code, court decision, or statute, may profitably be analyzed to determine the practical policies which lie behind it. The relative merits of such a law, aside from the technical quality of its drafting, may be described in terms of the validity and proper application of these policies. This necessarily involves critical analysis of the policies themselves, and such analysis is fundamental to any real understanding of the laws. However, despite this fact, critical review of economic and other policies is primarily within the province of economists and others rather than lawyers, and seems inappropriate here.

For this reason, the present discussion will not center on a detailed study of any particular law or set of laws or of the policies behind them. Its aim is much more fundamental. It concerns introductory discussion of a basic issue that faces every developing country: What sort of legal institutions, what "legal system" in the broad sense can best further policies of economic development? That is, can any of the elements of a legal system itself, considered in the abstract and

without reference to specific laws or economic policies, be identified
which will help the system as a whole induce economic development?[1]

ECONOMIC GOALS[2]

Just as specific, substantive laws are the product of political, social, and economic policies, so too are legal systems as a whole. The
discussion that follows is premised on certain economic goals, and
although these goals are not analyzed herein, they should at least be
mentioned. National economic development[3] is assumed a desirable
goal, as indeed it appears a desired goal in all developing nations.
Also, a significant measure of individual initiative is assumed to be desirable, that is, a legal system would endeavor to induce private individuals to enter into commercial effort or investment. Finally, the
assumption is made that the development sought includes participation in commercial activity by persons at all levels of the social and
economic scale, and that particularly in rural areas, greatly increased
participation by a broad segment of the population is hoped for.[4]

---

[1] It should be emphasized at the outset that a suitable legal system is only one
of many factors conducive to development. Some societies appear to have
attained such a legal system but nevertheless remain underdeveloped, and it
can be argued that some nations have achieved considerable development
without such a legal system. Within these limits, however, it certainly is
proper to analyze those elements of a legal system best designed to foster
economic development. Although much of what follows is applicable to
developing countries anywhere, the author's practical experience with legal
systems in such countries has been limited largely to Africa and more particularly to Ethiopia. For this reason, the discussion does not purport to bear
directly on the problems of countries outside Africa. Where appropriate,
references to the author's experiences and to specific legal sources are made
through these footnotes.

[2] The stated goals are not the only policies relevant to a discussion of legal
systems designed to aid economic development—there are, of course, an
almost infinite number of factors, values, and interests which mold any legal
system. The stated policies are singled out for attention for the limited purpose of this discussion only because they are sufficiently basic to be common
for nearly all developing countries. Their number is limited also to permit
a reasonably simple and coherent model for discussion. Full analysis of all or
most of the significant policy choices available and the various ramifications of
each for legal systems presents a task far too complex for treatment in a single
article.

[3] The definition of "economic development," although obviously relevant to
this paper, is not the subject matter of this study. Suffice it here to say that
the term includes a substantial and rapid increase in commercial activity and
trade as well as in measurable per capita income.

[4] Application of this discussion is thus limited to those societies in which at
least some measure of rather broadly based local private enterprise or foreign
investment is encouraged. It is not restricted to purely capitalistic economies;
it applies as well to these portions of mixed economies where private initiative
and investment is anticipated. However, the discussion is not directly applicable to a society which has decided, as a matter of policy choice, not to solicit
voluntary, private participation in any commercial activity.

ELEMENTS OF AN EFFECTIVE LEGAL SYSTEM

A preliminary issue to be discussed, as noted, concerns the essential elements that should be present in a legal system designed to augment economic growth, particularly with respect to the encouragement of individual initiative and investment. Of course, an exhaustive analysis of such an issue cannot be undertaken in a short chapter. What follows is, instead, a brief description of some of the more critical ingredients of what will be a successful system measured by the stated standards. The list is by no means exclusive; there is at least some degree of overlapping within it, and some of the factors discussed compete with others included; but the following are the basic requirements of an effective legal system for a developing country.

PREDICTABILITY

Perhaps the most important single feature for a legal system designed to foster economic growth must be that it makes as predictable as possible the consequences of commercial activity. The need for certainty is obvious: all sorts of economic initiative, from the efforts of the lowliest peasant to increase production of goods from his or another's land to the grand operations of the largest local or foreign entrepreneur, are discouraged unless the beneficial consequences of that intiative are able to be understood in advance. Therefore, if a legal system seeks to promote such initiative, it must strive to offer as much legal certainty as possible to all expected participants in commercial activity.

If a legal system is to afford a high measure of predictability to many persons, it must at the very least include substantive and procedural rules that are set down *in writing*. Even in a local context, oral legal traditions are far too ambiguous, too imprecise to permit fully advised commercial decisions to be made. On a regional or a national level the imprecision grows, because many more legal administrators with official authority are called upon to construe unwritten traditions, and thus the traditions are made subject to many more different interpretations.

A legal system should not only be reduced to writing, it should be *applied uniformly* throughout as wide a jurisdiction as possible. One of the consequences of giving effect to differing local laws and traditions is that the application of any national regulation or institution designed to speed economic growth is rendered relatively uncertain, so that the national measure cannot achieve its optimal impact. For instance, any national legislation designed to spur agricultural investment by providing means for the obtaining of security interests in farms and farm equipment will be considerably frustrated if various local traditions defining ownership of such assets are in force.[5] The application of any national secured interest legislation to each local district will remain in doubt until duly interpreted by an official with national authority which will be respected both by local and national courts, and the policies of the national legislation may well be denied by this interpretation when it is offered. The drafting of the national measure will be rendered immensely complex and difficult; and the beneficial effect of the measure will be postponed at best and at worst may be negated altogether.

For a written, uniformly applied legal system to achieve its full capacity as a predictor of the consequences of commercial activity, it should be as *thorough* and *complete* as possible. It should include *substantive* laws pertaining to every aspect of commerce. The draftsmen of the legal system should try to anticipate needs for legal certainty in areas of commercial activity in advance of the actual commencement of the activity, in order to hasten and encourage initiative. Moreover, to best promote commercial effort, a legal system should offer more than one basic method for organizing business activity and investment.[6] In many developing countries, the level of present commercial activity is such that few methods of business organization or operation are utilized, but the law should nevertheless provide for a wide range of alternatives to accommodate any potential investor of capital or effort. Thus, for example, more than just one or two forms of business association should be permitted;[7] and likewise, land tenure systems should permit the creation of a wide variety of interests in land.[8] A legal system which is too narrow in its scope un-

---

[5] Substantive differences among various local (tribal) land tenure systems have proven exceptionally difficult for national legal policymakers to deal with. In Ethiopia several important systems are in effect, and they are so different and have so rarely been studied and reported about in writing that relatively few people understand even their basic terms. For a description of some of these systems, see H. S. Mann, *Land Tenure in Chore* (Shoa), (Addis Ababa, Ethiopia, and Nairobi, Kenya: Institute of Ethiopian Studies and Faculty of Law, Haile Selassie 1 University, with Oxford University Press, 1965); *Field Study in Systems of Land Tenure and Landlord Tenant Relationships in Tabor Wereda (Sidamo)* (Addis Ababa, Ethiopia: Imperial Ethiopian Government, 1967).

[6] An example of substantive legislation which was omitted in Ethiopia's new legal codes is agricultural cooperatives, although the potential value of such an organization for aiding rural development is obvious. See Art. 212 of the *Commercial Code of Ethiopia* (1960).

[7] In Ethiopia, six kinds of business organizations are permitted: share company, private limited company, ordinary partnership, general partnership, limited partnership, and joint venture. See Art. 212 of the *Commercial Code of Ethiopia*. As noted above, however, cooperatives are not covered; nor are public or quasi-public development corporations, potentially a powerful tool for economic development. See Lawrence C. McQuade, "The Development Corporation in Africa," 10 *American Journal of Comparative Law* 188 (1961).

[8] A legal system may need to impose some restriction on ownership or use of land to ensure that land control not become too far removed from considerations of the market place or public policy. Thus, most jurisdictions in the United States now prohibit attempts to tie up land ownership for excessive

necessarily restricts the alternatives available for investors and thus tends to retard investment.

A legal system also should spell out very clearly the *procedure* necessary for the enforcement of legally protected rights and interests. A person cannot be expected to make investment of effort or capital merely on the assurance that under the substantive provisions of applicable law his effort should be rewarded. He must also be certain of his ability to enforce, or cause to be enforced, those provisions. Thus, he must be able to know in advance the judicial or administrative procedures available to him and the approximate cost to him of such procedures. This requires that judicial and administrative procedures be clearly and centrally set forth, both for trial and appellate levels, and that a national court system is afforded access to the prescribed procedures.

The requirement of predictability imposes another burden especially applicable to the legal systems of developing countries: The law must not only be uniform and complete, it must also be *made available* both to those who will enforce it and to those who will be guided by it. This means, first, that the laws and rules comprising the system must be widely distributed, at the least to legal administrators. Laws designed to encourage rural development, for instance, will obviously have but a limited effect if they are known only to a few persons in large towns. If it is asking too much that such laws be known and understood in advance by ordinary citizens in the countryside, these citizens should at minimum be afforded relatively convenient and inexpensive access to persons who can explain them. This requires the training of a substantial number of legal administrators and advisers and the creation, at the minimum, of regional libraries containing the laws themselves and suitable supporting materials.

Moreover, both substantive and procedural laws in developing countries must be made as *unambiguous* as possible. Simplicity of concept and clarity of expression are much more significant in such countries than in areas with well-educated and commercially experienced populations. For example, the economic and social policies that lie behind national taxing legislation are arguably just as complex and difficult in developing nations as they are in the United States. Yet it would be self-defeating if the tax laws for such countries were as intricate and complex as they are in this country. Here, the exhaustive statutory provisions and official comment provide a high degree of certainty concerning the tax consequences of all sorts of income producing activity. In a developing country, comparable

---

time periods. Similarly, public control over land use is reflected by legislation concerning zoning and eminent domain. Judicious use of the latter device can be an important tool for development in developing countries. See H. Dunning, "Law and Economic Development in Africa: The Law of Eminent Domain," 68 *Columbia Law Review* 1286 (1968).

treatment would rather reduce legal certainty because there would be so few persons available to understand and apply the law, on behalf of either the taxing authorities or taxpayers.[9] Introduction of laws that are too complex results in uneven application of the laws and an inability on the part of all affected to understand them, that is, to make accurate predictions concerning their laws' effect.

Thus, a legal system should strive to provide laws that are *simple* and *precise,* while at the same time offering coverage that is sufficiently comprehensive to minimize ambiguity. In a society comprised of persons with a limited educational background, laws may generate uncertainty as well if they are too long and complex as when they are too short and insufficiently detailed. In most developing countries there are groups of persons with relatively sophisticated commercial knowledge and experience. Laws which relate particularly to such groups can profitably be made more intricate than laws of general application. For instance, laws respecting national commercial monopolies need not be drafted with simplicity just because most persons in the country would have difficulty understanding them—most persons are unlikely ever to be regulated by such laws.[10] To some degree, it may even be possible to separate all "commercial" laws from other laws and to draft the former with more particularity.[11]

FAIRNESS

Legal systems designed to foster economic growth in developing countries need to place heavy emphasis on the relative "fairness" of the law.[12] As much as possible, laws should apply equally to all, regardless of the public connections or private power of affected parties. Again as much as possible, both substantive and procedural laws

---

[9] Compare the Ethiopian *Income Tax Proclamation,* Proclamation No. 173 of 1961, the *Income Tax (Amendment) Proclamation, 1967,* Proclamation No. 255 of 1967, and the *Income Tax Regulations, 1962,* Legal Notice 258 of 1962, with their United States counterparts, the *Internal Revenue Code* and *Income Tax Regulations* of the Treasury Department.

[10] The basic anti-trust laws of the United States, as contained in the Sherman Act and the Clayton Act, are themselves very brief—but they have engendered volumes of judicial and other review and interpretation.

[11] In Ethiopia, a Commercial Code has been adopted to cover, on a European model, broad areas of commerce. (See the definition of "traders," Art. 5, *Commercial Code of Ethiopia* [1960]). The practical application of the Commercial Code, however, is intended to extend to many participants in commerce who are without commercial or educational experience; and the terms of the Code are not stated with much more particularity than the terms of other codes of avowedly general application, such as the Civil Code.

[12] The concept of "fairness" is the course susceptible of much more intensive analysis than is here possible, and the meaning of the term will vary to some degree depending on the attitudes and aspirations of the persons, or nations, concerned. See Robert B. Seidman, "Law and Economic Development in Independent, English-Speaking Sub-Saharan Africa," *Wisconsin Law Review* 999 (1966).

should carefully preserve at least minimum notions of "due process," that is, of open and unrestricted access to public courts and administrative bodies for the airing of legal grievances and for the enforcement of legal rights.

The chief economic reason for the importance of maintaining traditions of fairness is that, regardless of any direct impact on economic growth, such traditions are instrumental in creating a social and political climate that is ripe for personal initiative. Above all, economic development reflects the state of mind of a population. History has demonstrated that abundant resources and available capital do not alone guarantee economic growth.[13] Conversely, growth can take place without one or both. But broad-based growth cannot be obtained where significant proportions of a population do not want it or are not sufficiently motivated to risk personal involvement to participate in it. A legal system can have much influence on the collective state of mind of a population. If it permits arbitrary exercise of power without legal recourse or tolerates unequal application of legal standards, it tends to induce passivity or resentment, or both, among those without political power. Neither condition is healthy for a people seeking to encourage widespread and enthusiastic participation in commercial activity. A legal system can help set the tone of life for a country, and thus it can have a profound effect on the capacity of the country for rapid economic development.

In addition to the subtle influence on the mood of a whole people which a reasonably fair and equitable legal system can have, it can have another important effect. Such a system also increases considerably the predictability of the law with consequent beneficial effect, as noted above. This is because to the degree that application of a system takes legal account of political or social power, results under the system necessarily depend upon the relative power of the parties involved. However, the relative power which will thus be at issue is rarely predictable—it is not usually well known with any precision and is not usually very stable.

RAPID ADJUDICATION

All too many of the world's legal systems, including our own,[14] appear to have an unfortunate propensity for nearly interminable

---

[13] Of course, resource exploitation can be highly beneficial. For a review of the impact of natural resources on emerging African economies, see Andrew M. Kamarck, "The Economics of African Development" (New York: Frederick A. Praeger, 1967). It is important that the law define clearly permissible processes of resource exploitation. See R. Berman, "Natural Resources: State Ownership and Control Based on Article 130 of the Revised Constitution," 3 *Journal of Ethiopian Law* 551 (1966).

[14] There is a case backlog of more than a year in most major American metropolitan centers, and in some instances the parties may have to wait for five years or more for adjudication of their dispute. Moreover, the process

delay before official litigation of any dispute can be completed. This, of course, is an impediment to initiative wherever it occurs. But it is particularly a luxury that cannot be afforded in developing countries where initiative is such a precious commodity. Thus, a legal system in such a country should pay special heed to creating procedures that permit rapid adjudication of disputes. This requires that formalized procedural rules be kept to a minimum and that a sufficient number of courts be established to handle anticipated litigation without undue delay. It also suggests the possibility that administrative procedures be established to solve some problems without time consuming and expensive recourse to the courts, and where practicable, that private adjudication, such as through prearranged arbitration, be encouraged.[15] One caveat to the utility of relatively informal administrative procedures should be noted, however. Unless the rules limiting and defining administrative authority are very clearly set forth and enforced, and unless the parties affected by administrative decision are protected by procedural safeguards, there is a very real danger that too many administrative actions will become arbitrary and thus will violate the standards of fairness previously set forth. The realization of this danger is the cause of increasing public clamor for reform in this country; and potential abuse of administrative discretion in developing countries is far more serious.[16]

SIMILARITY TO SYSTEMS OF DEVELOPED COUNTRIES

There are several reasons why the legal system of a developing country should bear some resemblance to the system of a developed country. One is that this will help to encourage foreign investment and aid in the former country.[17] In some instances, investment seems to be induced merely by the stirring of nationalistic feelings of paternalism and common identity directed toward countries with similar legal systems. More importantly, public and private investors from developed countries demand the same legal certainty and predictability that local investors do. That certainty may not be appre-

---

of appeal and retrial can consume additional years. Such delays in commercial litigation could prove fatal to a fragile entrepreneurial spirit in developing countries.

[15] Title XX, *Civil Code of Ethiopia* (1960), defining procedures for private compromise and arbitral submission.

[16] For a statement that the limits of authority of administrative bodies must be clearly set forth, lest all the substantive certainty and procedural due process sought after in a legal system be circumvented by decisions of autonomous administrative boards and agencies, see R. Means, "The Constitutional Right to Judicial Review of Administrative Proceedings: Threshold Questions," 3 *Journal of Ethiopian Law* 175 (1966).

[17] There are naturally more direct ways to attract foreign investment, including the offering of tax and other concessions on a broad scale. For an example of such legislation in Ethiopia, see the *Investment Decree of 1963*, Decree No. 51 of 1963.

ciated by the foreigners unless it is reflected in laws that include concepts and terminology that are relatively familiar. Experience has
shown that foreigners will rely on laws patterned after those of other
major commercial nations, but they are sometimes reluctant to rely
on laws based on unknown local concepts and traditions.[18]

Another advantage of a legal system which has similarity to
the system of a developed nation is that application of the law will
be rendered less ambiguous. In the first place, a law drawn from a
developed country is typically a law which has already gone through
several stages of refinement. Therefore, the very drafting of the law
is likely to be more careful than the independent drafting of a new
provision. Secondly, the meaning of laws and legal terms in developed countries has usually been the subject of litigation and study
for a long period of time. Out of this process a vast collection of
interpretive materials and explanation has developed. For instance, the word "possession," as used in various legal contexts, has
received long and careful judicial and scholarly attention in this
country, and its meaning has been exhaustively charted. If this same
word is used in the context of a law of another country and that
has as its source an American law, for example, the great body of
American experience with the word can be of considerable assistance
in interpreting the word as used in the other country's law. There
will be many reasons favoring a different interpretation, to be sure;
but the word will still have much more depth of meaning than it
would, or a comparable word would, if there were no connection with
an established legal tradition. Until a developing country has produced its own collection of supplementary materials and comments
and nurtured its own legal tradition, reference to the traditions of
other countries can provide a convenient and workable means of
adding body to the skeleton of a newly adopted legal system.[19]

SIMILARITY TO LOCAL TRADITIONS

It is axiomatic that no legal system can remain effective and
depart totally from the habits and traditions of the populace it
serves.[20] That the legal system of a developing country should strive
as much as possible to incorporate the legal and social customs of
the country's people follows. Unless this is done, the people may re-
sent or mistrust the law. Equally important, they will not be able to

---

[18] This is in part because lawyers of the major commercial nations have developed considerable knowledge of the laws of the other commercial nations,
and in part because there is usually much similarity in the basic commercial
laws of these countries in any case.

[19] George Krzeczunowicz, "Statutory Interpretation in Ethiopia," 1 *Journal of
Ethiopian Law* 315 (1964).

[20] Robert B. Seidman, "Law and Economic Development," *supra Wisconsin Law
Review* 1024 (1966).

understand much of the law. Indeed, even trained scholars will have only a limited opportunity to understand the law since it will have been separated from the local traditions which would give full meaning to its terms. Foreign jurisprudence might be available as a reference, but, by itself, this could never suffice fully to implement a legal system.

The requirement for the incorporation of local traditions into national legal systems poses a great dilemma for developing countries. Precisely these traditions often seem to retard development. Thus, some of these traditions must be deliberately ignored in a legal system designed to foster growth. The difficult question is which customs and traditions to discard. This is a question which cannot be answered in the abstract. The solution depends on the nature of the local tradition, on the damage it may cause to development, as opposed to the damage to development which may ensue if the public is forced to adopt a wholly new concept. One solution may be to introduce the new concept but limit its application to only a few commercially oriented persons with the hope that the concept will become more familiar and acceptable with the passage of time.[21] This is a choice, however, that may not be available with respect to matters of general application, such as ownership of personal property or common commercial activities, and in such cases, local traditions may be changed completely and abruptly, with resultant disruption of legal traditions and understanding.[22]

DIFFICULTIES FACED IN ESTABLISHING AN EFFECTIVE LEGAL SYSTEM

It is, of course, not enough to identify some of the basic elements of a legal system designed to help spur commercial growth. A much more difficult problem confronting developing countries is how to create such a system in the foreseeable future given the extreme and

---

[21] Preface to the *Commercial Code of Ethiopia* (1960).

[22] Much of Ethiopia's Commercial Code does completely ignore local customs and traditions, even though the laws involved will be applicable generally to all merchants. For this reason, the courts are faced with innumerable instances where the formalities required by the Code are not followed, for instance, with respect to books of account supposed to be kept by all traders. (See Art. 63, *Commercial Code of Ethiopia* [1960]). Even the Civil Code of Ethiopia preserves formalities practicable only in a developed country, such as the requirement of Art. 881, that a certain kind of will be made in writing and signed before four witnesses. In a case involving a will in proper form (a rare enough occurrence) but with two few witnesses, the Ethiopian courts showed a willingness to reach what they felt to be the only result consistent with all the policies applicable by construing the word "four" to mean "three." *Chake Avakian v. Artin Avakian*, reported in 1 *Journal of Ethiopian Law* 36 (1964). Where a legal system includes laws that are too far removed from local customs, such problems are inevitable and similar resulting ambiguity ensured.

unfavorable conditions of the present. All developing countries face a common problem in this regard: the very nature of their present conditions makes extremely difficult the implementation of even a moderately complex, comprehensive legal system. In addition, most developing nations face further grave problems imposed by tribal, religious, and political conditions. An understanding of the nature and magnitude of at least the more significant of these problems is an essential prerequisite to any reasoned attempt to mold an appropriate legal system for the country involved.

DIFFICULTIES ARISING OUT OF UNDERDEVELOPED CONDITIONS

Economic development itself, or the lack of it, produces and in turn is caused by the collective state of mind of the populace involved. In a typical instance, the conditions comprising underdevelopment serve also as a major impediment to the implementation of an effective legal system.

In the first place one of the characteristics common to developing countries, particularly those in Africa, is a general lack of formal education on the part of the great majority of the population. This educational deficiency has several important consequences. The most noticeable is that many of those who are affected by the applicable legal system cannot read or write. This means, of course, that much of the beneficial effect of reducing the legal system to writing is frustrated. If one of the essential elements of an effective system is that it enables all, or nearly all, to predict the legal consequences of their acts, the capacity of the system to accomplish its purpose by fairly detailed and elaborate writings is undermined unless all the population has reasonable access to those writings. This does not necessarily require that all people be literate; but it does mean that persons who can explain and interpret the law should be available for consultation. In many developing countries there are not enough literate people to fulfill this minimum requirement, especially in rural areas where formal education is often practically nonexistent.

The problem is intensified because the level of education required for an understanding of legal regulations is much higher than that required for mere literacy. By consensus in most developed countries, nearly twenty years of formal education, including several specifically devoted to either academic or apprentice legal study, is required to train competent lawyers. The cost of this training is such that few developing countries can afford it on anything more than a modest scale. The result of this is that in such countries few lawyers are available for service of any kind, fewer available for service as private practitioners, and practically none available for service outside larger cities.[23] Thus, there is no possible way for a person of ordinary means to ascertain the meaning of the law in rural portions of many countries. In these places, predictable operation of a legal system remains an unattainable goal for the present. No one is available to give competent advice on the law, no judge or administrator present to give consistent direction under the law, and in many instances, no copy of the law at hand for study.

The shortage of lawyers has ramifications that extend beyond the accessibility of the law to ordinary citizens. It also means that, for the present at least, there is little opportunity for legal study and review at any level, so that the present body of legal analysis and legal traditions cannot be significantly increased or changed. Lasting impact on a system of law largely dependent on judicial consideration of problems and cases relies in the first instance on a large number of written case reports widely distributed. This cannot be accomplished, of course, if there are few judges who submit written opinions based upon application of the written national law. Lasting impact on a system of law more dependent on legislative and scholarly analysis also relies on written studies concerning the law, and is likewise frustrated by the absence of trained lawyers and scholars. Thus, an important requirement necessary for the development of certainty and predictability of the law cannot satisfactorily be provided: complete and detailed review and commentary of all the written law cannot be achieved, and a full depth of understanding cannot be acquired, except in isolated areas of the law.

Another element common to most developing countries that restricts their ability to establish a legal system which will foster economic growth is the fact that their own legal traditions are sometimes ill-adapted for this purpose. Legal institutions can and do change, but the rate of change is slow, and thus, the magnitude of change required may defeat desires for rapid implementation of effective modern legal systems.

Traditional legal systems in developing countries tended to provide but a slight measure of commercial predictability. Many of the laws were unwritten, significant areas of modern commerce and trade were not covered at all by formal laws, and the laws were too often administered on a less than systematic basis by local leaders and

[23] In 1963, there were about twenty Ethiopian lawyers with an LL.B. degree available for service in any capacity in Ethiopia. This was approximately one academically trained lawyer for every million people, an obviously unworkable ratio. There are, of course, many more persons involved in the practice of law, directly and indirectly, but the shortage of well trained attorneys continues to be acute and to reduce greatly the beneficial impact of the country's modern codes. Nor is the shortage of trained lawyers a problem unique to Ethiopia. See Sir Sidney Littlewood, "The Legal Profession in African Territories" in *Changing Law in Developing Countries,* ed. J. N. D. Anderson (London: George Allen and Unwin, 1963), p. 154.

politicians. In many important areas of law, precision of interpretation was impossible even in one locality, and substantive laws could be completely different in neighboring areas.[24] In most of Africa, for instance, laws respecting land tenure were the result of rather vaguely defined tribal traditions and laws respecting the operation of commercial organizations were practically nonexistent.[25] The establishment of effective and uniform laws in these areas therefore requires an almost complete break with tradition, demanding a legal and cultural reorientation that just cannot be accomplished in a short period of time.

Perhaps even more significant than the state of traditional substantive law in many African countries is the procedural traditions that have been a part of the legal process in the past. The concept of universal submission to an ordered national legal system administered by an objective and impartial judiciary is central to the understanding of most developed societies, but this is a goal which has sometimes proved difficult for newly developing societies to attain. This has tended to undermine confidence in the law, thus discouraging investment of capital or effort where recourse to the courts might be necessary for the realization of rewards therefrom. It also tended to induce those regulated by commercial laws to achieve desired judicial or administrative approval by means addressed more to political power than social policy. Where legal consequences are in the largely unrestricted control of judges and administrators, the temptation to attain a favorable ruling by means of influence is correspondingly forceful. Where a legal system has fostered such an approach, and political or social traditions have encouraged it for a prolonged period, it is almost inevitable that effective and even-handed administration of the law will be considerably frustrated by arbitrary rulings and corruption. Many developing nations have been obliged to mount great efforts to reduce the debilitating impact of capriciousness and graft at all levels of legal administration.[26]

OTHER DIFFICULTIES TYPICALLY FACING DEVELOPING COUNTRIES

There are, of course, great differences among conditions which deter the establishment of a sound, commercially oriented legal sys-

---

[24] Antony Allott, *Essays in African Law* II and III (London: Butterworths, 1960).

[25] Note 5, *supra*, respecting Ethiopian systems of land tenure. In colonial territories, a further problem arose because of the existence of two separate systems of land tenure at the same time, one local and the other colonial. See Ann P. Munro, "Land Law in Kenya," *Wisconsin Law Review* 1071 (1966).

[26] In Ethiopia, the effort to formalize procedural rules and objectivity has led to the enactment of codes of civil procedure and criminal procedure as well as the organization of a nationwide federal court system with prescribed channels of appeal. Some of the benefits of these measures are precluded, however, by the lack of trained lawyers to serve as judges.

tem in developing nations. However, some of these conditions are sufficiently prevalent to warrant brief mention at this point.

One condition often noted is the existence of several tribal or regional groups within a single country. This fact adds immeasurably to the difficulty of creating a national legal system. In the first place, the groups often mistrust one another, so that full cooperation on any matter is rendered unlikely. In addition, group differences interpose several other obstacles to the establishment of a nationwide legal system. The first of these is the introduction of a very serious language problem. Too often, major portions of a country will not speak the official language or languages. Where the inability of people to be able to comprehend written law is already a problem because of a general lack of education, the added impact of such a language barrier is dramatic.[27] In addition, the existence of tribal or group differences means that cultural traditions and legal traditions may vary greatly within a country.[28] Consequently, the establishment of a legal system is made much more complicated and difficult, requiring more time and effort for its accomplishment.

Political (and sometimes religious) conditions in many countries also tend to impede the establishment of a desirable legal system.[29] In the first place, present day political conditions may merely reflect past relationships of power, with the result that the law may more often be a tool of the ruling forces than the servant of economic and social development. Moreover, political conditions are often rather unstable. This makes all the more difficult the task of guiding and planning for the development of a modern legal system when the dominant political policies of the future are unpredictable. Because of this, effective legal planning can proceed on only a temporary basis, with long-range goals for a legal system inadequately studied or reviewed.

----

[27] In Ethiopia, the official language is Amharic, spoken by perhaps one-fifth of the population. The new codes for the country originally were drafted in the language of their foreign draftsmen (usually French) and then translated into Amharic. Separate translations from the original were then made into English. Current languages of instruction in Ethiopian schools are Amharic and English, although only a small minority of students advance far enough to become truly proficient at the latter.

[28] For a description of the sources of traditional law in Ethiopia, the single African nation with a long national tradition, see Jacques Vanderlinden, "An Introduction to the Sources of Ethiopian Law from the 13th to the 20th Century," 3 *Journal of Ethiopian Law* 227 (1966).

[29] In Ethiopia, Christianity is the dominant religion, and has been for more than a millenium, but there are nearly equal numbers both of Muslims and adherents of local religions living in the country. In some instances, religious customs are given legal recognition. See, for instance, Art. 579 of the Civil Code respecting "religious marriages." The importance of retained recognition of religious traditions is not free from controversy. See George Krzeczunowicz, "Putting the Legal Clock Back?" 3 *Journal of Ethiopian Law* 621 (1966). For a discussion of Muslim Law elsewhere in Africa, see W. D. Anderson, "Islamic Law in Africa," in *Changing Law in Developing Countries, supra.*

EFFORTS TOWARD SOLUTION OF THE PROBLEMS

Many developing nations are well aware of the magnitude of problems facing them in their quest for legal systems that will assist in the struggle for economic development. They recognize that some traditional laws and customs are not well designed to foster this development. Many have shown a surprising willingness to alter and even completely discard the old legal systems, as well as make significant allocations of resources to provide for the necessary training and scholarly study to prepare for the directed evolution of effective new systems.

The first step typically taken has been to call for the introduction of totally new laws in practically every area, and particularly in commercial law.[30] Because of the pressing demands for instant creation of modern systems, most of the new laws had to come from the legislatures, not from the courts. If courts were to be relied upon, great numbers of judges would first have to be trained and instilled with respect for the broad social and economic policies thought best to foster development. Then many years of case decisions would be required before the body of law began to take recognizable shape, that is, before the law became certain and predictable. Developing countries could not afford the luxury of waiting for a measured legal development derived from decisions of their own courts—they could not wait for the full growth of indigenous legal traditions in the leisurely fashion that western common law countries could.

Nor were the developing countries prepared to wait for the rather slow and cautious development that typified the growth of legal traditions in most western civil law countries prior to codification. This process too took centuries of careful and piecemeal development; and it had to be followed by many years of exhaustive analysis and review after codification before a full legal system really could come into fruition.

Many developing countries have demanded a much swifter creation of entire legal systems suited to commercial development. This has necessitated massive and far-reaching action by those in power and resulted in heavy importation of legal doctrines, traditions and whole systems from more developed countries, whether in the form of codes and commentaries from civil law countries or statutes and court-made legal rules from common law countries, or sometimes from a mixture of both. Under such programs for rapid legal development, a government could proclaim the broad policies designed to encourage development and simultaneously translate these policies into specific substantive and procedural statutory enactments with immediate legal effect. This, of course, meant that the policy bases

---

[30] The Civil Code and Commercial Code of Ethiopia both were adopted by Proclamation (165 and 166, respectively) in 1960.

of the law would be codified into law without extended study and would be at least partially immunized from continuing review and revision. This was a clear cost of wholesale importation of foreign legal traditions; but it was a cost far outweighed by the benefits of immediate adoption of modern legal systems.

The new codes and statutes served admirably to accomplish some of the needs of the developing countries for modern legal systems. In the first place, the laws now were in written form. Moreover, they were at least nominally uniform throughout every part of a country. More importantly, they embodied the basic institutions that have served the developed countries: procedurally, a new degree of fairness, of due process of law as administered by a national court system, was incorporated into the law; substantively, whole areas of rules and laws designed to facilitate commerce and trade and to encourage initiative were created. New forms of commercial organization were allowed and the legal consequences of commercial activity were described in detail unknown before. Almost overnight, a new potential for legal predictability and fairness was created.

However, the complete, modern legal systems which were sought did not materialize solely out of the new laws; they could not, for the laws could not by themselves solve all the conditions described above, slowing legal development. The new laws were nearly complete on paper; but that is where they remained for most people. In order to provide the means of access to the new legal framework for a broad segment of populations, and in order for the careful analysis and review necessary to fill out that new framework, large numbers of thoroughly trained lawyers were required. Accordingly, many developing nations undertook to provide increased training for their future lawyers. In many cases, the future lawyers were sent abroad to study in the developed countries; and, several law schools and law study centers were established or expanded. These schools were usually staffed initially with lawyers and teachers drawn from abroad, with the expectation that these would be replaced as qualified local legal scholars became available.[31] Also, efforts were made to establish new processes or augment current ones for distributing in writing important case decisions made by the courts; and scholarly legal articles and code commentaries were encouraged.[32] The purpose of this was to provide at least the beginnings of the full body of supporting materials and reported judicial experience necessary to round out the legal framework borrowed from the developed countries.

---

[31] James C. N. Paul, "Third Annual Report from the Dean," 3 *Journal of Ethiopian Law* 591 (1966).

[32] Several new law journals concerning African countries appeared; one was the *Journal of Ethiopian Law*, combining commentaries on the law with a selected reporting of case decisions, the first system of case reporting ever made publicly available in Ethiopia.

LEGAL DEVELOPMENT IN THE FUTURE

The attempts by some developing countries to create legal systems conducive to economic development have gotten off to a good start. With the enactment of comprehensive substantive and procedural laws and the establishment of institutions designed to train lawyers and to contribute to ever-broadening legal studies, the tools for the development of full, modern legal systems have been created. This is not to suggest, however, that the job is over, or even that the development of suitable legal systems is near at hand. On the contrary, what has been accomplished thus far amounts chiefly to identification of the methods of solution to the problems impeding such development and the creation of the framework of a legal system (borrowed mostly from abroad) to fill the near vacuum that existed before. Comprehensive laws have been enacted; but the development of the legal traditions necessary for rational implementation of those laws has just begun. The real work lies ahead.

The task which now must be confronted especially by African countries, consists of two main efforts. One is to maintain and increase the difficult, expensive and slow process of training lawyers, judges, administrators, and legislators to interpret and operate the legal system. The other is to provide continuing review of the present laws and increased study of the economic and other policies which will determine the future direction of these laws. Neither of these efforts can possibly be successfully accomplished except over a long period of time. In both cases, the problems are much the same as those which the developing countries must deal with in other areas of economic development. The program for development must start from a low base, and for success, demands continued and concentrated efforts by fairly large numbers of highly qualified, expertly trained persons.

The training required to produce large numbers of lawyers and legal administrators is a time-consuming process in any society. In many developing nations, it becomes especially difficult to provide because of the intense competition for meager educational resources with other programs equally concerned with economic development and equally important to the national interest. The training required to produce not only lawyers but fully qualified policy makers and advisers, who are at home with both the law and economic policies and who can thus change the law and reform it as well as interpret or administer it, is even more difficult to provide—but nothing less than this can possibly suffice.[33]

Many years of dedicated effort will be required to make even the

---

[33] The same need for interdisciplinary training is receiving increasing recognition in developed countries, of course. For a description of the need in Africa, see Antony Allott, "Legal Development and Economic Growth in Africa," in *Changing Law in Developing Countries, supra.*

present systems of law truly effective throughout entire countries. The process of altering the present legal systems to meet identified national economic, political and social policies will take much longer. This will require the seasoned wisdom and effort of large numbers of law trained persons. Thus, years, perhaps generations, will be needed before many developing nations can achieve full growth of legal systems rationally structured to induce economic expansion. This, of course, is not to conclude that progress toward establishment of mature legal systems cannot be made in the immediate future. As existing lawyers and legal administrators deal with the law, it should steadily become more fully shaped, and this process should accelerate as and when more trained persons are worked into the system. But this has to be a lengthy process, and there is no way it can effectively be shortened. Until considerable numbers of trained legal personnel are made available to explain and apply a legal system to all concerned; and until all concerned are at least somewhat familiar with the basic policies of the law, the legal systems of many developing countries will remain less than perfect as vehicles for economic development.

CONCLUSION

In summary, legal systems do have a role to play in attempts to foster economic development. In order for the contribution of a legal system to be maximized, the system must enable persons involved in economic activity to predict the consequences of that activity. It must also create an economic and social climate of fairness, of equitable dealing among all persons to motivate as many as possible to enter into the commercial arena.

Measured by these standards, the legal traditions of many developing countries have not been well adapted to promote economic development. This, coupled with a lack of commercial understanding and general education, have combined to render establishment of workable legal systems very difficult. Attempts to overcome these difficulties have been made, particularly by the adoption of complete, written legal codes borrowed largely from developed societies.

The task now before many developing societies is to define the broad terms of the borrowed codes in detail and to modify the codes to meet local policies as well as reflect in some measure local traditions. This is a process that will require great effort by highly trained personnel, a process that cannot be well completed except over a long period of time. A legal system can serve as inducement to economic (and political and social) development. But to an unavoidable extent, the capacity for creation of such a system fully equipped to foster development is itself limited by some of the same factors that cause the present conditions of underdevelopment. A legal system designed ideally to induce economic growth can neither be drafted nor made operative until a fair measure of economic development and the educational and other capacities derived therefrom have already been attained.

DISCUSSION by MARSHALL HARRIS

THE TOPIC ASSIGNED Church was too large for the plausible alternatives: (1) a comparative analysis of the relationship of legal systems to economic development, or (2) the development of a philosophical-theoretical framework for guiding developing countries in formulating legal systems to encourage economic development. He chose to aim between the two targets, perhaps missing both, but nevertheless supplying much insight needed by those actively engaged in the formulation of more effective national laws in developing countries.

Probably the two greatest characteristics in United States procedural law are: (1) the division of responsibility at the national, state, and local levels, and (2) the checks and balances provided for in the triumvirate of legislative, executive, and judicial. Church's emphasis is on national law, with little emphasis on law promulgated at state or local levels. Some ideas on the distinctive roles of the three branches of government are explained, but the compelling notion of checks and balances barely emerges.

Perhaps the greatest single idea of United States law at its inception was equality. The simplicity and power of the idea has made it last to this day, and the struggle still exists to attain a satisfying degree of equality. In recent years, security has emerged as a complementary idea to equality. The more recent emphasis on civil rights is another crucial element in our desire to furnish maximum opportunity for economic development. The relation of such elements to economic development might well have been explained. Although expressing qualities of the law in general, these three ideas seem to furnish necessary guidelines. If they were supplemented by some additional procedurally related characteristics, they would strengthen the already enunciated principles. Procedural examples are: (1) the right to have legal counsel, (2) the protection against self-incrimination, and (3) the right of trial before one's peers.

Church's second and third elements are fairness and prompt

adjudication. The due process element is met where courts are accessible, but he recognized this is no guarantee of fairness. There seems to be an implicit faith, however, that justice will be done if there are lawyers and a court. The emphasis on administrative procedure in making the law effective is fraught with many dangers, as was recognized; arbitration was also mentioned. Few insights were revealed, however, as to the roles of administrative procedure and arbitration. The important role of the citizen could have been emphasized.

The last two elements of a legal system pose an unanswered, and probably an unanswerable, question: How much to borrow from the laws of developed countries and how little to depend upon local custom and tradition? The author has fallen into the trap that has plagued many social scientists (including lawyers) who have endeavored to be of service to developing countries. They have tried to impose our way of doing things upon unsuspecting populations, rather than building upon native custom and intelligence. There appears to be much faith in the belief that what is good for our economy will be good for developing countries. In Ethiopia, for example, those who drafted the decreed law depended heavily on civil law, with only belated borrowings from common law and local custom. What will be the court's process of Ethiopianizing the civil-common law hybrid, particularly at the local level?

The proposed process of improving the law seems to be too much revolutionary and too little evolutionary—there was not time for evolutionary processes to work out. This judgment is unquestioned, if the alternative is to let things evolve as they will. An alternative, however, is to aid and abet the evolutionary process by every appropriate means. My suggestion is to start with the country's legal system, however crude and rudimentary it may be.

This hypothesis is proposed: The fewer the lawyers, the less developed the courts, and the less literate the people, the more essential it is to build upon the existing legal system. The endeavor to give the developing country a modern, complex legal system and let uneducated people learn over the years how to operate it would seem to be self-defeating. Rather, it would seem better to build, step by step, from simplicity to complexity and from where people are to where they would like to be.

The next major section of the chapter is concerned with difficulties in establishing an effective legal system. Most of the difficulties are familiar, and many of them arise out of the endeavor to impose overnight a foreign system on a native population. There is every reason why a developing nation should be "suspicious of foreign laws" and should hold on to its tribal and religious customs and laws. We are too inclined to think that every developing nation should aspire to be like us. The Christian religion, free enterprise, rugged individualism, sole proprietorship, and corporate enterprise are a few elements that we are trying too hard to export to most developing countries in which we are rendering substantial assistance. "Doing our thing" may needlessly become a heavy burden on many developing countries. These cautions arise out of a conviction that I would not make the world over in our image even if I could—there is much room for great diversity.

Most of the difficulties indicate the wisdom of starting where people are and evolving a structure as they develop. What is the use of a finely drawn, complex legal system when there are few literate people? Admittedly, there are too few lawyers, judges, and administrators in many developing countries to give consistent legal direction to complex legal systems. Would it not be better to begin with tribal custom in developing a few commercial rules and regulations to encourage intertribal commerce? Can a highly developed legal system be sustained in the almost total absence of a correspondingly highly developed judicial system? How can a country overcome the formidable difficulties of distrust among tribal groups, of the lack of a common language, of religious beliefs not conducive to development of either a formal legal system or modern economic activities, and of a very unstable political situation? All of these conditions, so common to most developing countries, speak a mute testimony against an endeavor to leap with one stroke of the pen from tribal custom to a legal system of a modern industrialized, urbanized nation.

The section on efforts toward solution shows a lack of faith in the ways we developed our commercial law. Most laws designed to encourage economic development were the outgrowth of years of successful indigenous experience. Those designed to prevent the doing of certain things likewise were based on years of experience. The "trade" was prepared to help police and enforce the law when it became statutory; complete dependence on "the strong arm of the law" was seldom evident. It is not clear that "piecemeal formation of law by the courts," particularly with assistance of the legislative and executive branches of government, would be at a cost greater than that of the "wholesale importation of foreign legal traditions."

The proof by assertion that developing "countries could not wait" and that they demanded a swift creation of an entire legal system may be persuasive, but we should be quick to point out the fallacies of the position, unless we are convinced that the quick and easy way would prove to be efficacious. The "high expectations" perhaps should be mellowed by a modicum of realism. The sending abroad of students and the development of law schools locally seem essential, but this should have been done before the laws were put on the books. The law that is to be interpreted by native personnel should have been formulated in large part by native scholars. The process was reversed. The author recognized, however, that "the real work lies ahead." Perhaps the statesmen of tomorrow will be able to redo, reinterpret, and redirect the imported legal system until it meets the needs of the developing nation.

A concluding plea for highly trained personnel at every decision-making juncture seems appropriate. The utter necessity for patience over the long pull, while the "borrowed codes" are being interpreted and modified, likewise seems appropriate. So does the concluding sentence, "A legal system designed ideally to induce economic growth can neither be drafted nor made operative until a fair measure of economic development and the educational and other capacities derived therefrom have already been attained." These qualifying comments seem more perceptive than the bold assertion that the "legal systems conducive to economic development have gotten off to a good start."

DISCUSSION by H. W. HANNAH

PERHAPS the most striking things about this chapter are the idealistic description of a legal system appearing in the first part of the chapter, and the interesting, down to earth and cogent observations about legal systems in developing countries drawn largely from the author's Ethiopian experience appearing in the last part of the chapter. One feels that if he had chosen to deal in greater depth with the Ethiopian system and its history, his comments would have been even more useful. Certainly, any system of jurisprudence should be predictable, fair and swift, but in discussing the elements of predictability and fairness and particularly of swiftness, the author sets goals for developing countries that have not yet been reached in the developed countries.

The author feels that sophisticated, highly technical and hard to understand jargon should be kept out of laws in developing countries —the reason being that only a relatively small percent of the people being literate, only a small percent would ever understand the law. This prompts several thoughts—among them, that the literate American can also be confused by such laws and that the main reason more literate Americans are not confused is because they have not read the laws. There is some naivete in an expectation that large numbers of people will become familiar with the law, even if it is couched in the simplest of terms—and even if simple legal educational materials are disseminated in large quantities.

In assessing the impact of a legal system on economic development, the author has laid great stress on commercial law. He points out that to promote commerce and the flow of goods, particularly in volume, and more particularly between the developing country and other countries, there must be a firm, understandable, and at least somewhat currently accepted set of commercial laws. One would not quarrel with this, but finding a model is not easy. The fifty American jurisdictions have only within recent years got around to adopting uniform laws such as the Uniform Commercial Code. But that is only a beginning. Not only are there jurisdictions which still have not subscribed to all of the uniform laws which have been propounded over the last several decades, but once they are adopted the courts in a particular state make their own interpretations of the uniform law, so that over time, there may in fact be a great divergence from one jurisdiction to another.

Laws which clearly fall within the domain of a local jurisdiction (an American state, for example) seem to have an increasing impact outside the jurisdiction—professional licensing laws are a splendid example. A hundred years ago the separate licensing laws for medical doctors, veterinarians and dentists in California, Illinois, and New Jersey did not matter so much, if indeed they had laws on all these subjects at that time. But today, with the fluidity of movement in the professions as well as in nonprofessional callings, and in view of the relatively uniform standards which states have adopted for gaining admission to a profession, it seems rather ludicrous that one who is qualified to practice in one state cannot practice in another—unless he takes the examination given by that state or qualifies through the rather dubious and highly nonuniform reciprocity route. Hence, local laws in a developing country are likely to have a greater impact than the author ascribes to them.

Perhaps as the author suggests, two levels of jurisprudence are possible—one rather sophisticated and dealing with the commercial elements of the country—the other dealing with property, criminal laws and the everyday life of the people. This notion, however, makes me uneasy. It gives rise to the fear that this would preserve or perhaps even create a stratification which other elements of the development program are attempting to break down. Nigeria, for example, accumulated millions of pounds in the hands of government created marketing boards, but instead of these pounds being distributed back to producers, as one would suppose, they were regarded as uncommitted resources for doing whatever the decision-making machinery at the upper levels of government decided. Certainly, there was some sophistication in creating the marketing boards to insure a full price to producers, but the law did not carry all the way through, so that in the end the cocoa, palm oil, and ground nut producer could feel some tangible results.

Perhaps unavoidably, certain objectives of the writer seem in conflict. While on the one hand, he makes a plea for simple, clearly stated, written laws, both substantive and procedural, he on the other hand feels that the laws should provide for a wide range of business organizations and for a wide variety of legal interests in land.

No one would argue with reducing the rules of procedure to a written form which would insure due process, but the detailed spelling out of such rules, as suggested by the author, makes one fear that in a country lacking in legal talent there might grow an inflexibility which could deny substantial justice. The history of our English Common Law teaches us that this can happen.

The author feels the importance of retaining some local legal traditions, but recognizes that here, as well as in other facets of the people's lives, lies a dilemma. Who really has any good answers to the question: What customs and traditions in village life should be preserved while progress and development are being attained? Can anyone decide such a question? Is disruption to be avoided at all costs—even at the cost of the hope for progress itself? People in the villages in developing countries, like the people in our own country of two centuries ago, have an implicit faith in education and insist that their young have an opportunity to learn, but when their young do learn and become restive in the village and move to the cities where all kinds of social problems are created but not solved, they are saddened. Perhaps in a sense it is the same with the legal system. If the Panchayat in an Indian village settles most legal problems in an informal way and this supplies a quick and ready justice which the people accept, what will be the gain in formalizing such local procedures? Even if the day comes when there are a sufficient number of trained legal personnel to carry out a more formalized and sophisticated program, what assurance is there that it will result in a better dispensation of justice? On this point, the developed countries seem to have no advantage over the developing countries, as the writer points out. Crowded dockets, delays, costs, and an apparent inability to make justice move any faster causes many people to compromise their rights, to stay out of court—in short, to not get justice. The writer very wisely advocates wide use of arbitration and of administrative procedures. He points, however, to our own experience with administrative procedures, namely that unless formalized to the point where due process is reasonably assured, such forms can be poor dispensers of justice.

The author's discussion of difficulties in establishing an effective legal system is very much to the point, but on analysis, the roadblocks he names are the same as those which stand in the way of agricultural, industrial, educational, and social progress; namely illiteracy, tribal differences, language differences, religious differences, political conditions, the resentment of outside models, particularly if they come from a former colonial power, and sheer lack of resources to do many things which would be necessary to provide a more comprehensive legal system.

The author points to hopeful signs when he discusses the efforts that have been made toward solution. There is an awareness of the need and of the problems created by lack of a more uniform and reliable system; there are efforts to provide more legal education; and there has been a development of considerable importance in commercial law, particularly at that level necessary to foster international trade and the attraction of foreign capital. Apparently, the author feels that the seed has been sown, that a favorable climate exists and that a slow but sure process of growth is taking place in the legal systems in developing countries. He points out that all segments of the life of the people are interdependent and that the achievement of a mature and satisfactory legal system will be possible only after economic and social development in the country will support such.

INDEX

Abbott, John, 67
Adelman, Irma, 4
Adler, John H., quoted, 3–4
Africa, 47, 54, 147, 167, 228, 230: legal institutions in, fn. 219, 234; research institutions in, 140. *See also* West Africa
Agency for International Development, fn. 182
Agricultural credit institutions, 168–88: alternatives to, 185; and capital formation, 169–70; demand for, 175–80; and influencing institutions, 173–75; lender services, 180–82; objectives of, 170–71; role and significance of, 171–73, 183–84; and supply of agricultural credit, 180; and training of personnel, 182–83, 185
Agricultural development, 50, 107: and agricultural credit institutions, 170–73 *passim*, 186–87; complexity of, 58; conditions which stimulate, 42–43; and factor markets, 43–45, 57–58, 62; relation of research to, 45; role of agricultural institutions in, 3–13 *passim*
Agricultural Development Council, 186
Agricultural economics, 129–32, 137, 148
Agricultural experimental stations, 24
Agricultural institutions, and concept of layered constraints, 11–12; definition of, 9–13; role of in agricultural development, 3–13 *passim*. *See also* agricultural credit institutions, agricultural planning institutions, extension institutions, factor markets, land tenure institutions, legal institutions, product markets, research institutions, rural governing institutions, and teaching institutions.
Agricultural planning institutions, 91–105: aims of, 93–94; central planning agency of, 96; definition of, 91–92, 97–99; factors which reduce effectiveness of, 103–5; place of in agriculture, 94–96; problems of, 92–93; process of, 100–102, 105; programming units of, 96; reform methods for, 98, 99–100; and role of government in, 94–97, 103
Agricultural production, 5, 16, 17, 21, 32, 44
Agricultural Sciences in Latin America and Asia, 133

Agricultural scientists, 114–21 *passim*, 135, 140
Agricultural universities and colleges, 11, 24. *See also* land-grant system and teaching institutions
Agriculture, *passim*, 8, 19–24, 54–57, 63
AID-MIT Seminar, 42–43
Alliance for Progress, 121
American Agricultural Economic Association, 9
American Farm Economic Association Committee on New Orientations in Research, 131
American International Association, 158
Argentina, 64
Asia, 35, 47, 137, 138, 145, 147, 188
Asian Drama (book), 9
Assoçiaca de Credito e Assistencia Rural (ACAR), 158
Atkinson, J. H., quoted, 123
Ayub Khan, 197

Balance of payments, 21
Basic Democracies Order (East Pakistan), 197, 198
Belshaw, Cyril S., quoted, 65
Belshaw, Horace, quoted, 168
Beltsville, Maryland, Research Center, 146
Biafra, fn. 46
Bolivia, 36
Bombay Tenancy Act of 1948, 34
Boulding, Kenneth E., 65
Brazil, 46, 54, 148: agricultural planning institutions of, 103–5; extension institutions in, 157–59 *passim;* land tenure systems in, 35–40; teaching institutions in, 122–23
Breimyer, Harold F., 80, 83, 88, 90
Buritica, Carlos, fn. 160

Caja Agraria, Colombia, 49, 54
Campinas, Brazil, 46
Canada, 145
Capital rationing, 55–56
Chambers, Robert, 215, 216
Chapingo, Mexico, 146
Chen, Hsing-Yiu, 180
Chile, 17, 47
China, 7, 188
Church, W. Lawrence, 236
CIDA, 27

243